CM00740587

ATTACK ON THE SOMME

Attack on the Somme

1st Anzac Corps and the Battle of Pozières Ridge, 1916

Wolverhampton Military Studies No.19

Meleah Hampton

Helion & Company Limited

Helion & Company Limited
26 Willow Road
Solihull
West Midlands
B91 1UE
England
Tel. 0121 705 3393
Fax 0121 711 4075
Email: info@helion.co.uk
Website: www.helion.co.uk
Twitter: @helionbooks
Visit our blog http://blog.helion.co.uk/

Published by Helion & Company 2016
Designed and typeset by Mach 3 Solutions Ltd (www.mach3solutions.co.uk)
Cover designed by Paul Hewitt, Battlefield Design (www.battlefield-design.co.uk)
Printed by Gutenberg Press Limited, Tarxien, Malta

Text © Meleah Hampton 2016
Images © as individually credited
Maps © Luke Hampton 2015
Front cover: A working party of the 7th Brigade carrying empty sandbags past
Gibraltar on their way to the front line, 28 August 1916 (Australian War Memorial
EZ0098). The centre of Pozières on 28 August 1916. The trench on the left is
Centre Way, and the tram line is visible to its right. The soldier in the foreground is
looking towards the OG Lines (Australian War Memorial EZ0099).
Rear cover: Australian transport limbers returning down Sausage Valley at a gallop
(Australian War Memorial EZ0072).

ISBN 978-1-910777-65-7

British Library Cataloguing-in-Publication Data.
A catalogue record for this book is available from the British Library.

All rights reserved. No part of this publication may be reproduced, stored in
a retrieval system, or transmitted, in any form, or by any means, electronic,
mechanical, photocopying, recording or otherwise, without the express written
consent of Helion & Company Limited.

For details of other military history titles published by Helion & Company Limited
contact the above address, or visit our website: http://www.helion.co.uk.

We always welcome receiving book proposals from prospective authors.

Contents

List of Illustrations

List of Maps

The Wolverhampton Military Studies Series
Series Editor's Preface

As series editor, it is my great pleasure to introduce the *Wolverhampton Military Studies Series* to you. Our intention is that in this series of books you will find military history that is new and innovative, and academically rigorous with a strong basis in fact and in analytical research, but also is the kind of military history that is for all readers, whatever their particular interests, or their level of interest in the subject. To paraphrase an old aphorism: a military history book is not less important just because it is popular, and it is not more scholarly just because it is dull. With every one of our publications we want to bring you the kind of military history that you will want to read simply because it is a good and well-written book, as well as bringing new light, new perspectives, and new factual evidence to its subject.

In devising the *Wolverhampton Military Studies Series*, we gave much thought to the series title: this is a *military* series. We take the view that history is everything except the things that have not happened yet, and even then a good book about the military aspects of the future would find its way into this series. We are not bound to any particular time period or cut-off date. Writing military history often divides quite sharply into eras, from the modern through the early modern to the mediaeval and ancient; and into regions or continents, with a division between western military history and the military history of other countries and cultures being particularly marked. Inevitably, we have had to start somewhere, and the first books of the series deal with British military topics and events of the twentieth century and later nineteenth century. But this series is open to any book that challenges received and accepted ideas about any aspect of military history, and does so in a way that encourages its readers to enjoy the discovery.

In the same way, this series is not limited to being about wars, or about grand strategy, or wider defence matters, or the sociology of armed forces as institutions, or civilian society and culture at war. None of these are specifically excluded, and in some cases they play an important part in the books that comprise our series. But there are already many books in existence, some of them of the highest scholarly standards, which cater to these particular approaches. The main theme of the *Wolverhampton Military Studies Series* is the military aspects of wars, the preparation for wars or their prevention, and their aftermath. This includes some books whose main theme is the technical details of how armed forces have worked, some books on wars and battles, and some books that re-examine the evidence about the existing stories, to show in a different light what everyone thought they already knew and understood.

As series editor, together with my fellow editorial board members, and our publisher Duncan Rogers of Helion, I have found that we have known immediately and almost by instinct the kind of books that fit within this series. They are very much the kind of well-written and challenging books that my students at the University of Wolverhampton would want to read. They are books which enhance knowledge, and offer new perspectives. Also, they are books for anyone with an interest in military history and events, from expert scholars to occasional readers. One of the great benefits of the study of military history is that it includes a large and often committed section of the wider population, who want to read the best military history that they can find; our aim for this series is to provide it.

Stephen Badsey
University of Wolverhampton

Foreword

As I write this, we are just a few months away from the centenary of the Battle of the Somme. Most famous for its opening day, on 1 July 1916, and to a lesser extent for the debut of the tank on 15 September, the Somme offensive actually lasted until 18 November 1916. As Meleah Hampton accurately observes, it is the many, mostly forgotten days of fighting in between such large-scale set-piece actions that form the heart of the Battle of the Somme. In this fine book Dr Hampton subjects one such series of actions, fought by the Australian divisions of I ANZAC around Pozières in July-August 1916, to minute, forensic investigation. In the process she makes a very significant contribution, not only to our understanding of the Pozières/Mouquet Farm actions, but also of the Battle of the Somme itself.

When I was researching my scholarly article on the fighting around Pozières, published in 2002, I was surprised to find that it had received little attention from historians. After the publication of Charles Bean's 1916 volume of the Australian official history in 1929, it wasn't until 1986 when a book-length treatment appeared. Unfortunately Peter Charlton's popular account was tinged by a nationalistic interpretation and was firmly in the 'butchers and bunglers' camp. It did not represent an advance on Bean (although it boasted a splendidly frosty foreword by John Terraine, who clearly disliked the book but presumably was contractually obliged to produce some copy). Since then we have had further popular books, by Scott Bennett and Peter Fitzsimmons. Meleah Hampton's book, by contrast, is a genuinely original piece of historical scholarship.

One of the most important things about *Attack on the Somme* is that although it covers actions fought by Australian troops, and is written by an Australian historian based at the Australian War Memorial in Canberra, it does not adopt a narrowly nationalist perspective. Rather, Dr Hampton is at pains to place this case study in the wider context of the experience of the British Expeditionary Force (BEF). In these pages you will not find material on the Anzac legend, on the supposedly uniquely Australian quality of 'mateship', or side-swipes at British commanders because they were British. To all intents and purposes, the Australian divisions in France formed a contingent of the BEF, albeit a slightly unusual one, and Dr Hampton is right to treat them as such. In adopting this approach she is not, of course, alone. I am constantly struck by the disconnect between popular writers of Australian military history and professional academics. Certainly in the case of Australian scholarly historians of the First World War, the current generation is almost without exception careful to locate Australia's story in a broad context: of the anti-Central Powers coalition, Britain, and the British Empire. Jeffrey Grey, Robert Stevenson and David Stevens (to mention the authors of three books that I happen to have read recently) are cases in point.

Meleah Hampton's take on generalship on the Somme is sobering. Some years ago I wrote on the command performance of the top team at Reserve Army in 1916, and she provides further evidence of the poor quality of the generalship of Lieutenant-General Sir Hubert Gough and his Chief of Staff, Major-General Neill Malcolm. Whatever lip service they paid to the importance of proper preparation, they were far too inclined to rush subordinates into premature action. However, Lieutenant-General Sir William Birdwood at I ANZAC and his CoS, the latter much praised Brigadier-General Cyril Brudenell White also come in for trenchant criticism in these pages – one begins to see why Haig distrusted Birdwood. More surprising is that the performance of 'Hooky' Walker and H.V. Cox, the commanders of 1st and 4th Australian Divisions respectively also come in for fair and measured criticism. Dr Hampton's most damning comments concern the failure of commanders at all levels to link attacks into the bigger picture. It was pointless to launch (invariably costly) attacks that successfully gained ground, if the attacks did not contribute to the overall operational and strategic objective. One does not need to be a proponent of the 'bloody fools' school to think that the volunteers of 1916 deserved better from their commanders.

The third highlight of the book is its examination of learning in combat. As it happens, I am associated with the use of the term 'learning curve' as applied to the BEF. Of course I did not coin the term, or was even the first to use it in studies of the BEF. In any case, some people have taken it rather too literally. 'Learning curve' was never anything more than a piece of shorthand for the learning process (a term which is to be preferred) that went on. As Dr Hampton correctly observes, this simplistic interpretation is 'increasingly being discredited'; no one believes that there was a simple, steady upward curve in learning. It was a lot more complicated than that. *Attack on the Somme* argues that evidence that lessons were learned by I ANZAC and its subordinate formations, and lessons were then applied to subsequent operations, is singularly lacking. This is the most important finding of the book, and given the amount of primary evidence used, and the persuasiveness of Dr Hampton's analysis, it is not to be discarded lightly. This prompts at least three questions that lie beyond the scope of this monograph.

The first question is, *why* were lessons, which were certainly recorded in war diaries and the like, then ignored in planning for operations that took place only a few days or weeks later? Perhaps it relates to the fast tempo of operations, and the lack of time to sit back and process and disseminate the lessons; if so this might be an explanation, but it is not an excuse. Second, in some other cases, such as Major-General Sir Ivor Maxse's British 18th (Eastern) Division, there is clear evidence of lessons being learned during the early stages of Somme and applied to great effect later in the campaign. Is it ultimately about individuals making a difference? Was Maxse, one of the best trainers in the British army, who does seem to have fostered a culture of learning, the reason why lessons were learned and applied in this formation, and the lack of an Australian equivalent the reason for the failure to do so in I ANZAC? Third, a comparison of operations in the early stages of the Somme with the last phase in November 1916 (the Battle of the Ancre), still more with the BEF's performance at the Battle of Arras in April 1917, suggests that lessons had been learned and applied. Where does I ANZAC fit with this? Like all good history, *Attack on the Somme* is not an end in itself – it poses challenging questions that need to be addressed, and this book will certainly fuel the debate. These questions can only be addressed by further research in archival primary sources.

Attack on the Somme marks the debut of an innovative and original historian. I very much hope that Dr Hampton will continue her work in this field.

Gary Sheffield
Professor of War Studies
University of Wolverhampton
19 December 2015.

Notes

… on nomenclature

The usual form for naming formations and units is as follows: First Army, I Corps, 1st Division, 1 Brigade, 1st Battalion. However, I have chosen to use the naming conventions of the 1st Anzac Corps at the time of the fighting at Pozières and Mouquet Farm. The most notable difference comes with the name of 1st Anzac Corps itself – Anzac is an acronym and the name of the corps can be correctly rendered as I ANZAC. Corps headquarters most commonly referred to itself as I A. & N.Z.A. Corps in its own documents, but all divisions, brigades and units below referred to it almost invariably as "1st Anzac Corps" – hence the reason that this is the name in use in this book. The British corps on the flanks of the Australians preferred the use of the roman numeral, which is reflected in the text. Similarly, although "1 Brigade" is now considered the correct form of naming brigades, all documentation in the 1st Anzac Corps refers to its brigades as "1st Brigade, 2nd Brigade" etc, and that is again the form retained in the text.

… on quotations

While all quotations cited within this book are of course taken verbatim from the original source, in some cases I have modified the presentation of the words. Abbreviations have generally been rendered in full – for example, where the original writer has hurriedly scribbled 'Coy' or 'co.' for company, the full word is represented in text when quoted here. This is simply for ease of reading. The meaning of the word itself or the order of the wording of the message or quotation has not been altered in any way. Similarly, it was standard practice during the war to capitalise the names of places in the middle of text (handwritten or typescript) to minimise the chance of misreading during or after battle – for example 'the 4th Battalion will take DOT TRENCH tonight'. These capital letters have also been removed so as to avoid unintentional emphasis on certain words for the modern reader. These place names were misspelled in a colourful variety of ways – "Moquet Farm" and "Posiers" being favourites. Other writers preferred the French – notably for "Ferme du Mouquet". Different writers may variously use forms of words in messages or documents which even then were becoming archaic, for example "shew" for "show" or "to-night" for "tonight". In each of these cases, the modern variant was used or inserted. These and other spelling errors or inconsistencies have been corrected to the standardised, modern spelling and the English name used unless otherwise indicated.

Acknowledgements

This book is the result of five years of study for my PhD. Five years is a long time, and ends with lots of people to thank, most of whom I have no doubt I will forget. Sorry about that. But I am completely indebted to my PhD supervisors for their support, guidance and stimulating discussion during the process of writing this thesis. I would particularly like to thank Robin Prior as my principal supervisor for his advice, accessibility, generous knowledge, support and (with thanks to Heather, too) occasional lend of his cats. It has been a privilege to write most of this just two floors away from one of the great scholars of the First World War. Similarly Gary Sheffield as my co-supervisor has been extremely generous with his expansive knowledge, advice, time, and (with thanks to Viv, too) spare room on visits to the United Kingdom. I could not have had two better supervisors, and am glad to count them as friends and now colleagues.

I must thank the Army History Unit for their generous funding of my trip to the archives in London. The material I gathered there has been invaluable to my understanding of this topic. Without the 'Scheme F' papers this would be a very different study. I am also very grateful to Ade, Lanre, the officers of the East Street Baptist Church in South London and my very dear friends John and Deborah Woolley – and Jessica of course – for their assistance with accommodation and friendship during that time.

I am indebted to Andrew Richardson of the Army History Unit for doggedly tracking down a photograph of Ferdinand Medcalf for me. Thanks too to the Army Museum of Western Australia, and Ian Gill for their assistance in this matter. It is lovely and an unexpected pleasure to know what such a pivotal member of the 1st Anzac Corps looked like.

For the last year of my PhD, and the time since I have had the privilege of working in the Military History Section of the Australian War Memorial. I could not work with more supportive, knowledgeable and talented people. I am very grateful to Karl James, Aaron Pegram, and Lachlan Grant for their willingness to read the nightmare and make very sensible amendments and encouraging comments on a regular basis. I am greatly indebted to Ashley Ekins for his ongoing and enthusiastic support and mentorship, as well as access to his astonishing private collection from Lance Rhodes. Michael Kelly, Juliet Schyvens, Robert Nichols, Andrew McDonald and Christina

Zissis have also made the process so much better with their encouragement and cake (consumption if not provision). Colleagues from other institutions like Rhys Crawley, Nigel Steel and Michael Molkentin have been most encouraging and make me feel privileged to be allowed to call myself a military historian now!

My dad, Ken Ward, spent a great deal of time sorting out maps for me, as did my husband Luke Hampton. I am totally in their debt. My mother Meryn is always a marvellous source of support, although I suspect she's not that into having to deal with hysterical phone calls!

There are so many others to thank, in particular Meggie Hutchison for her friendship, support, shared academic angst (over a DECADE), coffee, drives around battlefields and mattresses on the floor. Miesje de Vogel has been both a material help both in getting to archives and commiserating on the pile of stuff to go through. To the folks at Adelaide Uni – Kylie Galbraith, Bodie Ashton, Daniel Ashdown, Jill Mackenzie, Alexia Moncrieff, and others – thanks for the good times and the angst-ridden, coffee-fueled nightmare. How fortunate I was to get a copy of *The Best 12 Anzac War Stories Ever!* commandoed into my letterbox one day.

And last but most, thanks to the amazing Luke, who wasn't around at the start, and is my husband at the end. He has been the best part of this whole process! This book is particularly for Jack, who is the baby I had after I had the thesis baby. *Cariad mawr* x

In memory of Matt Baird (1974-2015), who would have loved seeing his name in this book.

Introduction

... all we have to do is take a break
from researching the reports and plans of the generals
and look into the movements of those
hundred thousand men who were directly involved in the events themselves,
and all the apparently insoluble questions can be resolved once and for all
with extraordinary ease and simplicity.

Leo Tolstoy, *War and Peace*
Vol IV, Pt III, Chapter 19

The Battle of Pozières Ridge began on 23 July 1916 when the 1st Anzac Corps captured the small French village of Pozières. It ended on 3 September 1916 with 1st Anzac Corps' final attempt to take Mouquet Farm, just over one mile to the north west of Pozières. The battle lasted exactly six weeks, during which time the three divisions of 1st Anzac Corps rotated in and out of the line twice, each time conducting at least one offensive operation against heavily-defended German positions. These operations generally took place on an extremely narrow front and were easily seen by the Germans, who could pour accurate artillery and machine-gun fire onto the attacking troops from a number of different directions. The attacks were all generally conducted with the same basic structural approach of infantry advancing behind lifting artillery barrages, and from the same direction with very similar objectives. And yet this series of attacks demonstrates that this basic similarity in structure could be interpreted and applied in a variety of ways by divisional, brigade and even battalion commanders. This makes them an ideal candidate to understand the British tactical approach on the Somme, from the higher levels of command to the lowest, in all its complexity.

The Battle of the Somme, the major British offensive of 1916, is most often remembered for its 'big days' – the infamous 1 July with its huge numbers of casualties, the night attacks of 14-15 July, and the first use of tanks on 15 September. But there were another 138 days of the battle outside of these three operations. The bulk of the Somme campaign was a grim series of frontal assaults by the Allies and desperate counter-attacks by the Germans. On any given day only a small percentage of the line was engaged in fighting the enemy, almost invariably in the same kind of limited, set-piece attacks made by 1st Anzac Corps at Pozières and Mouquet Farm. Fourth Army, to the immediate right of the Australian sector and responsible for the greater part of the British offensives on the Somme, also conducted repeated relatively small-scale attacks on what has been called an "endless repetition of place names",[1] those such as Delville Wood and High Wood, largely through the use of similar uncoordinated, brutal frontal assaults. So, too, did other parts of Reserve Army, on the left of the Australians. Yet there have been very few studies of these ongoing, small-scale operations, and what they mean in the context of the campaign on the Somme, or in the context of the capability of any of the armies on the Western Front in 1916.

The attack in trench warfare was a more complicated matter than it had first seemed. Early attacks by infantry in either a single line or a series of closely spaced lines, such as in the battles along the Aisne and at Ypres in 1914, failed with heavy casualties. Infantry attacking in this manner proved ideal targets for entrenched machine-gunners and even riflemen. But the long, continuous nature of the Western Front meant that flanking manoeuvres were impossible and the only way of attacking the entrenched German invaders was by frontal assault. And so, as the simple approach was failing, some sophistication began to be introduced into the British art of attack. 1915 saw experimentation with a large variety of tactical methods with varying levels of success. Crucially it saw the rise to prominence of artillery support in the attack, and also the absorption of auxiliary arms such as trench mortars, Lewis guns, machine-gun barrages, gas, smoke screens, air observation and increasingly complex signals networks into a more integrated approach to the basic infantry attack.[2]

This gave commanders in 1916 a broader range of options for devising attacks than ever before, which is demonstrated by the variety of tactical approaches on the first day of the Somme. Some British divisions continued to attack in single lines while others adopted complex approaches in which the infantry advanced in widely spaced formations or even in waves. Some were given additional firepower in the form of machine guns and trench mortars to augment their rifles and bayonets, while others went forward under the cover of a lifting artillery barrage. But no matter what formation was adopted on 1 July 1916, almost all failed because of the simple fact that their main adversaries – distant artillery and well-emplaced machine-guns – had not been dealt with by the artillery. To the south, however, one or two divisional commanders had attempted to protect their troops by firing a heavy curtain of artillery shells in front of them. Here some ground was gained at reasonable cost. There were later successes, too. During the night of 14 July, Rawlinson's Fourth Army made some gains under the cover of darkness. These lessons did not go unappreciated, but in 1916 the British Army was still seeking consistency in approach and the ability to advance their lines in preparation for a major breakthrough attack.

1   John Terraine, *The Smoke and the Fire: Myths and Anti-Myths of War 1861-1945* (London: Sidgwick & Jackson, 1980), p. 122.
2   Paddy Griffith, *Battle Tactics of the Western Front: The British Army's Art of Attack 1916-18* (New Haven & London: Yale UP, 1994), p. 53.

The modern scholarly approach to study of the Battle of the Somme has taken one of two directions. This may seem an unusually small number of categories in which to place what is quite simply an enormous number of studies, but as Sir Michael Howard said in 1993, historians have:

> … let themselves be diverted, either upwards to a discussion of high strategy and a debate over the rationale for those operations; or downward to compiling battlefield memoirs and analysing the nature of trench warfare.[3]

The situation has hardly changed in the ensuing years, and the result of this is that almost all of the studies purporting to be of an operational nature undertake their subject from one of two perspectives – 'top-down', or 'bottom-up'. These two approaches can be best described by the questions they seek to answer. A top-down approach is concerned with understanding the role of high command in the operational conduct of the Somme. It remains analytical of the highest levels of command; the general staff, Army, corps, division and occasionally brigade and battalion level. It is also concerned with the role of the political leaders above these levels. The bottom-up approach asks different questions of its material. These works are concerned with the experience of the soldier and what it was like to be there, frequently avoiding an analysis of operations apart from those having a negative effect on the living conditions or life expectancy of the soldier. These two perspectives have dominated the study of the Somme for the last 90-odd years, at different times and with different results, but little innovation.

The simple vastness of the enterprise is one of the reasons that almost all operational studies of the British campaign take a top-down approach. The Somme was an enormous undertaking involving as many as 55 divisions of infantry along 18 miles of front. It lasted more than four months. The top-down approach concentrates on the largest of the formations of the British Army – Armies, corps, and divisions – to describe and analyse the battle. To attempt to get an overview of the battle without running to hundreds of volumes, this seems reasonable. But it limits knowledge of the battle to an understanding of the actions of a very few commanders. Events then seem to invariably be the consequences of their decisions. And, as Charles Bean found in writing the Official History of Australia in the war, commander's reports are prone to important inaccuracies. The top-down approach also provides a very simple reason for the focus on the three major operations within the Somme campaign. While the first day of the Somme involved a large number of divisions across a broad front, the rest of its days did not. The vast majority of the attacks made during the Somme campaign involved no more than one or two divisions – or fewer – across a mile or less of front. These small attacks can easily slip under the radar of a wider top-down approach to

---

3   Michael Howard, 'World War One: The Crisis in European History – The Role of the Military Historian', *The Journal of Military History*, 57:5 (October 1993), p. 137.

the war as seemingly insignificant to the bigger picture. Even Bean with his attention to detail struggled with the deterioration of scale in the fighting around Pozières Ridge, writing "the series of battles which ensued … cannot be described with the minuteness hitherto employed".[4] He still had a month of fighting to describe – nearly half of the campaign for 1st Anzac Corps. But rather than represent an insignificant part in the main battle, these 'insignificant days' *are* the battle. The days that are given the most prominence are in fact the least typical. And yet this is generally not recognised in the historiography.

The alternative to a top-down approach has been to move away from operational analysis altogether and take a bottom-up approach. This approach seeks to answer the question of the experience of the man in the field. What was it *like*? While this kind of approach sheds a great deal of light onto the experiences of individual soldiers, it does not link their experiences with the broader tactical and strategic plan. This is largely a result of the sources that this approach relies upon, namely the personal diaries and memoirs of lower levels of command during the war. This is a total departure from operational studies, because, in the words of one ex-serviceman, the ordinary soldier:

> … neither knew where he was, nor whither he was going, he could have no plan because he could foresee nothing … though his movements had to conform to those of others, spontaneously, as part of some infinitely flexible plan which he could not comprehend very clearly even in regard to its immediate object.[5]

An individual soldier was privy only to very specific information relating directly to the objectives he and his unit were to carry out. These bottom-up studies generally do not place the information these individuals were privy to into an extended understanding of the mechanics of the battlefield, but rather use their sources to discover the experience of the individual soldier – to describe the living conditions and experience of fighting during the First World War.

Similarly, studies of small-scale operations within campaigns – such as the Battle of Pozières Ridge as a part of the Battle of the Somme – have been largely avoided by academic historians. But while academia has paid little attention to these battles, others have been researching and writing about them. The focus of these publications is generally to tell the story of an event, usually with some kind of parochial motivation – that is, in order to give prominence to the story of a single unit or formation, or indeed a nation's involvement in the war. The limited number of popular histories on Pozières Ridge has tended to tell of the experience of the Australian formations and what those experiences meant for them *as Australians*. Too many works on Australia in the war fail to identify Australian formations as a part of a British Army, which they

---

4   C.E.W. Bean, *Official History of Australia in the War of 1914–1918: Vol. III. The A.I.F. in France* (Sydney: Angus & Robertson, 1929). p. 728.

5   Frederic Manning, *Her Privates, We* (London: Peter Davies, 1930) p. 14.

were; instead, all too often they are separate, unique and at the mercy of limited and inadequate British generals. But the fact is that these small-scale operations – even those by Dominion troops – have a great deal to say about the conduct of the war by the British Army in 1916.

One of the most important developments in the recent historiography of the First World War has been the development of the 'learning curve theory', which arose in the 1980s and 1990s among British historians. This is the idea that "the record of command during the war described a 'learning curve'," in other words, that a mixture of lessons taken from earlier battles like the Somme and Passchendaele combined with the 'wearing out' effects of the fighting on the German Army helped the Allies to achieve victory in 1918.[6] Historian Gary Sheffield has described it as viewing the Somme:

> … as a necessary, even an inevitable battle that hurt the Germans more than the British and pushed them towards making strategic decision that would eventually lose them the war … In this view, the Somme was the "muddy grave" of the Imperial German Army.[7]

A stronger assertion suggests that the Somme experience actually taught the British (and, of course, the French) valuable lessons for the future conduct of the war.[8] Robin Prior and Trevor Wilson, however, have concluded that if there was one, the learning curve was "an astonishingly uneven one".[9] Many tactical innovations were not GHQ-generated or endorsed ideas. Different tactics were tried, discarded, tried again and applied in a generally haphazard manner by different units at different times and – what is frequently overlooked – by different levels of command. The learning curve theory is increasingly being discredited because of too many examples of this unevenness. But while learning at all levels of command was irregular and stilted throughout the war, it is indisputable that by 1918 the British Army had put together a systematic approach to warfare that was able to break even the strongest German defences at will. There was learning and development going on somewhere within the British Army, but it does not necessarily stand to reason that the only manner in it could have happened was to have had its genesis with the highest levels of command before moving down to the lowest levels of the army.

What is missing between the top-down and the bottom-up approach, and indeed in the exploration of the learning curve theory, is an appreciation of the action and agency of mid to low levels of command in the military hierarchy during battle. The

6   Jay Winter & Antoine Prost. *The Great War in History: Debates and Controversies, 1914 to the Present.* (Cambridge: Cambridge UP, 2005), p. 75.
7   Sheffield, *The Somme*, (London: Cassell, 2003), p. xii.
8   William Philpott. *Bloody Victory: The Sacrifice on the Somme and the Making of the Twentieth Century.* (Great Britain: Little & Brown, 2009), pp.439 and following.
9   Winter & Prost, *Great War in History*, p. 75.

rapid and massive expansion the British Expeditionary Force had undergone since 1914 meant there were more levels of command between Haig as field marshal and the soldier in the field with bayonet in hand than there had ever been before. Almost all officers were in command of dramatically larger formations than they had been before the war, if they came from a military background at all. Orders had to pass through Army, corps, division, brigade and battalion headquarters before being issued to company commanders and onwards to platoons and their sections. Each of these levels of command had to adapt the orders given to become more specific to suit their unit, for the simple reason that the highest levels of command could not be responsible for every tactical manoeuvre over every small piece of ground. Each could therefore interpret orders given in a number of ways, having an impact on the end result of the battle, or at least the conduct thereof. And so it is not logical simply to draw a direct line between orders given by the highest levels of command and the end result of a battle.

Eventually the General Staff would issue pamphlets to disseminate these ideas BEF-wide, but in 1916 the practice of passing around tactical principles was in its early days; it was unevenly applied and frequently ignored by those who received the information. Developments often happened *in spite* of the actions or understanding of commanders at the upper levels. An example of this is General Sir Henry Horne, an artillery officer who commanded XV Corps in 1916. His corps was responsible for some of the earliest examples of creeping artillery barrages, and in fact fired one on 1 July with good effect. XV Corps went on consistently to develop their creeping barrage tactics, and apply them in future operations in order to provide their infantry protection in their advance. And yet Horne stated in September 1916 that he "could never follow what is the value of a creeping barrage."[10] Clearly appreciation of the value of the creeping barrage came from elsewhere within his corps; more importantly, this 'elsewhere' had the wherewithal to develop and apply this tactic without the understanding of the upper echelon of command. So the learning process was not a straightforward one, and not one that necessarily filtered from the strategy-makers at the top to the fighters at the bottom. How and where this tactical appreciation arose is precisely the kind of question that a continued top-down approach to the study of the First World War cannot answer.

The least common studies in First World War military history attempt to supply an appreciation of the action and agency of these mid to low levels of command in the military hierarchy. These studies are rare simply because in so many cases there are very few sources available at that level. The best way to overcome this so far has been to use sources such as the pre-war Field Service Regulations booklets and memoranda, training notes and other forms of information dissemination during the war. Paddy Griffith relied on these sources when writing *Battle Tactics of the Western Front: The British Army's Art of Attack 1916-18*, a work that stands almost alone in analysing

---

10   Prior & Wilson, *The Somme* (Sydney: University of New South Wales Press, 2005), p. 224.

lower level actions in the First World War. However, in testing principles derived from these sources he is generally constrained to the use of post-action reports generated at battalion level or higher, or from personal memoirs and recollections, bringing an edge of the top-down study to his work. Andy Simpson has studied the role of command at an intermediate level in his book *Directing Operations: British Corps Command on the Western Front 1914-18*. This book makes some important advances in our understanding of the increasing flexibility of the corps level of command during the war, but again avoids detailed operational analysis of lower levels to demonstrate how this worked in the field. Overall, however, these quality operational studies of lower-level units are few.

To really understand how battle worked at brigade or battalion level and below requires recourse to a layered and detailed qualitative study to produce a description of a battle to the lowest levels of command. In order to truly understand the process of not just fighting a battle, but of learning and development throughout a campaign, it is important to plumb the depths of the military hierarchy *during battle* to discover not only what army and corps commanders were ordering, but how those orders were taken up, developed and passed on by brigade and battalion commanders, and what battalion, company and even platoon commanders were doing with them in the field. With the unexpected stalemate on the Western Front, both technological and managerial problems either not encountered in warfare before, or at least not on the same scale, needed to be overcome by all armies. Part of the process of understanding how these managerial problems were overcome in the British Army is to study the entire managerial machine of the military. The upper levels have been described and debated in minute detail, but the debate now needs to move on to include lower levels of command.

Yet, as previously mentioned, there are generally very few sources available to write a detailed description of a battle, or to understand the role lower levels of command played in the overall adjustment to trench warfare conditions during the First World War. Battalion war diaries, particularly for British units in 1916, usually give only very brief daily summaries of events, and regularly do not contain reports or even orders. The records of the fighting around Pozières and Mouquet Farm are different, however. The Australian War Memorial in Canberra has a startling wealth of information on these battles, including some lower-level reports and, most importantly, more than 5,000 messages written in the field of battle. These messages were written by a variety of different men for the purposes of managing the battle. They range from the adjutant of the 7th Battalion advising the commanding officer of A Company to have his men dump their great coats when leaving the trench near Sunken Road,[11] to 1st Anzac Corps headquarters informing divisional commanders that Germans had been reported massing for counter-attack by neighbouring units.[12] In these messages,

---

11   Australian War Memorial (AWM): AWM 26/55/1: Bastin (Adj. 7th Bn) to OCs A & B Coys, 23 July 1916, 4.25am, Operations File Somme 1916, 3rd Infantry Brigade.
12   AWM: AWM 26/50/16: G.1263 1st Anzac Corps to 1st, 2nd & 4th Divs. & BGHA, 13

individual writers such as Captain Ferdinand Medcalf of the 11th Battalion or Captain Hugh Pulling of the 13th suddenly take on a great deal of importance in terms of the operational conduct of certain attacks where previously they have scarcely rated a mention in the literature. The messages are usually in the form of a pink message slip, but can be a mud-smeared corner of paper. Some are almost illegible due to the shaky hand writing them under heavy shellfire. They are generally signed, addressed, dated, and include the time they were written. These messages make it possible to reconstruct the Battle of Pozières Ridge in detail that has simply not been possible before.

These detailed records form the basis of this study. They have enabled a thorough study of the actions of the 1st Anzac Corps in a way that has not been done previously. The 1st Anzac Corps, comprising the 1st, 2nd and 4th Australian Divisions, conducted more than ten offensive operations against the Germans in the six week period from 23 July to 3 September 1916. Each division held the front line twice during this period, conducting attacks against the German line each time. All of these operations were conducted by the same basic means – a series of lifting artillery barrages behind which the infantry advanced onto either one or a series of objectives. They demonstrate some of the critical factors in battle that had to be appropriately ordered and executed for infantry units to have been able to function in the field – without a strong and appropriately paced artillery barrage, for example, the infantry could do very little. But they also demonstrate that with the appropriate framework, very small units of men, and even individuals, could have an impact on the course of an operation. Brigadiers or battalion commanders interpreted orders in a variety of different ways with impunity and again could make the difference between success or failure. However, without a solid foundation to the battle supplied in the artillery barrage and basic objectives in orders from Army or Corps, lower levels of command were much more restricted in what they could hope to achieve.

The most notable absence in this study is the German. The Germans used a variety of defences in the Pozières – Mouquet Farm area. In Pozières village they had strongly fortified houses, cellars and windmills. The German second line of defence, incorporating the OG Lines running to the north and east of the village, were prepared, deep trenches with deep dugouts. They also used a kind of early chequerboard defensive system in areas where trenches had been blown flat by the artillery by placing machine gun crews in shell holes at irregular intervals. At Mouquet Farm the Germans had deeper and more heavily fortified dugouts than Pozières village and could reinforce them via tunnels whose entrances were hundreds of yards to the north. The important factor in all of these methods of defence for the purposes of this study was that each type of defence was enormously successful, no matter what form it took. Well-placed machine guns with alert crews could stop any attack the 1st Australian Corps was capable of mounting without the careful planning, preparation and execution of a combined-arms attack.

August 1916, 11.15pm, Operations File Somme 1916, 1st Anzac Corps General Staff.

There were many German counter-attacks during this period as well, ranging from large-scale operations to short raids by twenty or so men. The British General Staff also recognised that "counter-attacks can be dealt with by the Artillery and Vickers Guns placed in rear covering gaps". The strength of defence was such that attacks were more likely to fail than not. Nevertheless, to fight on the Somme, the Allies had to attack these defences. The detailed paperwork left by 1st Anzac Corps and carefully conserved by Charles Bean means that the Battle of Pozières Ridge can be a critical case study of how they attempted to do it at all levels of command.

Despite experience from the Gallipoli campaign, Australian units were still taken by surprise by the conditions on the Western Front. Douglas Haig noted that "the situation seems all very new and strange to Australian H[ead] Q[uarters]. The fighting here and shellfire is much more severe than anything experienced at Gallipoli!"[13] This was true.The 1st Anzac Corps was like most of the British Army, struggling with the manner in which to conduct this new kind of warfare in 1916. There are more similarities between the Australians and formations of the new Kitchener Armies of the British Expeditionary Force than anything else. They were equally inexperienced, their training was based on British principles and their command structure was the same as the British. They were inserted into British Armies – in July, August and September 1916 1st Anzac Corps was a part of the newly-created Reserve Army under Lieutenant-General Sir Hubert Gough. This study should be considered more representative of the British Army in 1916 than of any form of Australian separateness or perceived superiority or inferiority, and it paints a concerning descent into chaos over the period of six weeks.

---

13   Gary Sheffield & John Bourne (eds.), *Douglas Haig: War Diaries and Letters 1914-1918*, (London: Weidenfeld & Nicolson, 2005), p. 209.

1

"A general confusion of units":
The Capture of Pozières by the 1st Australian Division, 23 July 1916

The Battle of Pozières Ridge began with an operation to capture the village after which the ridge was named. Today it hardly looks like a significant landmark among the gently rolling fields around Albert, but the small amount of advantage it gave in observation to the north and west was considerable in terms of trench warfare. Strategists noted that the position on the high ground around Pozières gave the enemy "a marked advantage in command and observation and cover[ed] from view a considerable part of his second line of defence."[1] Its capture would give the British an advantage in both artillery observation and a view into the German second and third lines of defence. Pozières was the first important obstacle in gaining control of the ridgeline in this particular sector. It was captured by the 1st Australian Division in an operation that began on 23 July 1916, and had secured the village within three days. While often held up as a sign of Australian military genius in the face of British bumbling, this battle reveals nothing could be farther from the truth on closer examination. Certainly it was successful, but at times there was a very definite danger of failure due to complicated battle plans and inexperienced troops. In many respects, the period 23-25 July at Pozières is the perfect example of how a few individuals were able to make a material difference to the outcome of an operation in the midst of a modern, technology-driven battlefield.

Pozières was bordered to the north- and south-east by the main trench lines of the German second line. In this sector these German defences were known as the OG – Old German – Lines. These were two roughly parallel trenches that were a part of the German second line of defence on the Somme. The nearest to the village was known as OG1 and the one furthest away, OG2. Several significant communication trenches ran from the village back to these main lines of defence as well as forward to advanced posts. Perpendicular to the OG Lines the main thoroughfare

1   Brigadier J.E. Edmonds (ed.), *Military Operations: France and Belgium, 1916. Appendices* (London: Macmillan, 1932), 'Plans for Offensive by the Fourth Army', 3 April 1916, p. 64.

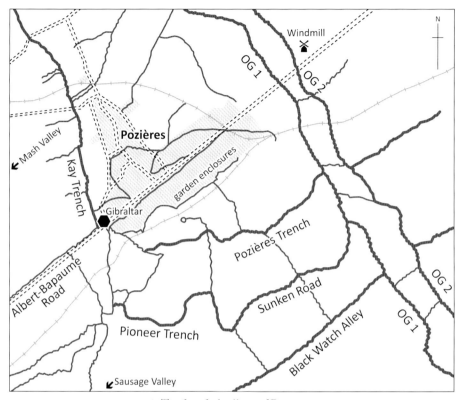

1 The fortified village of Pozières.

through the village, the Albert–Bapaume Road, ran from the south west to the north east through the southern edge of the town. To the north west of the road the main part of the village was home to an extensive German trench system. It was protected to the west by a strong trench covered by rows of barbed wire known to the British as K or Kay Trench. Along the south-eastern edge of the village, on the other side of the Albert–Bapaume Road, all of the garden enclosures behind the houses were entrenched and had strongpoints built into them. Some of the houses on the south-eastern sides of the road had fortified cellars, and the schoolhouse was home to a significant German strongpoint. At the south-west point of the village stood Gibraltar, another cellar with a heavily-fortified machine gun position which stood above the Albert–Bapaume Road. It gave a direct view down Sausage Valley, which formed the main thoroughfare into the sector. By the time Reserve Army was given the task of capturing it, the small French village was described to have been "very much knocked about by our artillery fire and all that remained undamaged

Pozières under German occupation. A German soldier stands by the pond which was outside the church in Pozières. (AWM J00217)

were cellars,"[2] but the deep underground fortifications and extensive trench network ensured the village continued to be a very formidable objective.

Preparation

At midnight on 17 July 1st Anzac Corps was transferred to the Reserve Army, which had been formed just two months before. The following day British General Headquarters issued an operation order to Fourth and Reserve Armies for an attack to take Pozières. This operation had been informally discussed on a number of previous occasions and was now formalised through the issue of Reserve Army Operation Order No. 11. This order also marked out a new boundary between the two armies. This new divide ran roughly north to south just over a quarter of a mile beyond the eastern edge of Pozières village. Here at the far right of Reserve Army's sector of operations, the 1st Anzac Corps was given responsibility for conducting the next major operation against Pozières.

The commander of Reserve Army was Lieutenant-General Hubert Gough, an impetuous and aggressive commander who had risen quickly to the level of army

2   AWM: AWM 4/1/42/18 Pt. 2: 'Short Account of the Taking of Pozières', 1st Australian Division General Staff War Diary.

commander, and could hardly resist rushing into battle immediately after receiving orders. Despite being required to negotiate the timing of his assault on Pozières with operations by Fourth Army on his right flank, Gough called spur of the moment conferences without representation from Fourth Army to begin planning for uncoordinated attacks within his sector. And yet 1st Anzac Corps was simply not ready, not as a result of any fault on its part, but because it was still in the process of moving into the sector. Gough had done what he could to move the process along by deliberately by-passing Corps command, taking direct control of the 1st Australian Division. This division was the first of 1st Anzac Corps' divisions to reach the sector and therefore the one assigned the task of taking Pozières. Gough issued a number of orders to attack for dates as early as 19, 20 or 21 July. But the Australian battalions of the 1st Division were only just entering the front line on the night of 18/19 July and the divisional artillery to be used in the attack was not even in position to start registering targets until 20 July, much less take part in an assault before 22 July. The very valid protestations of Major-General Harold Bridgwood Walker, the officer commanding 1st Division, as to the lack of preparedness of his troops meant that delay was inevitable.[3] The date of the attack was finally, after several conferences, compromises and withdrawn orders, settled for 23 July 1916.

This operation was to differ markedly from those conducted previously. Instead of attacking the village from the west or the southwest along the Albert–Bapaume Road, the Australians were to attack the village from the south east, at right angles to the Albert–Bapaume Road and parallel to the OG Lines. Both Gough, as army commander and Walker at divisional level claim responsibility for the change in direction but with no reference to what advantage they expected to achieve by doing this. Walker stated in his after-action report that he was given the choice of direction for his operation,[4] but Gough later indignantly denied this. In a letter to the British Official Historian years after the war he stated that:

> I gave Walker no choice in that matter … he got from me clear & definite orders what he was to do (to take Pozières) & how broadly he was to do it – only the details of the attack were left in his hands – and the details he carried out thoroughly well.[5]

3   For more on this, see G.D. Sheffield, 'Australians at Pozières: Command and Control on the Somme, 1916,' in David French and Brian Holden Reid (eds), *The British General Staff: Reform and Innovation c.1890-1939* (London, Cass, 2002), pp. 112-26

4   AWM: AWM 4/1/42/18 Pt. 2: 'Report on the Operations of First Australian Division at Pozières', 1st Australian Division General Staff War Diary.

5   TNA: CAB 45/134: Gough to Edmonds, 16 June 1938. Gough's strident denial would have held more clout had he not mixed up the directions – he claimed that he insisted on and carried that the attack would be from the south-west instead of from the south-east as the attack was conducted.

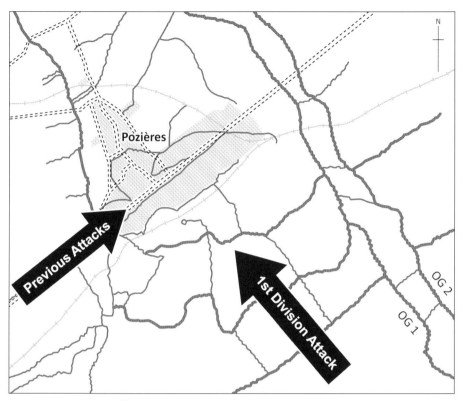

2 The change in direction at Pozières, 23 July 1916.

While the change in direction seems to have been considered a critical factor in success at Pozières, it also caused considerable complications. The first and most important of these was that it diverted the operation away from a frontal assault on the OG Lines in favour of an attack on the village. Instead of attacking the main defences in the area head on, this operation would take a swipe out of the German second line by focussing on an outpost to the main German line of defence – the village of Pozières rather than the OG Lines. These would be attacked in part, but were a secondary consideration to the village itself.

The second complication inherent in this change of direction was to do with the boundary between Reserve and Fourth Armies. Because the border ran behind and in parts almost parallel to the Australian front line, there was little to no depth in the back lines. All traffic into the battlefield had to filter along Black Watch Alley. The ground to the south-east of this trench was in Fourth Army's sector and could only be used by the 1st British Division. Due to the lack of depth behind the front line, waves of attacking infantry could not be evenly spaced behind each other waiting to jump off, but instead were spread out along Black Watch Alley and beyond to the village

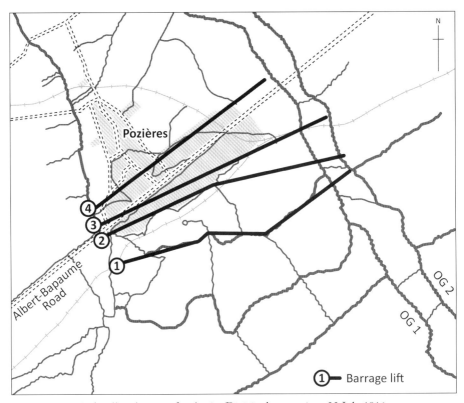

3 Artillery barrage for the 1st Division's operation, 23 July 1916.

of Albert waiting to move into jumping-off position as the lead troops attacked. The dominant features of Black Watch Alley were no more than shell holes and bodies which made judging the correct position from which to turn left into the fight difficult for those entering the battlefield. The extreme right of the line suffered most from this configuration, with formations having to move along a mile of trenches, behind and parallel to the front line and including the full length of Black Watch Alley, before turning left to enter their area of operations. Even troops positioned closest to the left flank arrived worn out from the march in. Positioning of troops took longer because the approach was so difficult. Late and lost troops, as well as those exhausted before they reached any point of combat, proved to be an ongoing problem.

The orders issued by Reserve Army were for an attack by the 1st Australian Division under cover of a lifting artillery barrage. This basic structure, with various modifications, formed the basis of all operations to follow. As with the other divisions in the corps, the 1st Division had yet to participate in a major operation on the Western Front, and were heavily reliant on guidance from Reserve Army headquarters for the tactical structure of the assault. And Reserve Army did not let the division down in

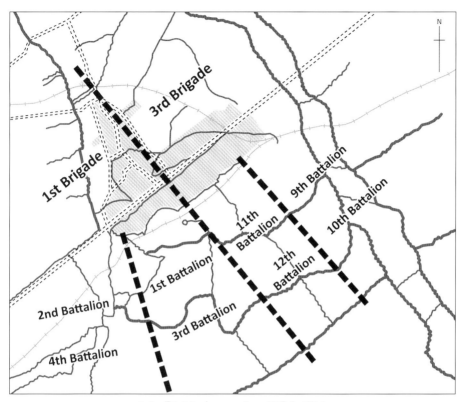

4 1st Division's operation, 23 July 1916.

its temporary role as both Army and corps command structures, providing clearly articulated plans for the lifting barrage. Hereafter barrage plans would be worked on between both Army and corps headquarters – Army would give the basic structure and instructions for the heavy artillery, but the lighter divisional artillery usually worked to a plan devised by Corps that was (hopefully) designed to integrate with the heavier barrage. On 23 July 1916, the artillery plan took the form of three lifts followed by a standing barrage. The first objective, Pozières Trench, was to be subjected to three minutes' fire. After this the barrage would lift onto the second objective, the back of the enclosures along the Albert–Bapaume Road just over 400 yards away, for half an hour. It would then move onto the third objective, the road itself which was 450-500 yards further on again, for another half an hour. Finally the barrage would fall onto the north side of the Albert–Bapaume Road for an extended period of time to protect the infantry, who were expected to be consolidating their gains at that time, from counter-attack. Each battery was allocated between two and five rounds per gun per minute of shrapnel in the preliminary barrage, slowing their rate of fire to two rounds per gun per minute, half shrapnel, half high explosive, for the three lifts of the barrage.[6] The artillery would provide the timetable for the entire attack, which was to begin with the bombardment on the first objective at 12.28am. This was a strictly limited-objective affair, with no move beyond the Albert–Bapaume Road to take place until further notice. In particular, the orders specify that the OG Lines had to be strongly held and consolidated before any advance into the village could be made.

The infantry for this operation were evenly deployed along the line. The 1st Australian Brigade was designated the left half of the line, the 3rd Australian Brigade the right, leaving the remaining brigade of the division, the 2nd, in reserve. Each brigade put two battalions across their front, with two behind. The infantry plan was inextricably linked with that of the artillery. A wave of troops was to ordered to take one of the artillery objective lines and consolidate it as the barrage lifted. So the troops detailed for the first objective, eight companies from four battalions, were to wait as closely as possible to the barrage, rush their objective as the barrage lifted from the first to the second objective, and stay there to consolidate the position. The second wave, also comprising eight companies, but with additional contingents of engineers, pioneers and at least four Vickers machine guns, moved up while this was happening, waiting to move through the first objective to rush the second. A third wave of troops would then move through the second in the same manner. Importantly, each of these waves of infantry were to stay on their objective and consolidate it into a strongly defended position rather than continue to push forward to the most forward positions. Divisional orders designated positions for at least eleven strongpoints to be constructed by the engineers and pioneers accompanying the second wave at various points in the advance. The most important thing to take from these plans is that the operation was intended to be conducted in depth. Three waves of infantry resulted in three captured lines being consolidated into deep defensive positions at the end of the attack. The expectation was that the artillery would pull the infantry forward through by creating space for them to work – the best case scenario was that the German defences would be destroyed and the defenders within killed, but even keeping Germans in their trenches, heads down and away from their machine guns and rifles was an advantage of the utmost importance. The three consolidated objective lines then meant that a German counter-attack was very unlikely to succeed in breaking through a newly-won line, and maximised the chances of success in this limited-objective operation.

The orders from Reserve Army had next to pass through 1st Australian Division Headquarters in order to gain another layer of detail for the brigades taking part. Walker and his staff presented a simple, straightforward interpretation and development of Reserve Army orders. But the two brigades most closely involved in the attack – the 1st and 3rd Brigades – passed on these uncomplicated divisional orders in two very different ways, which would have broader implications for the success

6   AWM: AWM 4/13/10/22: 'Table of Artillery Tasks attached to First Australian Divisional Artillery Order No. 31', 21 July 1916, 1st Australian Divisional Artillery War Diary.

of their combined assault. Both brigades were commanded by experienced British officers. The 1st Australian Brigade was commanded by Lieutenant-Colonel Nevill Maskelyne Smyth, a 47-year-old career soldier who had served in India, Egypt, the Sudan – where he won the Victoria Cross – and South Africa as well as more recently in the Gallipoli campaign. Lieutenant-Colonel Ewen George Sinclair-Maclagan, commanding the 3rd Australian Brigade, had also had experience in India and in South Africa – where he had been awarded the Distinguished Service Order – and the Dardanelles campaign. Both had attended conferences with Divisional command at least once, and both based their operations on the basic model of attack as outlined by Reserve Army and the 1st Australian Division.

By the time this tactical model passed through brigade headquarters, a second line of infantry had been added to each assault wave, or rather each assault wave was split into two. The first half of the wave would spearhead the attack, while the second half would follow up closely to provide support where needed. But while the basic form of attack prescribed by division is present in orders from both brigades, the manner in which it was applied was very different between the two. The most straightforward adaptation of tactical orders from division was made by Smyth at 1st Infantry Brigade headquarters on the left. In his assault, while the split waves were present, they featured no further in his orders in any practical way. The emphasis in his orders was on the waves as a whole, moving one by one through each other to their designated objective.

On the other hand the 3rd Brigade, under Sinclair-Maclagan, put much more emphasis the role of the lines within the waves. As a result 3rd Brigade orders quickly become confusing. It is broadly true that here on the right of the Australian line, the plan was to have each objective rushed by the first line of each wave, with the second coming behind to help consolidate gains. But Sinclair-Maclagan sometimes assigned infantry lines to attack objectives they did not belong to – for example, a line belonging to the second wave of infantry might be assigned to attack the third objective, or lines from the fourth wave, intended to provide reinforcement as needed, was committed to attack the third objective. This resulted in a ridiculously bewildering state of affairs in which the orders gave directions to the effect that the taking of the second objective would be "by 3rd and 4th [line], closely supported by 5th [line], the 6th [line] being used if necessary to push home the attack. This objective when gained will be consolidated by 3rd, 4th and 5th [lines]".[7] The confusion is surely self-evident – a and a pencil are essential to decipher who should be where, when. Command must also have been confusing. Here the third and fourth lines of infantry would be from

---

7   AWM: AWM 4/23/3/9: '3rd Infantry Brigade AIF Memo of Instructions with Brigade Operation Order No. 21' 22 July 1916, 3rd Brigade War Diary. The order reverses use of the terms 'wave' and 'line', so each objective would be attacked by a line of infantry comprising two waves. However, for the purposes of consistency later, I have reversed the terms here.

one battalion and the fifth and sixth from another. Who was in command of this? In particular, who decided if the 6th line would be used? How were they in contact? It is certainly not made clear in the orders. Managing a cross-over between lines and waves would have been bad enough within the one battalion without crossing over between battalion commands. How Sinclair-Maclagan expected this arrangement to be followed in the field is unclear. While both brigade plans follow the broader scheme laid down by division, the difference between the simple adherence applied by 1st Brigade and the intricate movements of small units in the interpretation of 3rd Brigade is enormous, and would have serious implications under battle conditions.

One thing to note at this point is the disposition of troops for this attack. The term 'divisional attack' would imply that around 12,000 men would attack the objective. This may be true in a very technical sense, but in reality the placement of formations at Pozières demonstrates that the spearhead of the line was much more thinly applied than would first seem. With the 2nd Brigade in reserve and as much as two or three miles from the front, only two thirds of the division was at the forefront of the attack. But because each of the two brigades in the front line was broken down into waves to effect the leapfrog manoeuvre, the number of men actually strung along the half mile-long front was just eight companies' worth. And with each line being broken into two waves – even in the simply-applied 1st Brigade plan – this is halved again. What this means is that effectively 1,000 men out of 12,000 of the division formed the foremost part of the line. Or, in other words, one battalions' worth of men out of the eight battalions of the leading brigades was directly opposite the German lines. But while the very front part of the line was thinly held, the emphasis here was always on depth. Another three lines of eight companies each were to follow, meaning that the front line would be about 6-800 yards deep and held by as many as 8,000 men. The attack plan was such that the imperative was on maintaining this depth. Every gain had to be strongly consolidated by improved trenches and the construction of strongpoints, and each wave of attacking infantry was specifically instructed not to move forward from their objective unless otherwise ordered.

The attack – 23 July 1916

The artillery barrage – "a treffic [sic] hail of shrapnel mixed with high explosive shell"[8] – began at 12.28am on 23 July 1916. Each of the lifts of the barrage took place on time and without any major problems. On the left, the simple attack plan of the 1st Brigade worked well. The sector had been divided into two halves. On the brigade's left, the 2nd Battalion provided the first and second waves of the attack, followed by the 4th Battalion forming the third and fourth waves. On the right of 1st Brigade's sector the 1st Battalion similarly formed the first and second waves, while the 3rd

8   AWM: AWM 4/1/42/18 Pt. 2: 'Short Account of the Taking of Pozières', 1st Australian Division General Staff War Diary.

Battalion followed up acting as the third and fourth waves. Each of the attacking lines of infantry moved forward as ordered and by 8.50am the three objective lines were in various states of consolidation and the brigade was seeking to move beyond the Albert–Bapaume Road.

But a simple explanation of events such as this belies the complexity of the battlefield here. To begin with, not all troops behaved according to orders given, in the infantry or in the artillery. On the extreme left end of the line, Captain S. R. Thurnhill of the 2nd Field Artillery Brigade pushed forward his 18 pounder gun from a position at the head of Sausage Valley to a location on the Bapaume Road. Most of the road is visible from the Gibraltar strong post, but Thurnhill chose the one small dip out of the line of direct fire available to the Germans. His crew then fired 115 rounds, starting at zero hour, enfilading the main road through the village and providing a kind of direct-fire horizontal barrage to protect the infantry and demolish enemy barricades. It seemed that its appearance was so unusual that the Germans did not manage to stop the gun, and it and its crew were later withdrawn to a crater without casualty. Despite the fact that this was completely outside of the artillery firing plan and seriously depleted his battery, the ad hoc plan seems to have been effective and Thurnhill earned himself and his crew nothing but admiration.[9]

All of the infantry formations did not necessarily attack from their prescribed positions, either. An aggressive policy by the 2nd Battalion on the far left put a platoon ahead of the first two objective lines to a position in which it was more or less on the Albert–Bapaume Road itself. In fact, it was probably positioned not far from Captain Thurnhill's gun. This platoon had managed to eject a German patrol from some old gun pits and maintained their situation because they were to the left and ahead of the first fall of the artillery barrage and therefore missed by it. But this unscheduled advance had mixed results. Certainly the fire from this platoon helped protect the flank of the 2nd Battalion as they rushed the Gibraltar strongpoint at the south-west end of the Albert–Bapaume Road. But their situation was too far forward of the line and completely unsupported on either flank. They had to be withdrawn when the third barrage hit their position. Oddly, at the time this was attributed to the heavy barrage falling short rather than the platoon being well ahead of their designated position, but there is little doubt they were positioned under the line of the third lift of the artillery barrage. The record does not show which company this platoon came from, or under whose authority they advanced to where they did. Most likely, as in the case of Captain Thurnhill, it was individual initiative that led to this group departing from the plan and acting alone.

But multiple acts of individual initiative without reference to the battle plan were not necessarily what was required. This was a set-piece attack with a strict timetable and detailed list of tasks to be achieved. It was to be made by large numbers of men working in lines in depth, and as such required group coordination. As previously

9   This event was widely reported – not a single negative comment on it was found.

mentioned, the first waves of attacking troops on the left of the divisional frontage were formed by companies of the 2nd Battalion which were leapfrogged through by the 4th Battalion, and from the 1st Battalion which were leapfrogged through by the 3rd. It would appear from messages that an informal arrangement was in place across the division whereby overall command of a sector was retained by the officer commanding the first battalion in the attack. So, for example, Lieutenant-Colonel Arthur Borlase Stevens, the officer commanding the 2nd Battalion at the far left of the divisional line, was to retain command of his sector even as the lines from his battalion had completed their attacks and companies from Lieutenant-Colonel Iven Giffard Mackay's 4th Battalion had moved through and were assaulting the third objective. But, just as the two brigades functioned in slightly different ways, so did the battalions in the two different sectors of the 1st Brigade's area of operations. And, informal arrangement or otherwise, Stevens did not work in conjunction with Mackay at all. In fact he did not seem even to consult with him in the field, but by-passed the need to deal with 4th Battalion headquarters altogether by requesting Brigade Headquarters to issue orders to Mackay on his behalf. So, for example, at 2.45am Stevens sent a request to 1st Brigade headquarters, saying, "to enable this operation to be successful can a company of 4th B[attalio]n be placed in between the 2nd and 3rd B[attalio]ns".[10] This worked both ways, because by the next day Stevens was complaining to Brigade headquarters that "nothing further can be obtained nor has any attempt been made to keep in touch with me",[11] which would indicate that there was little communication between his headquarters and others. Stevens gradually lost control of the situation through a lack of communication keeping him in close cooperation with his reserve formations.

Fortunately this sector, being at the extreme left of the 1st Australian Division's line, faced the least determined German defences. The main German line of defence at Pozières was the OG Lines; the village was itself merely an outpost to that main line. Although the 2nd and 4th Battalions had had to deal with the Gibraltar strongpoint in their sector, a German position that had caused many casualties in previous attacks on Pozières, this was the extreme end of the advanced fortifications of the German second line of defence, and the most likely to be evacuated by them in the case of a determined assault. Both commanders in this sector kept what control of their battalion they could, and enough cohesion was maintained in the attack which, when combined with a very strong advance on their right flank, ensured that this operation did not disintegrate in the confusion of battle and infighting of command.

On the right flank of 1st Brigade's sector the situation was completely different, and demonstrates how well the informal command arrangement could work. The

10   AWM: AWM 26/53/21: Stevens to 1st Bde, 23 July 1916, 2.45am and 6.47pm, Operations file Somme 1916, 1st Infantry Brigade.
11   AWM: AWM 26/53/21: Stevens to 1st Bde, 24 July 1916, 1.50am, Operations file Somme 1916, 1st Infantry Brigade.

Lieutenant-Colonel
Iven Giffard Mackay,
photographed as a captain in
1915. At Pozières Mackay
was in command of the
4th Battalion, and did not
cooperate with the other
battalion in his sector, the 2nd
Battalion, on the far right of
the operation on 23 July 1916.
(AWM DA13052)

A signed portrait of Lieutenant-
Colonel Arthur Borlase Stevens, officer
commanding the 2nd Battalion. He
and Lieutenant-Colonel Iven Mackay
did not cooperate well in their shared
sector at Pozières, leading to a smaller
advance than that experienced by
the other battalions in their brigade.
(AWM P05182.068)

Lieutenant-Colonel James
Heane, in command of the 1st
Battalion in 1915, standing
on the steps of 2nd Brigade
Headquarters in 1918.
(AWM E02266)

commanders in question were Lieutenant-Colonel James Heane in command of the 1st Battalion (and therefore the first two lines of attack and, informally, the sector), and Lieutenant-Colonel Owen Glendower Howell-Price commanding the 3rd Battalion, which would follow with the third and possibly fourth lines. These two commanders worked closely together, even sharing headquarters. Early in the battle the 1st Battalion was having problems receiving information as to troop locations. Heane took control of the situation by leaving headquarters together with a group of bombers, staff and signallers to go to the front line and find out the where his men were and what the state of the line was for himself. He left the 3rd Battalion commander, Howell-Price, at battalion headquarters with the remainder of his and Howell-Price's staff to exercise command over the sector. Heane found Lieutenant Richard Stewart Burstal in the German first line and sent him to the second and third lines to ascertain information about their situation and report back. Burstal complied and reported success in each line. On Heane's return to headquarters, Howell-Price handed back overall command. As a battalion commander Heane could be expected to use his headquarters as a central location, staying there to receive messages and issue orders. Heane's actions in going forward show individual initiative – but unlike that of Thurnhill and the unknown platoon of the 2nd Battalion, this initiative had the purpose of maintaining structure and cohesion of the fighting unit in order to advance the line.

In this sector strict attention was paid to structure in other ways as well, which is particularly evident in the assault by the 3rd Battalion. Before attacking the third objective, C and D Companies of the 3rd Battalion under Howell-Price paused about 100 yards short of it to form up into their two waves – the third and the fourth of the operation – and ensure that they were working in the right direction. Once the objective was taken, company commanders prioritised the creation of communication lines to the right and left, sending patrols forward to obtain information, and digging a communication trench to maintain contact with the rear. In the end the fourth wave (comprising reinforcements from the second half of the 3rd Battalion) did not have to advance at all as every objective was taken without complication. This meant that this final wave of infantry remained in its jumping-off position instead of moving through the first two objectives held by the 1st Battalion. Heane as sector commander again prioritised structure by reorganising the battlefield once all objectives had been taken. This meant moving the remainder of the 3rd Battalion forward while at the same time

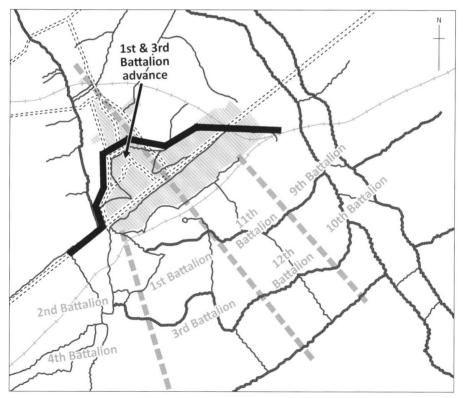

5 Situation at daybreak, 23 July 1916.

moving parts of the 1st Battalion back to eliminate this split and consolidate command structures in the field. Heane used initiative to create a strong web of communication and to confirm the command structure in his sector, making it clear to all what was expected and how communication was to be maintained. Unlike Stevens, he was able to consolidate his position as sector commander, establish firm control and make effective manoeuvres as needed on the battlefield while creating an effective working relationship with Howell-Price. It is telling to note that while the least resistance was met in the sector on the far left, that of the 2nd and 4th Battalions, the greatest gains were made in the right of 1st Brigade's sector, where Heane and Howell-Price of the 1st and 3rd Battalions paid strict attention to structure and cooperation.

By the end of the night, the 1st Brigade had taken all objectives and had pushed some patrols north of the Albert–Bapaume Road. With daylight to aid observation, messages were received that a German retreat was in evidence. A straightforward assault plan combined with a general adherence to structure meant that the 1st Brigade was organised enough to occupy the north side of the Albert–Bapaume Road when the opportunity presented itself. The advanced positions made it a straightforward matter to infiltrate the rest of the village, which was finally taken in its entirety within three days. The work of consolidation was carried out well, with trenches made habitable and deep enough to protect infantry from the firestorm of shellfire which continued unabated. Operations in the 1st Infantry Brigade's sector can be considered a complete success.

But while the attack by 1st Brigade was a success, but it was not matched on either flank. The 48th British Division on the left flank had placed the 5th Battalion Warwickshire Regiment of the 143rd Brigade on the boundary with the 1st Australian Division. This battalion had been given the task of keeping in touch with the Anzac troops "wherever possible".[12] It did not prove possible at all. Their attack approached the village from the west and, despite the belief of the 2nd Australian Battalion that they had joined up on both flanks within half an hour of zero hour – one flank of which must have been with the English – they had not. The Warwicks attacked on several occasions, sometimes using bombing parties or infantry armed with Stokes trench mortars; on two occasions with artillery cooperation, but they were held up by a German strongpoint and failed to join up with the Anzac line.[13] As a result the Australian left flank was 'in the air', the common term for being unconnected with flank units. The Australians were prevented from linking with the 5th Warwicks by strong fire from a trench running down the western side of the village and the strongpoint that the Warwicks had been unable to capture. While not a problem for the immediate situation, this strongpoint would prove to be a significant barrier to linking up in the future, as it held at least three machine guns and had approximately 300

12   TNA: WO 95/2755: Message BM.475, 23 July 1916, 1/5 Bn Royal Warwickshire Regiment War Diary.
13   TNA: WO 95/2755: 23 July 1916 1/5 Bn Royal Warwickshire Regiment War Diary.

men nearby, many of them in the western trench, to reinforce it. It should be noted, however, that any failure to advance on behalf of the Warwicks, had little, if any, impact on the capture of Pozières village.

On 1st Brigade's right flank the 3rd Brigade had had a much more difficult task. To start with, being situated at the furthest point from the entry to the battlefield, the men of the 3rd Brigade had to negotiate as much as a mile of pitted, destroyed ground before making the left turn to take their positions. This brigade was attacking the village in the same direction as the 1st Brigade, from the south-east to the north-west, but their advance was flanked by the main trenches in the German second line – the OG Lines. Here German strong posts had been constructed at the junction of the OG Lines and Sunken Road Trench, a British trench that lay mid-way between Black Watch Alley and the first objective, Pozières Trench. These strong posts had so far proven impervious to attack. Furthermore, the Germans put up a spirited defence of these lines, which was very different to their willingness to retreat in the face of the 1st Brigade attack at the far end of the outpost village. It was into this battlefield of well-established defences and determined opposition that Sinclair-Maclagan sent his Brigade with its extremely complicated plan of attack.

As previously stated, the main threat to the success of operations in this area was the German second line of defence – the OG Lines. These trenches were 3rd Brigade's to deal with, and they did not give them anything like the attention they deserved prior to the main assault. The first attempt to secure the OG Lines came on the night of 21 July, when they were attacked by just two raiding parties of the 9th Battalion. Each party consisted of 51 men and an officer, one group being assigned to OG1 and the other to OG2. Their aim was to capture the OG Lines to a point near the tramline. To get there each party would have to attack two heavily defended German strongpoints. In order to accomplish this formidable task each party of the 9th Battalion received a total of 14 mortar rounds and a light artillery barrage that failed to eventuate. And although they had only 40 yards to cover before reaching the enemy trenches, they were in full moonlight and under enemy shrapnel fire. Once in the enemy lines, both parties were met with a strong resistance from grenades, and their reserves were prevented from providing support by heavy machine-gun fire. Unsurprisingly, the raids failed with heavy casualties.

Yet, despite the detrimental effect this strongly-held pair of German trenches had just demonstrated they could have on an advance at Pozières, no further operation was conducted against them in the lead up to the main attack on the village. And while the preliminary assault on the OG Lines was a dismal failure, additional plans to take this position did not seem to recognise the serious threat the OG Lines posed at all. No significant additional fire- or man-power was assigned to their capture, and minimal emphasis was placed on their capture in orders. Sinclair-Maclagan ordered the 9th Battalion to designate just one company – no more than 250 men – from their first infantry wave for the major divisional attack to enter the OG Lines and ensure their capture. One company of the 10th Battalion would serve as a reserve to this force. They were given no extra help in the form of a special artillery barrage or mortar support, but were simply to enter the OG Lines and roll them up as a part of the main assault. Surely the conclusion must be that divisional and brigade command at least, if not Gough and Reserve Army staff, took the ostrich approach to this formidable obstacle. But hiding their heads in the sand by not providing an appropriate force to attack the OG Lines did not in any way lessen the threat from these strong German defences.

The 11th Battalion on the left and the 9th on the right provided the first and second waves of the attack of the 3rd Brigade. Both battalions formed up carefully in their waves and lines in the half hour before the artillery barrage began. But despite this initial attention to structure, the battlefield became seriously disorganised shortly after the first lift of the barrage. On the left of the sector, furthest from the OG Lines and where 3rd Brigade saw the most success, the 11th Battalion's first wave failed to establish a line on the first objective. Instead of consolidating their new position, the majority of men in the first wave rushed on to the second objective and into their own artillery barrage. Ill-disciplined groups of soldiers became further disorganised as they went after parties of Germans, chasing them through what was left of the village. While officers managed to pull some of them back to start establishing a defensive line, the second line of troops leapfrogging through them could not find their objective in the confusion and, as with the first wave, rushed into their own barrage, which was now falling on the south side of the Albert–Bapaume Road. The second objective corresponded to the back of the enclosures along the south side of the road and was almost impossible to locate among the pitted and shelled ground. When officers arrived with the third and fourth waves, they could not identify their location, or the trench line that supposedly ran along the back of the enclosed yards of the village. Lieutenant Walter Rewi Hallahan reported the best he could do was ensure "[a] line is being formed on the N[orth] E[ast] side of the wood. There was no line of trenches here at all".[14] At 1am 11th Battalion Headquarters reported:

> … a general confusion of units looking for [the second objective] trench. Lieutenant Rogerson sent back word he is trying to straighten out [the] tangle and entrench [the] northern side of [the] wood.[15]

Edward Rogerson was later recommended for decoration for his "untiring … efforts to consolidate positions as they were captured". During the process he was buried by shell bursts twice but continued on in his work until he was "rendered insensible by the burst of a very high explosive shell".[16] He was so badly shellshocked that he was

---

14 AWM: AWM 26/55/1: Report from Hallahan contained within Message from Hemingway (11th Bn) to 3rd Bde. 23 July 1916, 4.25am, Operations File Somme 1916, 3rd Infantry Brigade.

15 AWM: AWM 26/55/1: 11th Bn to 3rd Bde, 23 July 1916, 1.00am, Operations File Somme 1916, 3rd Infantry Brigade.

16 AWM: AWM 28/1/6: Recommendation File for Honours and Awards: 1st Australian Division.

eventually repatriated to Australia with severe neurasthenia, ending his war. Walter Hallahan was killed in 1918.

Rogerson's experience was quite typical for the 11th Battalion's company commanders and junior officers. Although in places the first and even second objectives were reported taken, a flurry of messages sent between 1.30 and 1.45am indicate a very high rate of officer casualties and a desperate need for reinforcement. At 1.30am 2/Lieutenant Reginald Hemingway sent a report to say "Campbell … is wounded. Wants reinforcements from 12th Battalion."[17] Ten minutes later he added, "Milner reports first line taken. He is wounded. Urge 12th Battalion be sent forward. Two Company commanders out of action."[18] At 1.45am another message came from the Lieutenant Elliott of D Company: "Captain Wathers and [my]self wounded. Former needs immediate attention."[19] By 2am Hemingway could only report to 3rd Brigade headquarters "regret nearly all my officers casualties."[20] Captain Leone Sextus Tollemache at 3rd Brigade headquarters was forced to request the nucleus of 11th Battalion officers left behind with 1st Division to be sent forward to make up for the losses. In the meantime, without officers to sort out the mess, units became badly muddled together. The third wave, comprising A and D companies of the 12th Battalion, left for the third objective around 2am, leaving B and C companies as a further reserve for this sector. Once they reached the front the officer commanding D Company, Captain Alan Vowles, found the line to be about 50 to 150 yards to the south of the road. Vowles found that the right flank, which should have been protected by the advance of the 9th and 10th Battalions, was completely in the air, and had to swing his company around to form a defensive flank facing the OG Lines. The reserve force of B and C Companies were committed to the battle shortly before 3am to try to reinforce this tenuous line. But while the units in the field were highly disorganised, and panicky messages were being sent back for reinforcements, some organisation had taken place and a continuous, if short, line was being held.

What had happened to the right of Vowles? This sector, the far right of the operation, was the one with the most potential setbacks at the outset of the assault. Here the 9th Battalion formed the first two waves of the attack, and the 10th Battalion the third and fourth. Troops attacking the line here had to travel the farthest up Black Watch Alley to reach their jumping-off point and had the OG Lines menacing their attack from the right. The 9th and 10th Battalions operating in this sector were never sure of their location, both on entering the battlefield and when attacking their

17   AWM: AWM: 26/55/1: Hemingway (11th Bn) to 3rd Bde, 23 July 1916, 1.30am, Operations File Somme 1916, 3rd Infantry Brigade.
18   AWM: AWM: 26/55/1: Hemingway (11th Bn) to 3rd Bde, 23 July 1916, 1.40am, Operations File Somme 1916, 3rd Infantry Brigade.
19   AWM: AWM: 26/55/1: Elliott, (OC D Coy 11th Bn) to OC 11th Bn, 23 July, 1.45am, Operations File Somme 1916, 3rd Infantry Brigade.
20   AWM: AWM: 26/55/1: Hemingway (11th Bn) to 3rd Bde, 23 July 1916, 2.00am, Operations File Somme 1916, 3rd Infantry Brigade.

objectives. Not only were Black Watch Alley and Pozières Trench severely knocked about by shellfire, OG2 had been so damaged that the party of the 9th Battalion charged with its capture could not identify it at all and became lost in the darkness. A further two parties were sent out and also failed to locate the trench. The party attacking OG1 had better success and were able to take the first German strongpoint when the barrage lifted, but their support was running late. The 10th Battalion group had been held up by a heavy barrage of gas and high explosive shells from the German artillery, which had made the arduous journey to their position even worse, and caused them to be over an hour late. The situation in OG1 by no means secure, A Company under Lieutenant William Francis James McCann of the 10th Battalion was immediately sent forward to help. McCann pushed on to within a few yards of the major strongpoint at the junction of OG1 and Pozières Trench, but was unable to advance further. Despite a party under command of Lieutenant Arthur Seaforth Blackburn coming to support this attack, and even a Victoria Cross awarded to Blackburn for his gallantry in this position, the post remained untaken. It would take another three days and a major advance through the village before the OG Lines were clear to the Albert–Bapaume Road.

Elsewhere in the 9th and 10th Battalion's sector, in the gap between the rest of the Brigade operating on the left and the small parties fruitlessly attacking the OG Lines on the right, there was a potential catastrophe pending. The rest of the 9th Battalion, attacking the objective lines in front of the village, had became disorganised quickly – the second wave could not even form up correctly and become jumbled before reaching the starting line – and suffered a high number of officer casualties. It was clear to Lieutenant-Colonel Stephen Harricks Roberts, the officer commanding the 11th Battalion that there was a serious problem on his right flank; at 4am his staff sent a message to 3rd Brigade to say:

> Am not in touch with 9th [Battalion] and can find out nothing about them. Am afraid something wrong there. Have you any word. Am concerned about there being no troops in this line.[21]

Darkness had caused a problem and the companies became disoriented, apparently veering away to the left. It would appear that most of the 9th Battalion ended up somewhere behind the 11th Battalion, leaving the right flank of the 11th and the left flank of the assault on the OG Lines dangerously without support. The 9th Battalion, through becoming lost and disorganised, had ceased to be an effective fighting unit within hours of the start of battle. By 4.30am all reserve troops immediately designated for the attack were committed to the battle, and a battalion of the 2nd Brigade (the 7th) had to be called up to act as reserve. The attack on Pozières is usually discussed in

---

21   AWM: AWM 26/55/1: Hemingway (11th Bn) to AZC 3rd Brigade, 23 July 1916, 4.00am, Operations File Somme 1916, 3rd Infantry Brigade.

terms of success, but on the right flank there was a huge drain on resources and still a large gap in the line within hours of the beginning of the operation, and success was far from guaranteed.

It was individual action that saved the enormous problems on this flank from causing the attack to break down completely, but not necessarily the sort of individual gallantry displayed by the Victoria Cross-winning Blackburn, or indeed the individual initiative shown by Captain Thurnhill. While the 9th Battalion was missing in action, the nucleus of officers from the 11th Battalion sent forward to replace officer casualties reached the front line. Several members of this group took it upon themselves to organise the line and establish firm communications with their headquarters in the rear. Captain Louis Leon Le Nay, the 11th Battalion Lewis gun officer, worked together with Lieutenant Sydney Trevorrow Forbes and Captain Walter Cheyne Belford to establish a line about half a mile in front of their original position. Forbes organised the line while Le Nay and Belford put in a strong post in front of it. Le Nay then sent a number of detailed situation reports which give as much information as he had to hand as to troop locations, and conducted several reconnaissance patrols.

Captain Ferdinand George Medcalf was another, and in fact became arguably the most important individual on the 3rd Brigade's front. He had been called in shortly before the attack went ahead to take over after the death of another officer in Black Watch Alley early in the bombardment. He had been in charge of a line of troops designated to take the first objective, but rather than rushing forward to the second objective as so many men of this line did, he reported that at 1.10am he was "holding and digging in first objective ... don't know anything of second or third objective."[22] After this line was established, he had word of a group of about 400 men of various battalions establishing a weak line further forward, and took it upon himself to go to it and take command. Once there, he reported, he "made a personal reconnaissance of the country to the north of the road and village", sending back a sketch of the land around him, and an indication that he intended to stay there and carry on the work of consolidation.[23] Medcalf became the primary conduit of messages into and out of the field in this sector for some considerable time after 5am on the 23rd. Roberts, commanding the 11th Battalion, even entrusted him with responsibility of acting on behalf of himself or Sinclair-Maclagan, sending messages such as the following sent at 5am:

> Orders have been given for 12th Battalion which are forwarded [they] are to push on and take their objective and consolidate it. Give them orders accordingly and say such are from the Brigadier ... Good luck. Thanks for your work.[24]

22   AWM: AWM 26/55/1: Medcalf to OC 11th Bn, 23 July 1916, 1.10am, Operations File Somme 1916, 3rd Infantry Brigade.
23   AWM: AWM 26/55/1: Message from Medcalf (top part of message containing address torn away), 23 July 1916, 4.45am, Operations File Somme 1916, 3rd Infantry Brigade.
24   AWM: AWM 26/55/1: Roberts (OC 11th Bn) to Medcalf, 23 July 1916, 5.00am, Operations File Somme 1916, 3rd Infantry Brigade.

Captain Ferdinand George Medcalf, 11th Battalion, became the primary conduit of messages into and out of the 3rd Brigade's sector at Pozières, 23 July 1916. (Photograph courtesy of the Army Museum of Western Australia)

Captain Louis Leon Le Nay, Lewis gun officer of the 11th Battalion, who, with just four or five officers and a few men established a shaky line between the solid gains in Pozières village on the left and the OG Lines on the right at Pozières, 23 July 1916. He was killed in action at Lihons on 10 August 1918. (AWM E01778, detail)

Messages for individuals were passed via Medcalf as the most reliable means of communication, and he in turn regularly supplied headquarters with full situation reports, often written from reconnaissance patrols he personally made into no man's land.[25] In this way one man among thousands could almost single-handedly be responsible for turning the tide of the battle.

Other men were also trying to consolidate positions at various points in or near the objectives. What made the actions of Medcalf, Forbes, Belford and Le Nay different was that they prioritised communication with their headquarters and their flanks. They established as firm a picture of the situation as possible and kept their headquarters updated, which put them into an ideal position to effect change when needed. Le Nay and Medcalf were given the responsibility between them, as the two men best apprised of the situation, to decide among themselves how machine guns were to be used in various strongpoints constructed in and near their positions.[26] Medcalf was later awarded the Military Cross for his gallant action in protecting defensive works from a German raiding party and repairing his trench. More importantly, he received the second highest gallantry award, the Distinguished Service Order, for his action at Pozières. General Birdwood later wrote to Medcalf, saying:

> This is a line to congratulate you most heartily upon the DSO which you have so thoroughly well-deserved for your conspicuous gallantry and devotion to duty when leading your company on the enemy's trenches before Pozières.

Not only had Medcalf taken it upon himself to reorganise a precarious position on the right, but he had attacked and put out of action a German machine gun crew. "Later on," Birdwood added in his congratulatory message:

> You were, I know, placed in charge of the firing line of the battalion, when you showed resource, and were untiring in your efforts to make good and hold the ground which you had taken, and I know, too, that your coolness under that heavy shelling inspired all the men with the greatest confidence.[27]

It was this, more than his acts of personal bravery, that had the biggest impact on the battle in that it enabled the restructuring of a battlefield that had become highly and dangerously disorganised. Le Nay, too, was recommended for a Military Cross, and although he was not awarded one, the citation, which was for "rendering valuable assistance in reorganising and placing detached parties and machine guns in position" and for being "untiring in his efforts to obtain information of the enemy and

25   AWM: AWM 28/1/5 Pt. 3: Recommendation File for Honours and Awards, 1st Australian Division.

26   AWM: AWM 26/55/1: Le Nay to Medcalf, 23 July 1916, 6.10pm, Operations File Somme 1916, 3rd Infantry Brigade.

27   'Captain F.G. Medcalf, D.S.O.', *The Daily News*, 13 November 1916, p.7.

submit[ting] valuable reports" demonstrates at least some recognition of the valuable work he did that day.[28]

The situation at day break on 23 July was not at all even across the front. The 1st Brigade had achieved its objectives and was in a good position to attack the rest of the village which lay to the north of the Albert–Bapaume Road. The 3rd Brigade, however, was still conducting small-scale attacks on the OG Lines, and had an extended gap in its line between these attacks and the 11th Battalion in the centre. As the morning brightened into day, the 1st Brigade spent time consolidating gains and pushing the line forward where possible, while the 3rd Brigade worked on closing the gap by extending the line from the 11th Battalion's stronger position towards the OG Lines. Consolidation work continued throughout the day of 23 July and the work of clearing Germans out of cellars was being carried out using phosphorus bombs. At all times the line was subjected to a German bombardment and work was carried out under heavy shellfire, but by 3.45pm on the 23rd all British and Australian artillery had stopped firing on the village of Pozières to allow the infantry to enter. This was a decision made by Reserve Army, which coordinated the infantry advance on the village with the lifting of the standing barrage. The troops to take the village were from the 8th Battalion, acting as a reserve for 1st Brigade. They attacked from the far left of the divisional line, largely as a result of the success in this position. The village of Pozières was now secured.

Follow-up operations – 25 July 1916

From this point the remaining objective was to secure the northern and western edges of the village and establish a perimeter. This, it was decided, was to involve another division-wide attack under cover of a hastily-arranged artillery barrage just forty eight hours after the initial attack on the village of Pozières. However, there were significant problems communicating these orders from division to brigade. A series of conferences between commanders at various levels were convened to discuss plans; but as to when and between whom these conferences were held is not clear. According to the 4th Battalion war diary, commanding officers were called to a conference at 1st Brigade Headquarters at 10pm on the night of 24 July to discuss plans to effect these orders, without formally issuing them.[29] Bean claims that the written order for this attack fixing the date for 26 July arrived during this meeting.[30] But the 8th Battalion's account records that at 8.20pm on the night of 24 July the commanding officer attending a meeting at brigade headquarters where battalion commanders "were given a general idea of operations to be carried out at 0320 the next morning."[31] The result, however, was that the 1st

28   AWM: AWM 28/1/5 Pt. 3: Recommendation File for Honours and Awards, 1st Australian Division.
29   AWM: AWM 4/23/21/17: 24 July 1916, 4th Battalion War Diary.
30   Bean, *Official History, Vol. III*, p. 571.
31   AWM: AWM 4/23/25/19: 24 July 1916, 8th Battalion War Diary.

Brigade commander, Smyth, was under the impression that the attack was to go ahead in the pre-dawn hours of the 26th, when in fact it was intended to go ahead in the early hours of the 25th. Ultimately the problem lay with the original divisional order, which contained the wrong date,[32] and a message to correct the problem that went astray. Sinclair-Maclagan messaged Smyth at 11.45pm on 24 July to confirm "Div[isional] Order No. 37 said operation 26th [of this month] but this was a mistake and was corrected to 25th in later message"– just hours before the assault was to begin.[33] This put Smyth on the back foot and a rush was on to recall the battalion commanders to brigade headquarters. The commanders of the 2nd and 3rd Battalions could not be found, and so the meeting was between the commanders of the 1st, 4th and 8th Battalions. The meeting was not concluded until 1.30am. The situation was a shambles. One half of the planned assault was almost completely unprepared – and it was the half of the line that had been the most organised, 1st Brigade's sector. Commanders of the 3rd Brigade's sector on the right, although aware of the attack, were still very poorly organised, and were equally hard pressed to effect preparations for the assault.

Despite being seriously handicapped by such late notice, it was the sector with prior organisation that saved the renewed operation. Because this sector's lines of communication were already established and working, and the front was well-manned and well-connected, the 1st Brigade's command structure could more efficiently send orders and effect organisation with little notice. In in fact the bulk of the village was taken by attackers from this side of the line moving northwards and then to the east to secure the right flank and make good the right side of the village up to the OG Lines. Once again, however, the 3rd Brigade struggled to advance in an assault on the right of the Australian line. They, too, had suffered from delays in issuing orders, but at a lower level. While Sinclair-Maclagan had reasonable notice of the time the attack was to go ahead – at least better than he could have had – he apparently lacked the ability to communicate that information to his battalion commanders in the field in anything like a timely fashion. Visual signalling was in use for only the most basic messages, and a runner took a minimum of an hour to get to battalion headquarters in the line. So the 11th Battalion did not receive notification of the time of the attack until forty minutes *after* the protective barrage had begun and the operation ostensibly gone ahead. Roberts later reported to 3rd Brigade headquarters:

> … time to attack received forty minutes after time – I can't get into touch with my units under thirty minutes. I did my very best but could not carry out the orders, so far as I can see no one but artillery had a chance.[34]

32   AWM: AWM 4/1/42/18 Pt. 2: '1st Australian Division Order No. 37', 24 July 1916, 1st Australian Division General Staff War Diary.
33   AWM: AWM 26/54/12: Sinclair-Maclagan (OC 3rd Bde) to 1st Bde, 24 July 1916, 11.45pm, Operations File Somme 1916, 3rd Infantry Brigade.
34   AWM: AWM: 26/55/1: Roberts (OC 11th Bn) to 3rd Bde, 25 July 1916 (untimed), Operations File Somme 1916, 3rd Infantry Brigade.

Illustration drawn by Major-General Nevill Smyth depicting a runner who had died
on the Albert–Bapaume Road, holding aloft his message so that it would reach its
destination. The picture accompanied a report on the event in the 2nd Battalion's war diary.
(AWM 4/23/19/15)

The assault on the far right was to be carried out by the 5th Battalion and two companies of the 7th Battalion, under the protection of the same artillery barrage. Most of the 7th Battalion did not arrive to their position until 2.20am – twenty minutes after the attack was supposed to have started. Traffic policing caused significant problems for 7th Battalion's companies – the 5th Battalion began filing out early and blocked the 7th from moving in their allotted time period. They could not begin to move until ten minutes after the assault was supposed to begin, and as a result they had to rush into the battle without forming up in assembly positions or giving definite directions for the attack. These two companies quickly became lost and disorganised, and took no further part in the assault. The 5th Battalion, having bought some extra time by gaining the advantage on the roads, arrived in better time and were able to make their way into what was now a lightly defended position in OG1. But too many men who had been designated for consolidating this objective excitedly rushed on to attack OG2, and the battalion became disorganised. In the end a German withdrawal left the Australian troops in control of the position in OG1, but with a thinly held line of no more than 130 men.

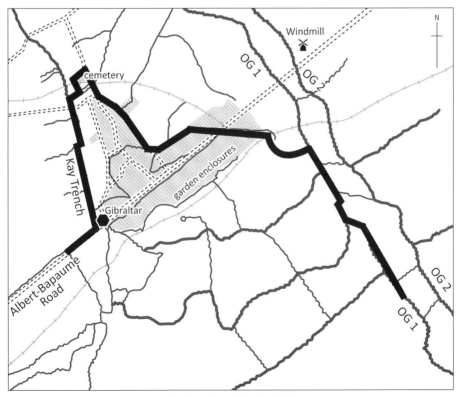

6   Front line, 25 July 1916.

The Battle of Pozières resulted in the capture of a tactically valuable village which offered an improved range of vision for British artillery observers, and a good jumping-off point for further attacks. But, contrary to what a higher-level examination of this battle can demonstrate, the capture of the village was not a straightforward matter of one unified division attacking and capturing all objectives. There were a number of significant problems during the battle both caused by and dealt with at lower levels of command that caused the attack to seriously falter and resulted in an uneven, gap-ridden line. Despite being 'only' a divisional attack, both preparation and execution of the operation were incredibly complicated, and even simple traffic control and movement of units in and out of the field could cause significant problems. Communication problems became apparent from as early as 1.30am on 23 July, an hour into the first operation. While telephone lines between brigades and artillery batteries remained intact, almost all lines forward of this level of command, that is, to battalion headquarters, liaison officers and forward observation officers, were severed and heavy shellfire meant that any repairs were short lived. Despite the best efforts of signallers to continue to repair the wire, all stocks of telephone wire had run out by 8.22am without consistent communications ever having been established. Divisional Headquarters was advised by a visual station during the night which could not function during the day, and struggled to handle complicated situation reports. Shellfire, smoke and haze also interfered with lamp signalling, and in fact, some success with pigeons notwithstanding, the only truly reliable means of communication proved to be runners. Messages were frequently sent in duplicate by separate runners as the casualty rate among these men was extremely high. There were a number of examples of runners arriving only to succumb to wounds received on the way, and others arrived with addenda to their messages asking that they might receive a meal or rest as they had made the dangerous journey a number of times and were on the point of exhaustion. Commanding officers forward in the field did not always prioritise communication with their commanding officers and higher command continually struggled for a picture of what was happening. Some lag was to be expected, but as communication was almost always inconsistent and unreliable, it was more difficult than it needed to be.

But there was another way to control the battlefield, and that was reliance on structure and planning. The sector with the most success, the left, made it a priority to keep structure as closely as possible, and follow the orders given. So in this sector there seems to be a much lower incidence of men rushing on to an objective beyond the one they were given. Commanders on the left, too, gave a high priority to maintaining their troop structure in the field and establishing a strong, consolidated line wherever possible. Here battalions were able to attack at relatively short notice because of established infantry lines, with well-established communication routes. They were aware of where they were, and where they should be going. That is not to say that they were not somewhat muddled – not every individual in this sector remained with his company – but company commanders found company-sized groups of men and made them a cohesive unit in order to carry out their orders. It should be remembered that the left of the line was attacking lightly held trenches and had the easiest approach to their sector, and so arrived in a lesser state of exhaustion. This may have made it easier to maintain these structures and links, but at all times they also demonstrated a concern for actively maintaining them that it helped their effort immeasurably.

It is in the matter of structure that individuals could make the most difference to the conduct of the battle overall. While Arthur Blackburn won a Victoria Cross and many other medals were won that day for very brave deeds, none was more important than the awards won by Ferdinand Medcalf. He is an excellent example of the impact of an individual who prioritised communication and structure could have on the conduct of the battle. Without him and the unit of men he collected and organised, the right sector of the battlefield would have been in worse disarray than it was, and higher command would have lost one of their major conduits of information, often their only source of information, into and out of the battlefield. The first move in the Battle of Pozières Ridge demonstrates just how critical attention to structure and communication was in battles in 1916.

The assault on the village of Pozières on 23 July was secondary to what had become the main thrust of the Somme Offensive, which was being conducted by Fourth Army to the south and east. The attack did not directly contend with the main defences on the Pozières Ridge, but rather took a swipe out of them by having its main thrust virtually parallel to these primary German lines of defence. Despite this, the village of Pozières was a clearly and oft-stated objective of the British Army, and its capture was somewhat of a triumph for Gough and Reserve Army. It had been conducted under Haig's policy of 'keeping the enemy occupied' in the north while the main attack was going on to the south. With this objective in mind, the capture of the village was deemed to have been successful – not only did it gain "a considerable amount of ground," it also "fulfilled its role of holding the enemy to his positions, and by causing him to anticipate an attack has prevented him from withdrawing troops or guns for action against the Fourth Army."[35] The foundation for the ongoing use of the 1st Anzac Corps in operations in this sector had been laid.

35   AWM: AWM 26/43/37: 'Summary of Operations of Reserve Army up to 6pm on 28th July, 1916,' 29 July 1916, Operations file Somme 1916, Reserve Army Summaries of Operations.

2

"Met with very heavy machine gun fire":
Gordon Legge, the 2nd Australian Division and the OG Lines

Now that the village of Pozières was secure, the British General Staff began to toy with the idea of expanding operations from the Thiepval-Ginchy-Morval line, which mostly fell within Fourth Army's sector of operations. Investigations began for an extension of the general assault to the north. On 30 July the Reserve Army was ordered to "make all necessary preparations for delivering an attack on the front River Ancre–Serre" about the middle of August.[1] This represented a significant departure from the previous position of the General Staff. Before now any action by Reserve Army came second to the main assault conducted by Fourth Army. But from the end of July the attacks on this front began to be seen as an end in themselves, and an important step in this proposed northwards extension of the area of operations on the Somme. The extended plan required on II Corps and 1st Anzac Corps to break through the OG Lines before cutting off the German garrison at Thiepval by circling it and attacking from the north. Both these Corps were in Reserve Army, and, given the importance of this action to future plans, they now found themselves with a central role. Gough's Army no longer had to fit in with action conducted by Fourth Army, but was preparing to take on an increasingly important and autonomous part in the future projections of the British General Staff.

In the end this broad extension of the line to the north was not to eventuate for some months. However, it did leave the fighting in the Pozières-Mouquet Farm-Thiepval area with a much greater degree of importance than it had had when it was simply "keeping the enemy fully occupied" north of Contalmaison.[2] Reserve Army was no longer acting as an adjunct to action by the Fourth Army, but had its own, independent objectives. In fact, Reserve Army's front had become so important that the General Staff allocated half of all future consignments of rifle grenades, light

---

1 TNA: WO 158/333: OAD 87, Kiggell to Reserve and Third Armies, 30th July 1916, Scheme "D".
2 TNA: WO 158/21: Haig, to Robertson, 8 July 1916, War Office Correspondence.

signals, flares and other armaments to be divided equally between Fourth and Reserve Armies, even though Fourth Army held at least twice the length of line than that held by Reserve Army. Although not able to expand into the broad-fronted assault envisaged by optimists in the highest levels of command, Reserve Army's offensive did gradually expand to the left, away from the boundary with Fourth Army. The focus of operations moved away from 1st Anzac Corps' sector to their left where II Corps had three divisions in the front line.

As a part of this shift, Gough stated that his new intention was "that the centre and left [of II Corps] shall both be brought forward as the right [division of the corps] advances."[3] This meant that the main thrust of this new plan would be conducted by II Corps' 12th Division, holding the line to 1st Anzac Corps' immediate left. Their task would be to work their way "methodically northwards", past Mouquet Farm, to a point directly north of Thiepval, and then circle back around to their left to assault that village from the east and north. Their advance would pull both 1st Anzac Corps on their right, and the other divisions of II Corps on their left "steadily forward" with them.[4] The Australian position on the Somme was no longer primarily in support of Fourth Army, but increasingly in support of the 12th Division.

It is important to note that this is simply a change in aspiration – it did not look very different in terms of action on the ground. The 12th Division struggled to advance as much as 1st Anzac Corps did, and did not come close to encircling Thiepval or attacking it from the rear. But even while 1st Anzac Corps was supposed to cooperate more with its left flank from early August, the danger posed by the OG Lines and Munster Alley to their right claimed their attention for some time. Nevertheless, it is equally important to note the small disconnect between Reserve Army and Fourth Army at this stage, and to understand the shift in 1st Anzac Corps' importance to Reserve Army. They were no longer the only means available to Gough of conducting an attack within the broader strategy of the Somme Offensive. Given Gough's freedom to expand his area of operations, 1st Anzac Corps' sector was now becoming a support to what was hoped would become a larger attack on the left. The point of what 1st Anzac Corps was doing was slowly being lost in the shift from left to right.

Preparation

In the meantime, as mentioned, 1st Anzac Corps faced the immediate problem of the threat posed by strong German positions on their right flank. The observation the Germans had from OG 1 and 2, and the windmill to the northeast of the village, continued to give them a considerable advantage. Reserve Army General Staff considered that:

---

3   TNA: WO 158/334: SG.406/171 Malcolm to II Corps, 30 July 1916, Scheme "F".
4   TNA: WO 158/334: 'Outline of Plan of Attack on Thiepval,' II Corps, 28 July 1916, Scheme "F".

> … the capture of Pozières … is an important gain, but the Windmill N[orth] E[ast] of it and the high ground about OG 1 and 2 must be secured in order to obtain observation for ourselves and to deny it to the enemy. This must be considered the next task of the Reserve Army, and when completed will greatly assist the troops on our right as well as our own forward movement.[5]

Accordingly, preparations for taking these positions began. The 1st Australian Division, exhausted by the operation to capture Pozières, was relieved by the 2nd Australian Division. Commanded by Major-General James Gordon Legge, this division was ordered to press on with the advance as soon as possible. Legge took over command of the line at 9am on 27 July 1916, and quickly put together plans for an attack on the OG Lines. Three Battalions of the 7th Infantry Brigade would form the spearhead to this attack, assaulting OG1 and OG2 on a front of about 900 yards to the north of the Albert–Bapaume Road. To their left, flank protection would be provided by a battalion of the 6th Brigade attacking at right angles to the main advance. On the right, one battalion of the 5th Brigade would support the 7th Brigade attack by assaulting the OG Lines south of the Albert–Bapaume Road. This would be the first major operation of the 2nd Division on the Western Front.

On the surface, 2nd Division's orders for attacking the OG Lines look very similar to those given by the 1st Division for the attack on Pozières. Planned for just after midnight on 29 July 1916, the basic structure of this attack was for four lines of infantry to advance on a staggered set of limited objectives, at night, behind a lifting artillery barrage, with emphasis placed on consolidation of ground gained. However, a closer look at the plans will demonstrate that this similarity is only superficial. The emphasis of the 1st Division's attack was depth and firepower, with the artillery plan central to the assault. The 1st Division's infantry held the front line lightly, with just eight companies spread along the front of attack, but in depth, because another three waves of infantry with the same composition followed. This assault was carefully crafted to take advantage of previous success, and used technology to advance the infantry as far as their set objective and no further. As will become clear, this was not the case with the plans of the 2nd Australian Division.

This first assault of the 2nd Division was timed to come less than forty hours after Legge assumed command of the front line. This divisional commander proved much less resistant to pressure from Reserve Army than Walker had been, and went along with hastily issued orders to attack the OG Lines. Legge was not the only one to fail to argue for more preparation time for this assault. 1st Anzac Corps headquarters had taken back its rightful place in between Army and division in the chain of command at noon on 23 July 1916, but its commanding officer, Lieutenant-General Sir William

---

5   AWM: AWM 26/43/37: 'Summary of Operations of Reserve Army up to 6pm on 28th July, 1916,' 29 July 1916, Operations File Somme 1916, Reserve Army Summaries of Operations.

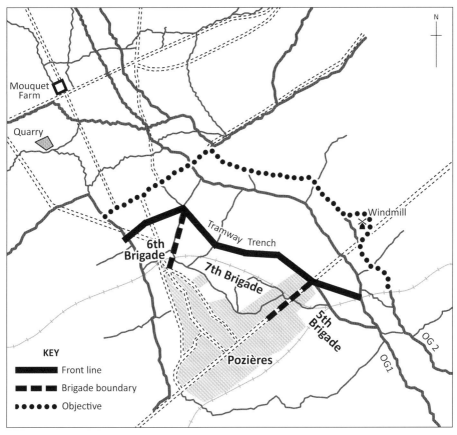

7 2nd Division's operation, 29 July 1916.

Birdwood, did not voice concern over the short period of time allowed for preparation either. While 1st Anzac Corps had not been involved in the planning and execution of the initial attack on Pozières, as a result of Gough refusing to wait for their arrival from the north, Birdwood himself was in Albert and spoke to Gough about his plans several times in the days preceding the operation.[6] He would continue to be in regular contact both with Gough and Malcolm, and his divisional and battalion commanders. Birdwood and his staff had had some input into the capture of the village itself by the 8th Battalion, but that movement had come as much from infantry on the ground taking advantage of the tactical situation before them as any planned operation from higher levels. Now 1st Anzac Corps headquarters was called on to conduct some

6   AWM: AWM 3DRL/3376: 19-22 July 1916, Personal diary of Field Marshal Lord
     William Birdwood.

serious staff work. Gough sent through only a very sketchy artillery plan, leaving the orders for "wire cutting, preliminary bombardment and subsequent artillery lifts"[7] up to 1st Anzac Corps – a significant body of work for a staff with yet minimal experience on the Western Front. The short amount of preparation time for a complicated attack is generally thought to be the principal problem with this operation, which would fail with heavy casualties. But are other factors to blame?

To begin with, the artillery plan produced was woefully inadequate. The preliminary bombardment was aimed at OG1, the first objective, and was timed to last only a single minute. Worse, the plan directed that the infantry had to be in position before it was fired, which involved leaving Tramway Trench and moving as close as possible towards the first objective, OG1. They had to do this without any form of a protective artillery barrage. The men would then have to lie out in the open to wait for the preliminary barrage to start and hopefully neutralise the German threat within its allotted 60 seconds, then rush the trench when the barrage lifted on to the next objective. The artillery would then fire a barrage on to the second objective, OG2, for ten minutes, during which time those that had survived getting into position and reaching OG1 had to capture and secure it with enough time for the second wave of infantry to move into position for the next artillery lift. In fact another two minor lifts would take place within the next five minutes, giving the second wave of infantry a (small) chance to attack OG2 before the final standing barrage fell 200 yards beyond them. This barrage programme was not only shorter – lasting only 16 minutes in total before reaching the standing barrage – and further away from the infantry, but lighter than that of 1st Division, too, at a rate of only a maximum of two rounds per gun per minute, instead of two to five rounds. By any standards, this was nothing like the strong artillery barrage of the 1st Australian Division.

There is some indication that a "number of alterations" were made to the artillery orders, delaying their issue until 5.15pm on the 28th.[8] In official records these alterations remain unspecified. Could Legge or Birdwood have tried to shore up the artillery support for the attack? Sadly, no. Haig's diary reveals that the already inadequate artillery orders were almost thrown out altogether by Legge before the operation went ahead. This problem was caught just in time by Major-General Noel Birch, Haig's artillery adviser at British GHQ. Haig recorded in his diary for 28 July 1916:

> General Birch in the evening reported that the Australians had at the last moment said that they would attack without artillery support and that "they did not believe machine gun fire could do them much harm"! Birch at once saw

7   TNA: WO 95/518 'Artillery Arrangements No. 2 Reserve Army,' attached to Reserve Army Operation Order No. 15, 28 July 1916, Headquarters Branches & Services: General Staff.

8   AWM: AWM 26/53/2: 28 July 1916, 1st Australian Divisional Artillery War Diary.

Gough who arranged that the original artillery programme should be carried out.[9]

Haig – or at least the artillery adviser appointed to his headquarters by him – certainly saw the value of artillery support in an infantry attack on the Somme, which is made clear by this episode. Yet at the same time, the original artillery programme that was hastily reinstated was also inadequate. It is unclear whether Birch or Haig enquired further as to the nature of this original programme. A failure to recognise the problem would have deadly consequences.

Pozières at this time was the centre of an artillery duel that rained shellfire on the village and its immediate vicinity almost constantly. Reserve Army batteries tried to engage their German counterparts around Le Sars and Courcelette, and although the Army claimed this "reduced to some extent the hostile bombardment of Pozières and vicinity",[10] this was not felt by those in the front line, or indeed anywhere in or near the village. The newly-won Australian position in Pozières was constantly under threat as a simple result of very accurate, ongoing artillery fire from the German artillery. The Australian artillery – still that of the unrelieved 1st Australian Divisional Artillery – found it difficult to establish observation posts in the village as a result. Shellfire prevented communication to batteries from the front line almost entirely, offering little hope of a speedy response from the big guns to specific threats and problems. This accurate German fire was probably guided from observation posts in the OG Lines and the Windmill, which made the capture of these positions before moving on to Thiepval all the more important. However, in the meantime this same fire was continuing to hamper preparations for the coming battle. New communication trenches were regularly rendered useless, destroyed by artillery fire before they could be completed. In most places the front line consisted of no more than a few unconnected trenches and strongpoints. Not only that, but the men of the newly-arrived 2nd Division were unfamiliar with the ground and commonly became lost before they could arrive at a location to work, and there were no large-scale maps of the new trench systems to assist. The only answer lay in familiarisation and the use of guides from the 5th Brigade who had been in the line longer, but all of this took time and meant that preparations were not as advanced as they could have been when the assault took place.[11]

The lack of decent observation posts meant that the 2nd Division's preliminary artillery bombardments to cut the German barbed wire emplacements were based on scanty information. Patrols were sent out as soon as 2nd Division took over the

9   Sheffield & Bourne (eds.), *Douglas Haig: War Diaries and Letters*, p. 210.
10   AWM: AWM 26/43/37: 'Summary of Operations of Reserve Army up to 6pm on 28th July, 1916,' 29 July 1916, Operations File Somme 1916, Reserve Army Summaries of Operations.
11   AWM: AWM 26/56/4: 'Report on Action of 28th/29th July. Part I,' 14 August 1916, Operations File Somme 1916, 2nd Australian Division General Staff.

One of the many aerial photographs of Pozières taken for the purposes of reconnaissance and mapping.

line to try to help Divisional Headquarters "to ascertain the condition of the enemy's wire and the extent to which the bombardment has been effective."[12] These reports returned with mixed messages. In some cases the information gathered indicated that parts of the wire had been effectively destroyed, but in other cases, messages specified that equally large tracts of wire remained untouched. Most reports concluded that the wire, although "knocked about,"[13] was "still an obstacle."[14] And yet the fact that *some* wire had been destroyed seems to have resulted in an unwarranted sense of optimism at Divisional Headquarters. Legge simply continued on as planned in the hope that further wire-cutting activities "would have increased the gaps and made new ones" by the time the operation was set to begin.[15] But observation of the wire

12   AWM: AWM 26/56/4: G.1/87 2nd Australian Division memorandum, 27 July 1916, Operations File Somme 1916, 2nd Australian Division General Staff.
13   AWM: AWM 26/56/4: 'Report on Action of 28th/29th July. Part I,' 14 August 1916, Operations File Somme 1916, 2nd Australian Division General Staff.
14   AWM: AWM 26/50/15: G.250 2nd Australian Division to 1st Anzac Corps, 11.55am, in 'Summary of Operation Messages. Midnight July 27th to Midnight July 28th, 1916,' Operations File Somme 1916, 1st Anzac Corps General Staff.
15   AWM: AWM 26/56/4: 'Report on Action of 28th/29th July. Part I', 14 August 1916, Operations File Somme 1916, 2nd Australian Division General Staff.

simply could not be obtained by artillery observation officers and so there was ongoing official uncertainty as to whether the wire had been cut further. Despite continuing suggestions from patrol reports that the wire would cause a problem, no attempt was made to increase or modify the barrage in places where the wire was noted to be particularly strong, nor was more time allocated for the establishment of appropriate observation posts to get more accurate information on the situation. And in fact the post-battle reports proved that the optimistic attitude that the wire would be cut in the end was wrong, stating that "the wire had not been cut in very many places" at all, and portions of the line had not even been touched by shellfire in any way.[16] The barricade of German wire was a serious problem that needed much more attention than it received.

While artillery plans for 2nd Australian Division's operations were markedly dissimilar to 1st Australian Division's assault, Legge was somewhat limited in his ability to modify the arrangements, particularly after Haig and Birch became involved. However, his division's infantry plan, for which he was responsible, was also very different from that of the 1st Australian Division. Like 1st Division's attack it was based on four waves of infantry advancing on staggered objectives, with orders to consolidate gains taken. But unlike 1st Division, the four waves would all start from the same trench, Tramway Trench, instead of being staggered one behind the other. And instead of three objectives as at Pozières, here there were only two, OG1 being the first and OG2 the second. Waves 'one' and 'two' were both assigned to take the first objective together and waves 'three' and 'four' were assigned together to the second. In a way each wave of infantry acted as the lines had during 1st Division's attack on Pozières. All four of these waves were to leave Tramway Trench at midnight with no more than 50 yards between them at the same time, and move to within 150 yards of first objective before the preliminary barrage took place. In practice this plan meant that each infantry wave was two to four times as densely populated as any used by the 1st Division. Even worse, each heavily populated wave of infantry was almost on top of the other, causing confusion before the battle could even begin.

If this was not bad enough, there was a further complication. In the 1st Division's attack one company belonged to one wave and worked as a single unit. With the 2nd Division, however, one company was divided into four to provide all of the waves assaulting single part of the German line. So, for example, A Company of the 26th Battalion was given the task of attacking the extreme left of 7th Brigade's sector. A Company would form all four infantry waves in this sector, attacking both OG1 and OG2. To do this each platoon from A Company would form a wave, and the four lines would follow each other closely into battle. Command of this arrangement was much more complicated because the company commander was expected to maintain

16   AWM: AWM 26/58/9: 'Attack on German Trenches on the Ridge North of Pozières by the 7th Australian Infantry Brigade on the Night of the 28th/29th July,' 29 July 1916, Operations File Somme 1916, 7th Infantry Brigade & Battalions.

control of both waves as they completed different tasks. The way Legge deployed his infantry seriously inhibited his brigade and battalion commanders' abilities to modify divisional orders to suit their formations. For example, Smyth would have had no scope to apply his straightforward infantry plan here. Instead every brigade of the 2nd Division was faced with carrying out the sorts of complicated orders which had so recently proved problematic.

In the case of an infantry disaster, reserves were not necessarily near at hand, either, according to this plan. The 6th Brigade on the left had a good supply of reserves. A force comprising half of the 22nd Battalion and half of the 24th Battalion under the command of Lieutenant-Colonel Robert Smith, the commanding officer of the 22nd Battalion, was waiting in Kay Trench, within easy reach of 6th Brigade's front lines. But the 7th Brigade, which was conducting the lion's share of the attack, had placed their reserve, the 27th Battalion, in Sausage Valley – well over half a mile from the front line. They were therefore not in close support, nor were they able to be easily or quickly organised into a support role since most of the battalion was occupied with carrying duties immediately before and during the operation. On the right of the line, the 20th Battalion conducted most of 5th Brigade's small-scale assault on the remaining uncaptured part of the OG Lines. The supply of reinforcements was uneven across the line, and again demonstrated some problems in the preparation for the coming battle.

Australian transport limbers returning down Sausage Valley at a gallop. Although Sausage Valley afforded some protection as an entry point to the battlefield, it was very shallow indeed.

And so there was an essential disparity between the action of the 1st Australian Division and the plans of the 2nd Australian Division that went beyond the simple matter of approaching things differently. Certainly both battles were based firmly on a series of basic, prescribed battle elements – a lifting artillery barrage, infantry attacking in lines and so on – but the incorporation of these elements into an infantry plan is completely different. This demonstrates that commanders could take a basic, standardised approach to battle and interpret and apply it differently on the Western Front in 1916. However, it also gives some indication that there was little or no information shared between the two divisions, despite their being in the same Corps. There was little time for assessment and formal reporting of 'lessons learned', but neither is there evidence of informal information gathering on the part of Legge in the way that Walker had done before his operation on 23 July. Furthermore, there were some demonstrable inconsistencies in the headquarters of 1st Anzac Corps. Although not involved at the outset of the operation against Pozières, Birdwood must have had access to the orders and plans for that first attack. Certainly he met with Gough several times during the planning phase of that operation. Yet he still seems to have failed to notice the huge disparity between the two attacks, or in particular recognise the problems inherent in the second. The fundamental difference was that the first attack relied heavily on firepower to advance the infantry in the field – the 1st Australian Division's emphasis was on a strong barrage with thin but deep infantry formations. The 2nd Australian Division's gave much more prominence to manpower, featuring a light, quick barrage with two thickly populated infantry lines making the main thrust of the assault. This is an important distinction. The operation of the 2nd Australian Division to take the windmill and the OG Lines is a straightforward infantry assault, not a coordinated, combined-arms attack, and no matter how much more time there had been allowed for preparation, this plan in any form, if fundamentally unchanged, would have gone on to cause problems.

The attack – 29 July 1916

In the last few hours of 28 July 1916, all battalions seem to have arrived in position in good time and in good order, notwithstanding the problems associated with finalising preparations under such heavy artillery fire. It was a difficult and complicated task to assemble battalions of as many as 1,000 men in forward lines at the right time, all the while in the dark under fire, and so what seems to be only a small success should be emphasised. In part this was the result of battalions sending company commanders to visit the ground over which the attack was to take place, to ensure they were as familiar with the ground as possible. At 12.14am on 29 July the artillery, too, proved able to begin its barrage on time. It went on to make all its projected lifts on time and without problems. But the infantry operation that followed at 12.15am did not succeed. On the left the 6th Brigade made some gains, but the assaults of both the 7th Brigade in the centre and the 5th Brigade on the right failed completely, and with heavy casualties. The 7th Brigade's attack was the main thrust of the entire operation.

When this central assault began to fail, the progress of the supporting attack by the 6th Brigade on the left faltered, and only partial success was achieved. On the right, where even more problems were encountered with intact wire and alert enemy fire, the 5th Brigade failed even to reach the first objective. So what went wrong?

One of the first indications of trouble came from the Germans. Their unceasing fire soon made it clear that most of the Australian forces forming up in the forward lines had been discovered by German observers in advanced listening posts. This was evident all along the line. On the far left, 6th Brigade headquarters reported that the Germans "were well aware of our attack from the first"[17] and "the first wave moved forward preceded by patrols under heavy machine gun fire, rifle and shrapnel fire, while a large number of flares were used by the enemy".[18] In the centre, the 7th Brigade found that "while waiting to advance there were indications that the enemy had his suspicions aroused".[19] As they advanced the Germans "met them with flares and heavy m[achine] g[un] fire from five to eight minutes before 12.15am".[20] The 26th Battalion reported that "enemy flares were sent up continuously from 11.42pm onwards and that it was impossible to move without being seen".[21] Only one battalion, the 25th, reported that they had assembled undetected. All along the rest of the line the alerted Germans let off a large number of flares and put assaulting troops under unceasing fire. Fortunately, in most cases this fire did not have much practical effect on either the 6th or 7th Brigades, because it was generally too high to find a target among the infantry, and was as such more a nuisance. Nevertheless, it was a dangerous indicator that the German defenders would be alert and ready as the operation went ahead. On the right the situation was worse. Reports state that:

> … the 20th Battalion, on leaving their trenches to form up in no man's land shortly after 11pm were evidently observed by the enemy for they came under heavy machine gun fire, and about a quarter of an hour later under artillery fire in which gas shells were used … meanwhile the 17th Battalion were also discovered by the enemy after two waves had moved out: the ground moreover was so lit up by German flares that their fire was very effective.[22]

---

17 AWM: AWM 26/57/27: 'Report on Operations 28/29 July 1916,', 29 July 1916, Operations File Somme 1916, 6th Infantry Brigade & Battalions.

18 AWM: AWM 26/57/27: 'Brief Report on Operation Carried Out on 28/29th July 1916. 29 July 1916,' Operations File Somme 1916, 6th Infantry Brigade & Battalions.

19 AWM: AWM 26/58/9: 'Report of Attack Carried Out by 26th Battalion AIF on Night of 28th/29th July 1916,' Operations File Somme 1916, 7th Infantry Brigade & Battalions.

20 AWM: AWM 26/56/4: 'Report on Action of 28/29th July Part I,' 14 August 1916, Operations File Somme 1916, 2nd Australian Division General Staff.

21 Ibid.

22 Ibid.

This caused heavy casualties before companies could even reach their jumping-off places.

The significance of this observation by the Germans – and the ongoing hostile fire in particular – is that it is a good indication that the artillery barrage was inadequate. Not only was the role of the artillery here to cut defensive wire emplacements, but the barrage was intended to keep the German defenders sheltering in dugouts and trenches, rather than locating attackers and firing machine guns at them. Prior to the one-minute preliminary barrage, there had been "a certain amount of bombardment in order to avoid there being a very remarkable silence prior to the intense bombardment," although this fire was not planned to be heavy.[23] Perhaps a very remarkable silence was avoided, but in every other capacity this artillery fire proved to be completely useless. Not only was it too light to keep the enemy under cover – troops reported that "up to 14 minutes past twelve [the artillery fire] was not heavy enough to keep [the] enemy down"[24] – but it also failed to fool the Germans into thinking nothing unusual was happening. At every part of the line the Germans began a defensive fire before or immediately following the one-minute preliminary bombardment, which in many cases actually grew stronger as the attack went on. This was proof that the artillery had had no impact at all in protecting the advancing infantry of the 2nd Australian Division or in preventing the German infantry from defending their position.

The most important part of this operation was in the centre, where the 7th Brigade made the greatest part of the attack against the OG Lines. The 26th Battalion was on the far left of the sector, the 25th in the centre, and the 28th on the right. The commanding officer of the 7th Brigade, Brigadier-General James Paton was able to report that "the difficult and complicated task of assembling the three Battalions concerned in the attack at the appointed place at the right time was most successfully carried out." The "four waves had passed through [Tramway Trench on their way to the front line] in almost perfect order … [leaving] no doubt whatever that the attack was successfully launched."[25] However, although the attack may have launched successfully, in some places it did little more.

The one part of the line that experienced the most success was the left, where troops of the 7th Brigade could benefit from the 6th Brigade's push on towards Mouquet Farm. Next to them, the 26th Battalion got forward, as did part of the 25th Battalion. Both of these battalions reported that the wire had not been cut in many places, but crucially there were enough gaps in it to enable them to get into their first objective,

23   AWM: AWM 26/56/5: Bridges (GSO1 2nd Division) to 7th Bde, 28 July 1916, 5.35pm, Operations File Somme 1916, 2nd Australian Division General Staff.

24   AWM: AWM 26/58/9: 'Report on operations of 25th Battalion,' 9 August 1916, Operations File Somme 1916, 7th Infantry Brigade & Battalions.

25   AWM: AWM 26/58/9: 'Attack on German Trenches on the Ridge North of Pozières by the 7th Australian Infantry Brigade on the Night of the 28th/29th July,' Operations File Somme 1916, 7th Infantry Brigade and Battalions.

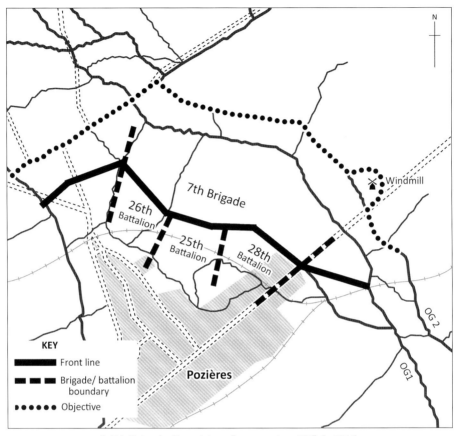

8 7th Brigade dispositions for operation, 29 July 1916.

OG1, with minimal resistance. But trouble arose when the second wave of men moved through to take the second objective. The second wave of the 26th Battalion found that the enemy wire in front of OG2 was almost entirely undamaged, and a significant obstacle. Not only that, but this trench was strongly held and actively defended by alert machine gun crews. Isolated groups of the four companies of the 26th Battalion got no further than the wire in front of OG2 before they were forced to retire. Lieutenant-Colonel James Walker, commanding the 25th Battalion, also reported that his men reached the first objective "without very much trouble or many casualties", but they found it "very shallow, only about three feet deep, [which] caused some confusion as to whether it was the real objective or not".[26] In fact, parties from the 25th Battalion

26   AWM: AWM 26/58/9: Walker (OC 25th Bn) to 7th Bde, 29 July 1916, 2.29am, Operations File Somme 1916, 7th Infantry Brigade & Battalions.

found themselves faced with little or no wire to negotiate here, with OG1 itself only lightly held and without defensive machine gun fire coming from it. But again, as the second wave moved through they encountered staunch resistance from OG2. The 25th Battalion's B Company under command of Captain John Edward Nix came into trouble only five yards from OG2. Later reports state that his company was:

> … met with very heavy machine gun fire which caused a great number of casualties. The waves approached to within about five yards of second objective when in addition to machine gun fire a considerable number of bombs were thrown. Capt[ain] Nix tried to re-organise this line to assault second objective but had not sufficient men left as they were being shot down fast so the order to fall back on to first objective was given. On reaching first objective again he had no men left at all and had to come back to position held by 6th Brigade. Captain Nix thinks that the best part of his Company are casualties.[27]

A small party from C Company of the 25th Battalion did actually succeed in entering OG2 through gaps they had managed to cut in the wire, but again were forced to retire to OG1 when they realised that the rest of the line had not been entered. Otherwise, all attempts to take OG2 by the 25th and 26th Battalions failed.

But a bigger problem soon became evident on the left of the line. The boundary between the 7th Brigade and the unit to their left, the 6th Brigade, was a perpendicular angle. The join came where the OG Lines met with the trench known as Tom's Cut and a road that would soon be named for Major Edward Brind, a company commander of the 23rd Battalion. To account for this angle in the objective line, the battalion at the far left of the 7th Brigade's sector, the 26th Battalion, was obliged to turn to the north west as they advanced. But a significant portion of the 26th Battalion lost direction because, as the intelligence report states, having to "go off at an angle, [they] soon made the angle too big".[28] Two companies on the left of the 26th Battalion became mixed in with troops of the 6th Brigade. As the attack went on, more and more of the 26th Battalion moved too far to the left, with units continuing to get lost in the rough ground and machine gun fire, until the trend to drift to the left began to affect companies of the 25th Battalion. Most of the 26th Battalion ended up more than two-thirds of the way into 6th Brigade's sector, from where they were later withdrawn.

In this part of the line the 23rd Battalion of the 6th Brigade had also managed to launch their operation on time. Their first wave was preceded by patrols, and despite coming under heavy fire from machine guns, rifles and artillery, they encountered

27   AWM: AWM 26/58/9: Walker (OC 25th Bn) to 7th Bde, 29 July 1916, 2.29am, Operations File Somme 1916, 7th Infantry Brigade & Battalions.
28   AWM: AWM 26/58/9: 'Intelligence Report on attack of night 28th 29th July 1916,' Operations File Somme 1916, 7th Infantry Brigade & Battalions.

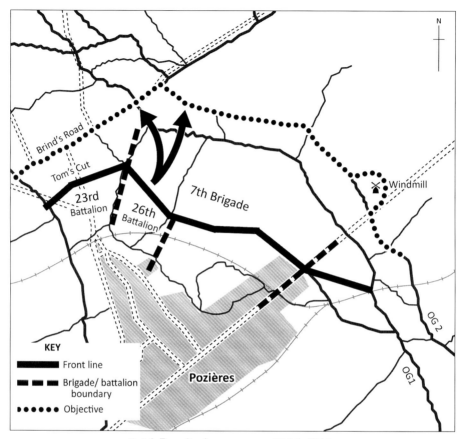

9 6th Battalion's manoeuvre, 29 July 1916.

demolished wire in front of their attack and reportedly took the first objective without difficulty. The first platoons reached the second objective within half an hour and even those that lagged behind were occupying the second objective around 2am. They were materially assisted in their efforts to consolidate their positions by the companies of the 7th Brigade that were drifting to the left. Nevertheless, the inability of the 26th and 25th Battalions to make good OG2 on the right, and the serious thinning of their line caused by their own drift to the left, meant that the 23rd Battalion's right flank was dangerously exposed. Efforts were made to plug the gap with companies from the 22nd and 24th Battalions, but the situation in 7th Brigade's sector was too serious. Within hours of the start of the attack, the two right battalions of the 7th Brigade were scattered across two sectors and suffering badly from heavy casualties, and the battalion of the 6th Brigade conducting their operation had been able to hold only a small advance.

If the situation was not ideal on the left, it was catastrophic on the right. The 28th Battalion on the far right of 7th Brigade's attack had reached their jumping-off position at 11.30 without casualty. As with the other parts of the operation, before the assault could begin the German troops opened up a heavy artillery and machine gun fire which caused a number of casualties. Despite this, the infantry of the 28th were able to move forward in reasonable order. But they soon discovered that the wire defences on their front had not been touched by the artillery barrage at all, even in front of OG1. They were all completely intact. The men of the 28th Battalion were forced to stand out in the open in no man's land trying to cut or force a path through the wire, and suffered many casualties from heavy rifle, machine gun and artillery fire. These were solid defences – the wire was staked up to a height of 3 feet in some places. As each wave of the 28th advanced it came upon the same problem, causing crowding and confusion in the heavy fire. The 1st Australian Divisional Artillery were firing short into their own infantry here as well, causing some of the casualties and accounting for the untouched state of the wire. Communication was impossible due to a heavy and effective German barrage between the front line and brigade headquarters, and it was not until some wounded men made it back far enough to send a report some time later that word of the failure reached battalion headquarters. There is no recorded instance of any opening being found in the wire and no troops made it into even the first objective.

To the south of the Albert – Bapaume Road, the 5th Brigade was in an even worse predicament. Bizarrely, they had not been allocated any part of the artillery barrage, and were supposed to rely on trench mortars to support their attack. But even this inadequate fire support was not supposed to be, as the unit that was supposed to support them, the Australian Light Trench Mortar Battery, later reported that it had been "placed in reserve, and took no active part in the operation".[29] And so the absent trench mortars had not been able to silence the enemy machine guns at all, and the infantry were left without any heavy firepower in support. The brigade conducted the assault with the 20th and 17th Battalions. Their advance to the jumping-off line had also been observed by the enemy and came under heavy machine gun and artillery fire which included gas shells. They managed to reach their allocated position by the jumping-off time of 12.15am, but flares lit the attacking troops so well that German fire was deadly accurate. It caused the infantry to become disorganised even before they could form up appropriately. The first two waves made it out of the trenches but failed to reach OG1 as a result of the hostile fire. The third failed as they left their trench when "heavy cross machine gun fire was opened and immense numbers of flares thrown", causing heavy casualties before they moved any distance at all.[30] Eventually

29   AWM: AWM 26/58/9: Australian Light Trench Mortar Battery to 7th Brigade, 9 August 1916, Operations File Somme 1916, 7th Infantry Brigade & Battalions.
30   AWM: AWM 26/56/4: 'Report on Action of 28th/29th July. Part I,' 14 August 1916, Operations File Somme 1916, 2nd Australian Division General Staff.

an officer from the 20th Battalion reported that they were unable to continue the attack, and as the 17th Battalion, at the extreme right end of the operation needed the support from their flank, the 5th Brigade's assault was at an end. The 28th Battalion, too, was gradually withdrawn from just after 2am, their attack an abject failure.[31]

The kind of individual initiative that had been able to have such dramatic consequences in the attack on Pozières had no effect here. There are examples of men taking remarkably brave steps to facilitate an advance. Even an examination of a single battalion gives examples of men like Lieutenant Victor Thomas Symes Warry, a company commander of the 25th who was commended for bravery in leading his men to a gap in the wire and standing in the open to direct more through. There were others too, like his fellow company commander Lieutenant John Lyall Smith, who had also managed to find one of the two narrow gaps in the wire before pausing to direct his men to it. Platoon commanders 2/Lieutenant Louis Walter Teitzel, 2/Lieutenant Thomas Joseph Carey, 2/Lieutenant Robert Stuart O'Hea, 2/Lieutenant Aaron McIntyre and 2/Lieutenant James Monteagle Brown were all mentioned in despatches for "great gallantry in leading their platoons on [the] night of 28/29th July in the attack on Pozières Ridge" with particular mention of the fact that "they were seen organizing the men as much as possible and encouraging them on".[32] This is exactly what Medcalf and Le Nay had done so effectively for the 3rd Brigade only days previously but with one important difference – at the end of the attack, all of these men were dead. Individual initiative and attention to organisation could not function in battle on the Western Front outside of a framework of carefully applied firepower. Without cut wire and an effective protective barrage, all of the bravery and initiative in the world could not protect men from alert defenders and accurate machine gun fire.

This absolute failure on the right spread to the left of the line, where the situation was more successful, if precarious. Then, somewhere in the vicinity of the 26th Battalion, the order to retire was given. The origin of this order could not be identified, although Paton, commanding the 7th Brigade, suspected "it may have been given by an officer who did not live to return".[33] The 2nd Australian Division had banned the use of the word 'retire' in any context, and so this order should not have been generated from any official source, and certainly the men had been told that it should not be acted on under any circumstances. But the situation was so perilous, and the line was so strongly defended, that the men retired anyway. Paton refused to accept it until he had clearly identified that the left flank of the 26th Battalion was far out of position to the left, but his confirmation of the order came long after the main body of the 26th

31   AWM: AWM 4/23/5/13: 28 July 1916, 5th Brigade War Diary.
32   AWM: AWM 28/1/69: Recommendation file for honours and awards, 2nd Australian Division.
33   AWM: AWM 26/56/4: 'Report on Action of 28th/29th July. Part I,' 14 August 1916, Operations File Somme 1916, 2nd Australian Division General Staff.

was in advanced retirement. In the 6th Brigade area, rumours of a general retirement were prevalent, but the commander of the centre company of the attack, a Captain Smith (probably Robert Frederick Maberley Smith, later awarded the Military Cross for his actions), declined to withdraw. Until he received confirmation from Brigade headquarters, he continued to consolidate his isolated position and make situation reports. Eventually though, given that the 7th Brigade was unable to make another attempt on the OG Lines, the 6th Brigade commander, Lieutenant-Colonel Wilfred Kent Fethers, issued an official order for withdrawal. And with that action, the entire attack was over, and a failure.

Consequences

Haig famously stated after this unsuccessful attempt that some of the divisional generals in the Anzac Corps were "so ignorant and (like many Colonials) so conceited, that they cannot be trusted to work out unaided the plans of attack".[34] While the apparent slight on 'colonials' has attracted much debate, there is another point to be made here, which is that Haig clearly expected divisional generals to be able to work out plans for operations themselves, or at least with the aid of no more than their own staff. Although plans were usually submitted for approval by the next most senior level – at all levels of army command – it would appear that there was still a requirement for self-sufficiency in the eyes of GHQ. This was about to change for the 2nd Australian Division. Legge and his apparent over-confidence had (not unfairly) been identified as the main fault in the 2nd Division's disastrous attack by the General Staff, and he was to be closely supervised the next time. Haig himself would become involved in preparations. Birdwood and the Brigadier-General of the 1st Anzac Corps, Cyril Brudenell White, also began a close supervision of Legge through a series of instructional letters and memoranda. Reserve Army took a much firmer stance in refusing to allow their artillery plans to be materially changed by either 1st Anzac Corps or Division. But there was no possibility of relief, and the 2nd Division would have to conduct another operation to secure the OG Lines. Haig went to visit 1st Anzac Corps' headquarters at Contay, where he informed Birdwood and White that "you're not fighting Bashi-Bazouks now – this is serious, scientific war, and you're up against the most scientific and most military nation in Europe".[35] Something in 2nd Division's approach would need to change.

The next operation, therefore, would be deliberately undertaken, meaning that the date of this attack would be determined by the progress of its preparation instead of being rushed through. This time the divisional attack would be coordinated with a

34   Robert Blake (ed.). *The Private Papers of Douglas Haig 1914-1919* (London: Eyre & Spottiswoode, 1952), p. 156.
35   C.E.W. Bean, *Two Men I Knew: William Bridges and Brudenell White, Founders of the AIF* (Sydney: Angus & Robertson, 1957), p. 137.

wider operation to be conducted by with the 12th Division of II Corps on the left, which was attacking Ration Trench, and the 23rd Division of III Corps on the right, which would be assaulting Munster Alley. But although coordinated as to time, the direction in which the series of attacks would take place indicated that these operations were not really connected. Corps commanders simply were not required to coordinate their methods across corps boundaries, or indeed even to match up their objectives or the direction of their operations with their neighbours. 12th Division's attack in particular was to take place *behind* the Australian operation, on a trench the 1st Anzac Corps had long since passed the entrance to. 'Coordination' then had little more benefit than stretching the German response more thinly, and existed only in the time the operations would take place.

The preparation undertaken by the 2nd Australian Division was based on what the divisional staff perceived were the major problems with their recent failed attack. They clearly identified three main problems – namely, that the assault had been at night with little preparation, that in many places the wire was uncut, and that the operation had been discovered by the Germans before it could be launched. The first of these was dealt with simply by timing the next assault for 9.15 in the evening, which in the late French summer was still light enough to see without being full daylight. The other two problems were more complex, and would take more time to work through.

To try to resolve the problem of insufficient artillery preparation and uncut enemy wire, the artillery would be given more time to prepare the ground for the next assault, both with wire cutting work and general demolition of enemy positions. Better observation of the wire enabled the General Officer Commanding the Royal Artillery (GOCRA) at 1st Anzac Corps, Brigadier-General William Napier, to make better judgements of the efforts required to destroy the wire entanglements that had caused so many problems for the 2nd Division. He concluded that 4,800 rounds of heavy howitzer ammunition would be needed against the two OG trenches and estimated this could be done "by 9 batteries averaging 540 rounds each, and could be done in one day".[36] Even more than this was used in the event. Four preliminary bombardments were ordered in which roughly a third of Napier's projected totals would be fired each time. Each bombardment was fired over an hour-long period, one on 31 July, two on 1 August and another on 2 August. With accurate ranging, and a period for observation between bombardments, the artillery preparations were much more adequate for destroying wire than they had been before.

The third problem identified by the 2nd Australian Division, the discovery of the operation by the German defenders, was to be dealt with by the construction of a new forward line to facilitate the assault. This was intended to reduce the amount of open ground the infantry would have to cover between their jumping-off point and the first objective. The new forward line was intended, Bridges noted, "to hold the troops

---

36   AWM: AWM 26/52/17: Memorandum S.498 from William Napier, BGRA, 30 July
      1916, Operations File Somme 1916, 1st Anzac Corps GOCRA.

required for the capture of OG1, [that is] the first two or three 'waves',", while subsequent waves would form up along the tramline further back.[37] A well-established jumping-off point had not been available for the previous attack, leaving infantry to assemble in the open and causing the operation to be discovered early, and so this answer seemed to be a reasonable solution. As mentioned, Haig was closely observing – if not supervising – this next operation, and so his observations formed the basis of a number of changes. His observations of the previous attack were that failure was the result of a general "want of thorough preparation", and he also considered that among other causes, the fact that "[t]he attacking troops were not formed up square opposite their objective" caused major problems.[38] As a result, the next front of attack was not only shorter, but omitted the angle between the 6th Brigade's front and that of the 7th Brigade. As before the 6th Brigade would attack on the left with a single battalion, all of the 7th Brigade would assault the middle of the line and two battalions of the 5th Brigade would advance on the right. This time all brigades making the new assault would attack in the same direction, towards Courcelette, instead of the 6th Brigade making their assault towards Thiepval, or in other words, at ninety degrees to the others. As such, the OG Lines formed the only objective for the new operation.

To deal with Legge's apparent over-confidence, Haig made a point of emphasising to Gough and his senior staff officer Neill Malcolm "that they must supervise more closely the plans of the Anzac Corps".[39] Haig was concerned about the weakness of the artillery bombardments accompanying the attack, particularly the minute-long preliminary bombardment. He made moves to rectify this for future actions by visiting Birdwood and his Brigadier-General, Cyril Brudenell White. He very clearly drew parallels between the operation of the 1st and 2nd Divisions, pointing out that "Pozières village had been captured thanks to a very thorough artillery preparation", and requested 2nd Division pay attention to this when working on the next operation.[40] While Haig may have been misinformed about some of the details of events of 29 July,[41] he demonstrated a clear understanding of some of the main problems of that operation, and took responsible steps to rectify them through sensible recommendations and open discussions with all of the relevant subordinates.

37   AWM: AWM 26/56/5: Bridges (GSO1 2nd Division) to 7th Bde, 1 August 1916, 5.00pm, Operations File Somme 1916, 2nd Australian Division.
38   Sheffield & Bourne (eds.). *Douglas Haig: War Diaries & Letters*, p. 210.
39   Ibid., p. 211.
40   Ibid.
41   Bean noted that when Haig had finished going through "the supposed defects in the preparations" for the previous attack, White went through them and "showed that the course of events was almost completely different". Haig apparently ended the meeting with a kindly "perhaps you are right", but some of his points at least were taking into consideration. Bean, *Two Men I Knew,* p. 137.

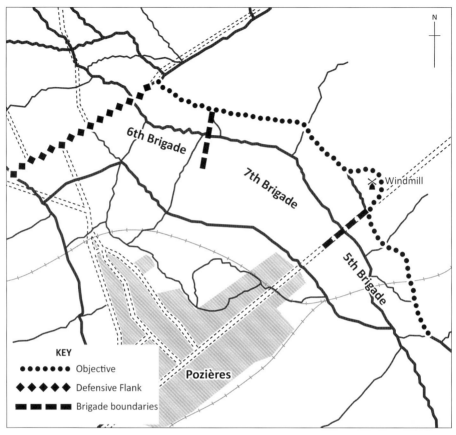

10 2nd Division's renewed operation, 4 August 1916.

Preparation

The preparations of the 2nd Division received a great deal of scrutiny at 1st Anzac Corps Headquarters, too. Generally most of the early operational arrangements for attacks on the Somme were made in person by generals making rounds of each other's headquarters, and so, in the absence of precise written records, just how close the supervision was will never be known. However, Birdwood's diary shows a great deal of regular visitation between he, Gough and Legge, and a number of memoranda from 1st Anzac Corps to Legge exist in the archives, demonstrating that Birdwood and White regularly visited 2nd Division to give instructions, request detailed information on proposals for offensive and defensive works, and make assessments of the divisional staff work even in matters as small as the supply of flares. Gough put a great deal of pressure from Army level to set an early date, but the prerequisite for this assault was the completion of all preparation tasks. For the first time Birdwood deliberately resisted pressure from Gough and Malcolm to hurry along in order to ensure the appropriate conditions were met, although there were concerns. Lieutenant-Colonel A.H. Bridges, GSO1 of 2nd Division, wrote to the 7th Brigade to say "after due consideration the corps commander has recommended to the Army commander that the attack be postponed … this gives us a bit more time for preparation and more time to the Bosche too!!".[42] There was an extended delay in executing the plans, however. The first serious date set for an assault was 2 August 1916, but that had to be delayed because 2nd Division's preparations were not advanced enough, causing the wider operation on the flanks to also be postponed.

The main cause for the delay was construction of the new forward line, which was painfully slow. Each night work parties went forward, but the work they were doing was hampered by severe artillery fire, and subsequently the casualty rate in working parties was extremely high, both when the men were moving forward and when they were labouring on the new position. This was not helped by 2nd Division again relying heavily on manpower and designating much larger parties to do the work than necessary, attracting enemy shellfire and its attendant casualties. This shellfire also destroyed much of the new construction, which then had to be done again under the same trying conditions. Working parties were sometimes seriously delayed through becoming lost in the featureless landscape, and on occasion retired without ever reaching the right position and beginning work. These conditions were not necessarily understood by those at a higher level of command. Legge wrote to Paton at 7th Brigade headquarters to complain about a trench under construction, stating:

> This trench to be dug tonight is most important, and I do not think your officers quite realised it last night. I would like you to put a senior officer in charge tonight and see the thing through. We may have to put up with some casualties, but all ranks should know that the work is to save our men in the attack.[43]

The unfair idea that the delay was no more than the result of forward officers slacking off was widespread at 2nd Division headquarters. Bridges also wrote to the 7th Brigade to stress that working parties should be commanded by a battalion commander because "[t]he work is important and a senior officer is necessary to push it in spite of obstacles".[44] Battalion commanders struggled to manage with unreasonable orders under the difficult conditions. Some ignored the size of working parties stipulated in orders, and sent smaller groups forward to limit casualties, which was tolerated as long as the work was demonstrably advanced. Under ongoing pressure, the

---

42   AWM: AWM 26/56/5: Bridges (GSO1 2nd Division) to 7th Bde, 2 August 1916, 11.40pm, Operations File Somme 1916, 2nd Australian Division General Staff.

43   AWM: AWM 26/56/5: Legge to Paton, 1 August 1916, 4.15pm, Operations File Somme 1916, 2nd Australian Division General Staff.

44   AWM: AWM 26/56/5: Bridges to 7th Bde, 1 August 1916, 5pm, Operations File Somme 1916, 2nd Australian Division General Staff.

new forward line was more or less completed by 2 August, but continued to require ongoing maintenance to repair the relentless destruction of heavy shellfire until the operation could go ahead.

The problem of unbroken enemy wire emplacements also continued. Preparations were taking place during hot, fine weather, which was suitable for aeroplane observation once the morning mist had burned off about 11am. These conditions were ideal for aircraft to monitor the artillery's attempts at wire cutting. Napier reported that early accounts from aircraft and infantry patrols showed that neither of the OG Lines had yet "been sufficiently done in" by artillery fire, particularly in front of OG2, where there was "good deal of wire still standing".[45] Patrols just north of the Bapaume Road found that the wire was in good condition, "following no definite pattern and [was] running from 2 to 6 feet high and approximately 30 yards wide".[46] This wire was taut and staked as much as 6 feet high, and showed signs of being regularly re-positioned. To deal with this even more artillery ammunition was allotted – all medium and heavy howitzer ammunition left over from the daily allotment was now to be used against the unbroken wire. In fact, any unused ammunition required an explanation given to the Army commander himself; not using enough ammunition was now considered as bad as using too much. By the time the jumping-off trench was completed on 2 August, some reports from aeroplanes and Forward Observation Officers indicated that wire-cutting work was good, with low, regular shell bursts in the right area. But it took some time for the positive reports to be confirmed. For example, on 1 August aerial photographs seemed to show that "the whole of the second line trench (OG2) … has been obliterated" to the extent that it was felt that it would "be sufficient for strong patrols with Lewis Guns to go forward and occupy" it.[47] Yet a day later reports were made that the wire in front of OG1 was still uncut in places and 18 pounder fire was reported to be falling short of it. Other reports indicated widespread destruction of the wire, with only small patches intact. Forward Observation Officers had a difficult task in observing the wire – while they could report that "the bursts were low and regular", they could not see the effect of the fire on the wire itself, especially at more distant locations like OG2.[48] But the artillery preparations were much more adequate for destroying barbed wire emplacements than they had been before. And higher command was willing (albeit very reluctantly) to wait for more positive reports before launching an operation. The extended effort put into the job of wire cutting eventually

45   AWM: AWM 26/52/17: Memorandum S.498 dated 30 July 1916, Operations File Somme 1916, 1st Anzac Corps GOCRA.

46   AWM: AWM 26/56/5: 'Extracts from Patrol reports', 31 July 1916, Operations File Somme 1916, 2nd Australian Division General Staff.

47   AWM: AWM 26/42/1: SG 406/187 Reserve Army to 1st Anzac Corps, 1 August 1916, Operations File Somme 1916, Reserve Army General Staff.

48   AWM: AWM 26/52/17: 'Report of Operations from 12.0 noon 1st August to 12.0 noon 2nd August 1916,' 2 August 1916, Operations File Somme 1916, 1st Anzac Corps GOCRA.

began to pay off, and despite a number of delayed starts, it was felt eventually that the wire was in such a condition as permitted the conduct of an assault on the enemy line.

Reserve Army had coordinated most of the preliminary artillery preparations, including a number of barrages designed to get the German defenders used to a pattern of shelling that could then be used to mask the next assault. Artillery instructions explained:

> The object of the[se] bombardments is not so much to kill the enemy, although that is fervently hoped for, but to "drill" him and get him thoroughly accustomed to a certain set procedure which in the ordinary course of events leads to nothing. Then, when the proper moment arrives, certain novelties will be introduced which may cause complete surprise.[49]

These 'novelties' consisted primarily of a lifting barrage followed closely by lines of infantry, as in all of the attacks by the Australians in this area so far. To match up with this habituation, all fire on OG1 and 2 would cease fifteen minutes before zero hour on the night of the next operation against the lines. It was hoped that the German defenders would stay in their shelters, unsuspecting and unprepared for an assault.

Finally preparations for battle were deemed sufficient to renew the offensive, and an operation was confirmed for the evening of 4 August 1916. The bombardment programme, which would as usual dictate the timing of this operation, was drawn up under Gough's close supervision. Gough's chief of staff, Neill Malcolm, warned Birdwood to guard against "the risk that Legge may want a different time of bombardment to that which has been drawn up in outline here".[50] The first barrage of shells was to fall on the first objective, OG1, for three minutes. After that the first lift would take the artillery barrage to OG2, the second objective for ten minutes, while the infantry followed, attacking OG1. Following that there would be three short lifts of fire every two minutes until the barrage finally fell 300 yards beyond OG2 while the second wave of infantry were attacking this objective. Each lift of the barrage was about as strong as the 1st Division's attack in terms of the quantity of shells fired per minute, but the actual artillery programme itself was again much shorter – only seventeen minutes would elapse before the barrage reached its final position. In comparison, each lift of the 1st Division's barrage lasted half an hour – longer than the entire programme here. So while there is a demonstrable recognition that artillery was important to advance the infantry, and a major part of the adjustment of the plan for the renewed 2nd Division attack, there seems to be little standardisation in barrage patterns from one assault to the next. This barrage benefitted from an extended period

49   AWM: AWM 26/52/17: 'Artillery Instructions No. 6,' 31 July 1916, Operations File Somme 1916, 1st Anzac Corps GOCRA.
50   AWM: AWM 26/42/1: Malcolm to Brudenell White, 30 July, 1916, Operations File Somme 1916, Reserve Army General Staff.

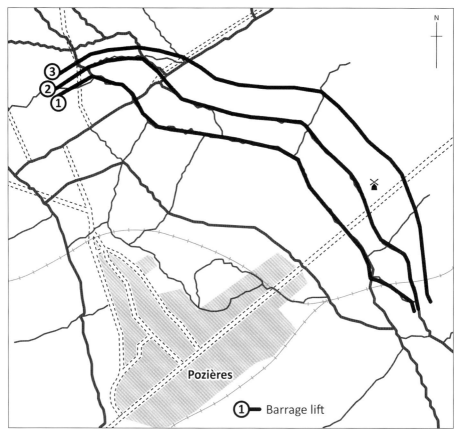

11 Artillery barrage for the 2nd Division operation, 4 August 1916.

of time and good weather for observation and ranging, and was, if not as strong as the barrage at Pozières, at least considerably stronger than the one that had preceded it.

While changes had been made to the original plan in the form of an extended preparation time and strengthened artillery barrage, the plan for the infantry itself changed very little. This was again Legge's responsibility, although the plan should at least have been monitored by Birdwood at corps headquarters. The infantry once more were assigned four lines, which as before operated in practice as two main waves against the two objectives. And yet again each of the brigades conducting the assault showed remarkably little variation in their method of attack. As before, this was the result of 2nd Division's staff work which once more showed a marked tendency to rely on manpower to forward their advance. The infantry lines were even more thickly populated than before, with the length of line previously attacked by three battalions of the 7th Brigade now being assaulted by four – three battalions of the 7th Brigade plus another of the 6th. This represented an increase in infantry in each attacking wave of 25 percent. This time the companies were better arranged, with one company per wave, or in other words being deployed in breadth not in depth. But very little else had changed, except to make the trenches even more crowded and the infantry an even greater target for German artillery and machine guns.

The attack – 4 August 1916

On 4 August at 9.15pm the artillery began its barrage, and fired all lifts on time. Without exception, none of the attacking battalions found wire emplacements strong enough to form an obstacle in front of them. As a result, in almost all cases the both objectives were taken without a prolonged struggle. Importantly, the German soldiers that the attacking Australian infantry came across were found while they were still in or were just leaving their shelters and dugouts in the trenches. The habituation barrages had been completely successful in creating a false sense of security among the defenders, and therefore had achieved the goal of ensuring the Germans were unprepared. However, the German artillery caused some problems for the attackers. The 22nd Battalion on the far left came under heavy shellfire as they deployed, and suffered considerable casualties. This barrage did not prevent the battalion from reaching the assembly trenches, but it did delay their attack slightly. The first wave was late in launching its attack by three minutes. The second wave of the 7th Brigade assault suffered under a heavy German barrage, too, with heavy casualties. In neither case were the attacking troops prevented from taking either objective, in spite of the high casualty rate. Nor was this German shellfire in response to the attack being discovered before it could be launched. The German infantry was almost entirely unprepared for attack and were therefore extremely unlikely to have called in emergency artillery support. By the early hours of 5 August, the OG Lines had been secured, and the work of consolidating the ground gained was well underway. A German counter-attack around 4am on 5 August was easily repelled from the newly-consolidated positions despite being conducted in force. This operation, although extremely costly in lives, could be considered a success.

Higher levels of command had accurately pinpointed some of the biggest problems – the lack of time to construct appropriate jumping-off places, discovery of the assault, an extremely weak artillery barrage and an inconsistent line of objective. Haig, Gough and Birdwood had all worked towards ameliorating some of these problems – Haig made recommendations as to the front to be attacked; Gough coordinated the preliminary artillery barrages; Birdwood (or his staff) designed the lifting bombardment. And with these changes, the assault succeeded. The preliminary bombardment destroyed most of the German wire and habituated the defenders into staying down instead of preparing for an attack. The lifting barrage was accurate enough for the infantry to follow closely, and prevented German machine gunners from manning their posts in time to stop the infantry. But while this operation was a success, it was not an unmitigated one. The 2nd Australian Division suffered a huge number of casualties – in fact in twelve days in the line they lost 6,848 officers and men, a casualty

A photograph of a destroyed portion of OG1 taken in October 1916. The trench was so destroyed that rifles resting in the trench were buried still resting vertically on the back wall of the trench. The very ends of the muzzles are just visible by the soldier's hand.
(AWM E00011

rate that would not be matched by another Australian division in one spell in the front line for the rest of the war.[51] For the second time in a week the 2nd Australian Division had conducted an infantry-heavy assault, made by two heavily populated waves of soldiers.

Staff of the 2nd Division had drawn the right conclusion following their first attack, reporting that "it is a mistake to crowd many men into a line after it has been captured".[52] But this advice should have been applied to the line *during* the attack as well, and anyway, they did not heed their own advice, so on 4 August the lines were even more crowded than they had been on 29 July. The plan seems to have been to thin the line once the objectives were secure, and to that end orders were given around 7.30 on the morning of 5 August, but only to send men back when it was possible. The definition of 'possible' was left to front line commanders. Forward commanders proved

51   C.D. Coulthard-Clark. *No Australian Need Apply: The Troubled Career of Lieutenant-General Gordon Legge* (Sydney: Allen & Unwin, 1988), p.151.
52   AWM: AWM 26/56/4: 'Report on Action of 28th/29th July. Part I,' 14 August 1916, Operations File Somme 1916, 2nd Australian Division General Staff.

resistant to this order, and many showed a marked preference for using large working parties to consolidate new forward positions instead of thinning the line before all the work was done. At more than one man per yard of trench in each infantry wave, it was almost impossible for the German barrage to miss, and so this reliance on manpower of the 2nd Division was directly responsible for the huge casualty rate suffered both during the attack and during the consolidation phases of the operation. They could recognise that it was a mistake to crowd too many men into a line, but in practical application, the 2nd Division had failed to draw many practical lessons from that first failed operation at all.

Yet although this overcrowding and reliance on manpower was one of the primary reasons for 2nd Division's high casualty rate, it was not the problem for which Legge drew criticism. Instead it was the delay in preparation, materially responsible for the positive result of the operation, that drew fire from Reserve Army. Before the second operation had even begun Army had launched an enquiry into the cause of the delay. Birdwood deferred answering Gough's queries as much as possible in order to give Legge the best chance of planning the new assault without additional pressure. In explaining the delay, Legge reported:

> … the very heavy barrage put on by the hostile guns so disorganised the work [of preparation] and damaged the trenches as to cause serious delay, and the constant destruction of our communications accentuated the difficulty.[53]

He had already said as much to Birdwood, who had reported the conversation to Reserve Army before Legge's short report. But, Birdwood added:

> I regret the delay which has occurred and the inconvenience caused at Army Headquarters and to other Corps by changes in artillery programmes. In all probability under a more experienced commander the operation would have been more expeditiously effected.[54]

Birdwood had identified an accurate source of the problems in Legge, albeit an inaccurate reason for them. Yet Legge's position was saved, but not by a defence of his capability. Birdwood, while making it clear it was not his intention "of retaining any officer in high command who is proved unfitted" – despite his own suggestions that Legge was proving exactly so – also made it clear that he should be "given full opportunity to prove his capability for command" solely because he was one of only two Australian senior officers at the time. He wrote that Legge:

---

53   AWM: AWM 26/50/15: Legge to Birdwood, 6 August 1916, Operations File Somme 1916, 1st Anzac Corps General Staff.
54   AWM: AWM 26/50/15: Birdwood to Reserve Army, 4 August 1916, Operations File Somme 1916, 1st Anzac Corps General Staff.

… was appointed to a divisional command in succession to the late Major-General W.T. Bridges by the Australian Government, and I am anxious that he should be given full opportunity to prove his capability for command. The Commonwealth Government are very desirous that Australian officers should, if they are found capable, be given the opportunity of filling higher commands.[55]

Legge was not blamed for an infantry plan that seriously overcrowded both the jumping-off position and the attacking waves. He was, however, in serious trouble as a result of the slow progress his division made in preparing for operations. But there would be no consequences for now, simply because it would be best to retain the confidence of the Australian Government in British Command by giving Legge what Birdwood termed "a fair trial".

An assessment of the actions of the 2nd Australian Division has more often than not been mixed together with allegations of bungled British generalship and discrimination against Australian officers.[56] But this should not be allowed to cloud what was going on here. Most of the problems evident in the first assault by the 2nd Australian Division were generated at divisional level, and were insurmountable at lower levels. While some problems were corrected at higher levels, particularly regarding artillery barrages, others, such as the overcrowded infantry plan, were not. Even when corps and Army took a much more managerial approach to the second assault, these problems were not recognised, much less resolved, and went on to cause further operational complications. The sheer number of infantry used to effect both the first and especially the second operation are inextricably linked to the enormous casualty figures for the 2nd Division's first period in the line. Whether or not Legge and his staff had learnt that lesson, or any others, would remain to be seen with their return to active operations later in August.

---

55 Ibid.
56 See Bean, *Two Men I Knew*, Charlton *Australians on the Somme*, Coulthard-Clark *No Australian Need Apply*, or for an account riddled with inaccuracies, John Laffin *British Butchers and Bunglers of World War One* (Gloucester & Wolfeboro: Sutton Publishing, 1992).

3

"Without rest or relief":
4th Australian Brigade's Rush of Smaller Operations

The 2nd Australian Division was exhausted at the end of its second operation, and its relief was imperative. At 9am on 7 August 1916 the 4th Australian Division, under the command of Major-General Herbert Vaughan Cox, took over the front line. This, the last untried division in 1st Anzac Corps, spent just over a week in the line and was pressed into immediate and constant service from the moment it arrived. This was in part due to the increasing impact of the German policy to counter-attack and retake lost ground at all costs, meaning the defensive role of 1st Anzac Corps was more and more necessary. But offensively, too, this division was the most active so far. In fact, the story of the 4th Australian Division's first spell in the front line is very complicated indeed. At least twice they participated in larger operations ordered by Reserve Army, but corps, division and even battalion commanders took their own initiative to conduct operations on a number of separate occasions, in some cases nightly. The division conducted more than six battalion-sized or larger offensive operations in their eight days in the front line, and as many smaller ones. At the same time, their situation in the front line was the most precarious the three divisions had yet faced.

Reserve Army's plan for a general movement to the north by II Corps and 1st Anzac Corps had resulted in a reasonably pronounced salient in the Australian sector. The point of this bulge into German territory was almost directly north of the village and left the Australians with more than half a mile of trenches on either side protruding into German-held territory before leading back to a connection with the British 12th Division of Reserve Army on their left, and the 23rd Division of Fourth Army on their right. The 4th Australian Division was dangerously exposed to German machine gun and shellfire, which could pour into its position from three sides. This salient presented a distinct strategic problem that required coordination by Reserve Army, if not GHQ, to ensure it did not continue to push out further and endanger those holding it even more. That coordination was not to eventuate. Instead, Gough issued a memorandum on 3 August 1916 which did quite the opposite. The importance of this short memorandum cannot be overstated. The document, signed by Gough's chief of staff Neill Malcolm, stated:

… it is important that Corps Commanders should impress upon their subordinate leaders the necessity for the energetic measures and offensive action which
the present situation requires … It is imperative to press the enemy constantly
and to continue to gain ground as rapidly as possible. This can only be done by
vigorous leadership, by plans comprehensively prepared to bring into play by
surprise a concentration of all the means at our disposal, especially Artillery and
Trench Mortars, and by the execution of those plans with resolution and energy.[1]

That the results of the 1st Anzac Corps were uppermost in his mind as he wrote is
evident from the second point in the memo, which directed that:

… where Divisions are not acting offensively for the moment more energy is
required in the execution of work which will assist a future attack so that there
should be no delay directly the time for such attack arrives. It is conceded that
preparation must be thorough and careful, but once that condition has been
fulfilled, it must be impressed on all leaders that rapidity, energy and offensive
action are now of the utmost importance to our cause. Every yard of ground
gained has great consequences, both material and moral.[2]

But the answer to success on the Somme, which Gough called "a great and decisive
battle and not … ordinary trench warfare" was not in careful preparation – conces-
sions that preparations must be thorough and careful notwithstanding – but was to be
found in haste and constant activity. Malcolm added:

At present there is a tendency to undue delay and to wasting precious time owing
to lack of foresight – days pass without plans being matured – to wasting time by
using too small forces in the hope of avoiding loss and then having to repeat the
attack later – platoons are sent to carry out operations which require a company,
and companies to do that which requires a battalion. Relentless pressure must be
exercised everywhere and always Subordinate Commanders must think out and
suggest enterprises instead of waiting *for* orders from above, which is entirely the
case at present.[3]

This plan left little if any space for a broader coordination of effort. Instead of
bringing together a broad-fronted attack targeted to manage his front and lessen the
threat to areas such as 1st Anzac Corps' salient, Gough was rushing his units into
hasty and ill-thought out enterprises which were to be initiated far below his level of

1   AWM: AWM 26/42/1: Reserve Army SG.43/0/1, 3 August 1916, Operations File
     Somme 1916, Reserve Army General Staff.
2   Ibid.
3   Ibid.

command. Gough had effectively removed himself from organising a broad operational strategy in favour of urging haste on a small, disjointed scale.

At the same time, this memorandum demonstrates an understanding of some of the factors that had caused so many problems for 1st Anzac Corps in its recent operations. Although almost completely negated by the imperative to rush given in the document, the need to carefully prepare for an operation rated a mention. The memo also identifies that the systematic use of weaponry was important by indicating that success would come through combining the heavy firepower of the artillery and trench mortars with the infantry. And yet at the same time, Gough failed to recognise the overemphasis on manpower prevalent in 2nd Division's operations when he urged that the use of "too small forces" should be avoided. The fear of avoiding loss was becoming more prevalent in the horror of counting casualties by the thousands, but Legge had filled his lines rather than thinning them out. Gough should have been urging the use of appropriate sized forces, rather than recommending what amounted to an almost automatic upsizing. Reserve Army staff seem to have had the impression that the front was manned by a group of lazy, indolent procrastinators. The document almost universally fails to recognise the difficult, slow nature of preparation under shellfire, despite the fact that it was being clearly reported regularly to divisional and corps commanders. But it cannot be avoided that Gough, while paying lip service to what were proving to be critical factors in successful attacking on the Somme – firepower and preparation – was in fact promoting the opposite – hasty assaults using large concentrations of troops in a small area to bludgeon the German defences no matter the cost of life.

Preparation

The 4th Australian Division was the first to be in the front line under this new directive. The formation arrived at a time when the major obstacles in the area – the fortified village of Pozières and the OG Lines – were under control, but the entire area was still under ongoing heavy artillery fire. To make matters worse, the position of German guns in Thiepval made enemy shellfire appear to be coming from the rear on the left of the Australian line. An increasing determination of the Germans to re-capture lost ground saw the 4th Division compelled to defend against numerous German counter-attacks in sizes from twenty men to two thousand during their time in the front line. Parts of the line, particularly on the flanks, repeatedly changed hands, although usually only by a matter of yards. This territorial uncertainty was made worse by the fact that the 1st and 2nd Australian Division's operations had brought the 1st Anzac Corps' line to the edge of the known landscape. The German defences facing the 4th Australian Division were almost completely unknown. Aerial photographs could identify the major obstacles and newly dug trenches, but in many cases the Germans' positions were as tenuous as the Australians' own. Letters found on German prisoners described a trench system so blown up by shellfire it had ceased to exist in places. One prisoner was found to have written "it is indeed not to be called a trench, it is more of a sap. We have always to lie or sit, we must not stand, for then we can be seen".[4] Another observed:

> … now for the eleventh day we have been sitting in this horrible filth and have been waiting day after day for the longed for relief … each of us is crouched in a little hole that he has dug out for himself as a protection against possible splinters and stares at nothing but the sky and the back wall of the trench and the airmen circle over us and try to do some damage.[5]

The vast majority of these destroyed trench lines and advanced positions could not be identified from the air with any certainty, and so the 4th Division were forced to send out patrols continually to the landscape and identify German strongpoints and potential targets.

With the OG Lines under control, most of the 4th Australian Division's offensive focus was on the left of the line where it faced Mouquet Farm. This was in accordance with Reserve Army's overarching plan for 1st Anzac Corps to advance to the north. The 4th Division, comprising the 4th, 12th and 13th Brigades, deployed the 4th Brigade on the left of their sector, and the 12th Brigade on the right. In the sector on the right, which largely ran along the OG Lines, the 12th Brigade was quite active during this time. However, its operations were either in response to German counter-attacks or in support of Fourth Army operations. Defensively the division held the front line with thinned out units armed with Lewis guns, calling on artillery to break up any massed formations of German soldiers seen preparing to attack. The cooperation with flank units on the right usually only happened informally as the result of the commanding officer of the battalion on the boundary noticing the attacking formations were hard pressed and volunteering his men to assist the British. None of these operations will be examined here. The 4th Australian Divisional headquarters always focussed on the operations on the left of the line, which formed the only part of their sector deliberately fulfilling their offensive strategy. As such the attacks in that area are the most important examples of their work in the early part of August 1916 in the context of this study. Nevertheless, during this period operations on the right continually sapped the strength of the battalions of the 12th Brigade, almost always to no good purpose.

The first operation conducted by the 4th Australian Division was on 8 August 1916, one day after Cox took over command of the line. Reserve Army had ordered 1st Anzac Corps to make an attack while Fourth Army was assaulting the French village of Guillemont. It was clearly stated that this operation was to be conducted in order

---

4   AWM: AWM 4/1/30/7 Pt. 2: 'First Anzac Intelligence Summary No. 24, from 6pm on 16th to 6pm on 17th August 1916. Part II, Information from Other Sources', 1st Anzac Corps Intelligence War Diary.
5   Ibid.

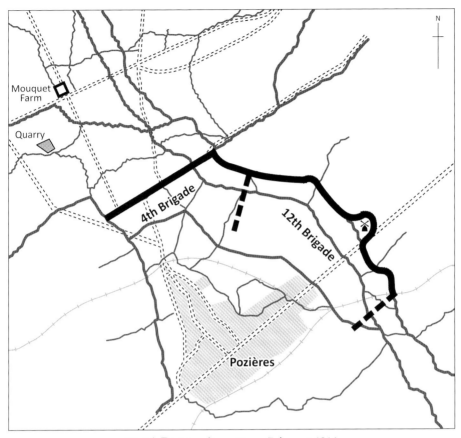

12 4th Division dispositions, 7 August 1916.

"to distract the enemy's attention from the point of attack [at Guillemont] and to diminish hostile artillery fire at that point".[6] Guillemont was just over five miles away to the east of the Australian line. Along the rest of Fourth Army's front artillery bombardments would also be fired with the intent of distracting the enemy, but no active infantry operations would be conducted between the Fourth Army attack on Guillemont and any operation conducted by Reserve Army. This operation, then, was intended to be little more than a diversionary tactic and should not be considered an extension of the Guillemont attack in any other way.

The new objective was a German trench known to the British as Park Lane which, at its furthest, was no more than roughly 250 yards from the Australian jumping-off

6   AWM: AWM 26/42/3: 'Reserve Army Operation Order No. 17,' 7 August 1916, Operations File Somme 1916, Reserve Army General Staff.

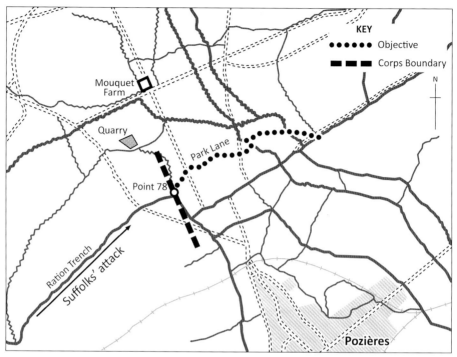

13 15th Battalion's operation, 8 August 1916.

trench. The operation itself was small, on a front of around 900 yards, but it received a reasonable amount of preparation and artillery support. On the left the 7th (Service) Battalion of the Suffolk Regiment would support the operation by attacking a German strongpoint on their boundary with 1st Anzac Corps. These two assaults were designed to be simultaneous. There would be no need for cooperation on the right flank because the Australian operation did not extend across the entire front of 1st Anzac Corps' sector. Park Lane was a useful objective for future operations towards Mouquet Farm in that it was more or less parallel to the road running in front of the farm buildings and was consistent with any future advance the 1st Anzac Corps would take to the north, if Reserve Army's strategic vision was realised. But it was no more than that – a step on the way, and a very minor one at that. The objective was not a particular source of German resistance, nor did it represent a major advance. The primary reason for this operation was as a diversion – the capture of Park Lane would merely be an added bonus.

Birdwood, however, seemed to see the plan as a much greater opportunity for his corps than it actually was, and was remarkably optimistic about his chances for success over and above the objective given. He indicated to Gough that he may well be able to push on to Mouquet Farm, well beyond the objective line. This caused some consternation in Reserve Army and in the end Gough's chief of staff rang 1st Anzac Corps headquarters to say that the "Army Commander does not wish us to push on further than the objective given in last Reserve Army order … as II Corps is not in position to go further".[7] In reality, Birdwood's talk of pushing on was no more just that – talk. Certainly there were no concrete plans in place for an operation that went further than Park Lane. And yet just days before subordinate commanders were ordered to "think out and suggest enterprises". Surely Birdwood's plans to push on to Mouquet Farm, if they had been more than talk, could be included in this directive? Surely Reserve Army would have to keep a very careful eye on their subordinate commanders, otherwise they had the potential to press ahead with operations that disadvantaged other units within the Army, destroyed men and materiel destined for further large-scale operations, or simply failed to follow the operational strategy of the sector in the future. And yet the directive to push on with 'enterprises' continued to stand, and would have a serious impact on the men of the 4th Australian Division.

The operation designed for 8 August was assigned to the 4th Infantry Brigade, which had until quite recently been led by Brigadier-General John Monash. Monash already showed the marked inclination towards instilling a high degree of organisation and detailed preparation into his troops which would so characterise his later military career, both in training and in preparation for operations. He had also instilled a culture of collaboration within the brigade, and so its battalions, the 13th, 14th, 15th and 16th, tended to share ideas, experiences and, if possible, equipment among each other to ensure problems were not repeated or compounded. The brigade was highly unified and well-trained. Following Monash's promotion to command the 3rd Division in mid-1916, temporary Brigadier-General Charles Henry Brand carried on this tradition of meticulous preparation. He took "minute care and soldierly thoroughness [in] his methods of training his new brigade",[8] and made a point of personally supervising battalions on the training field as they practiced in dummy trenches under actual artillery barrages. Each of the battalions was made familiar with the processes of forming up in jumping-off trenches, moving into the attack as the barrage lifted, advancing in waves and leapfrogging through each other. Importantly, all of the specialist roles, including scouts, wire cutters, wiring parties, Lewis guns, bombers, stretcher bearers and runners, were specifically taught and drilled in their roles as a part of these larger exercises. Every man was taught grenade throwing and how to dig silently and rapidly in the dark. By the time it arrived in the field, the 4th Brigade was as well prepared for battle on the Western Front as it could hope for.

This attention to detail is quite evident in the preparations of the 4th Brigade for the operation on 8 August. Officers made a careful reconnaissance of the position to be attacked while it was still daylight and in turn made sure that "all ranks were thoroughly acquainted with landmarks which defined their objectives and direction

7   AWM: AWM 26/50/16: Handwritten note re telephone call signed RHS, 7 August 1916, Operations File Somme 1916, 1st Anzac Corps General Staff.
8   Bean, *Official History, Vol. III*, p.707.

The centre of Pozières village on 28 August 1916. The trench on the left is Centre Way, with the tram line visible to its right. The man in the foreground is looking towards the OG Lines. (AWM EZ0099)

of attack, also distances to objectives" as far as time permitted.[9] There was a steady bombardment of the German trenches carried out during the 7th and 8th, and two further heavy bombardments were ordered on the trenches leading to Courcelette, the most observed source of German reinforcement. This operation was to take ground in a north-westerly direction, a shift in focus from 2nd Division's attacks to the northeast just days earlier. So instead of attacking towards Courcelette, 1st Anzac Corps turned ninety degrees to the left and attacked towards Thiepval. This change of direction seemed to take the Germans by surprise, and they did not use their artillery to harass preparations as ruthlessly as they had for the 2nd Division's recent assaults on their line. Despite the 4th Brigade facing a number of small counter-attacks in which the Germans used flamethrowers and bombs, preparation was able to continue reasonably unhindered.

Once again, this operation was based on the basic formula of an artillery barrage supporting a closely integrated infantry operation. But once more the 4th Australian Division showed that a division in the British army was more or less free to interpret the basic barrage model in its own way. The artillery barrage for the attack of 8 August 1916 was the strongest yet fired on 1st Anzac Corps' front. The barrage would fall

9   AWM: AWM 26/60/6; entry for 15th Bn, 8 August 1916, Operations File Somme 1916, 4th Australian Brigade.

on Park Lane, the objective of this operation, for three minutes, before lifting away to a second artillery objective line. It would then stay on the second objective for ten minutes before lifting to a final line between 150 and 300 yard from the infantry's objective. Instead of lifting from objective to objective in one jump, the barrage was to pause midway for a two to five minutes. So while the artillery barrage of the 1st Division during the capture of Pozières moved around 100 yards with each lift, these 'half' lifts meant that the barrage lifted no more than 50 yards each time. Ostensibly this would mean that the infantry could stay much closer to the protective curtain of shells – but for one critical factor. The artillery barrage started *on* the only objective for the operation. The infantry could not attack this objective until the artillery lifted away from it, and so every artillery lift after the preliminary bombardment on the objective line was outside of their area of operations. What appeared on the surface to be a sensible, well-constructed lifting barrage for the purpose of infantry coordination was in practical terms for naught. The artillery's sophisticated lifts benefited nobody because there was no reason to follow them. They did not lead up to the objective, they led away from it. The 4th Division, seemingly having proved so far to be the most reliant of the three divisions of 1st Anzac Corps on firepower to advance, in fact failed to demonstrate an understanding of the fundamental reason for a lifting barrage – an integrated plan that used the firepower of the artillery to protect the infantry as they crossed no man's land, *taking* them to the objective.

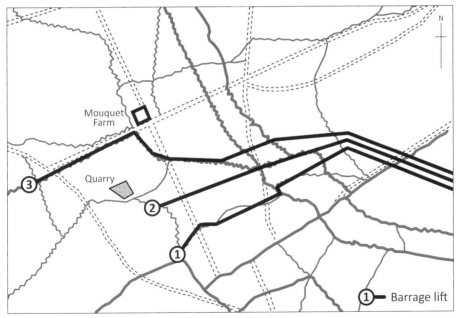

14 Artillery barrage for the 15th Battalion's operation, 8 August 1916.

The 4th Infantry Brigade's infantry plan for 8 August was much weaker than previous operations, again demonstrating the divergence in approach between divisions. The narrow front on which the assault was to be conducted was assigned to a single battalion, the 15th, under the command of Lieutenant-Colonel James Cannan, with the support of a single company of the 16th Battalion. The modest objective gave no opportunity for a series of infantry advances. Instead they would have to capture Park Lane in a single rush. To do this, Cannan deployed his infantry in waves. His orders do not survive in archives, but the 15th Battalion war diary noted:

> … the attack was launched in three waves – two platoons of each company in first wave, one platoon of each company in second and third wave. [The] first wave was accompanied by a proportion of Lewis Guns and preceded by scouts.[10]

In preparation for the assault, the first two waves were formed up in no man's land "on an alignment parallel to [the] objective prior to [the] commencement of our intense bombardment".[11] It is not possible to tell from existing sources how far apart these waves were from each other on deployment, or the distance they were meant to maintain from each other in the attack. However, it seems that each of these waves were intended to reinforce each other as they reached the single objective line. This is in direct contrast to the waves of infantry in 1st Division's attack on 23 July, in which each wave attacked one objective of a series, maintaining a succession of defended lines once the attack was over. Once this final line was secured and it had been consolidated it was to be held as lightly as possible, its defence reliant on Lewis Guns pushed out into no man's land, with no series of defended trenches behind. In the context of the extremely limited operation planned – really only just more substantial than a raid – this limited use of infantry was reasonable. Nevertheless, the plan was a substantial departure from recent experience. From 1st Division's three objectives for artillery and infantry, to the 2nd Division's two objectives, this operation was being conducted against a single objective line. It took a weak series of three waves of infantry and deposited them into a single objective in strength (it was hoped), before thinning them out for defence of the newly-captured line. There was no depth to this attack, and although there was an increase in the strength of the artillery support for it, there was little need for complex coordination between arms. The blunt force of the artillery was hoped to carry the infantry through, providing an adequate diversion to the Guillemont operation and a small territorial gain to 1st Anzac Corps.

10   AWM: AWM 4/23/32/17: 8 August 1916, 15th Battalion War Diary.
11   Ibid.

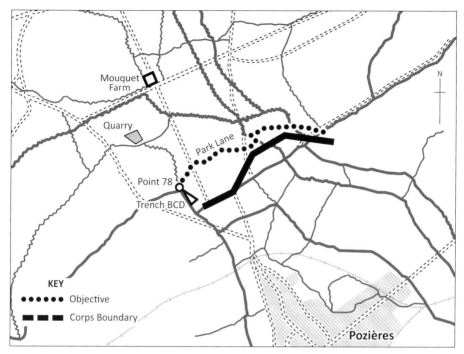

15 15th Battalion's situation, 9 August 1916.

The attack – 8 August 1916

The operation went ahead as timed at 9.20pm. The 15th Battalion, well prepared with officers and other ranks "thoroughly acquainted with landmarks which defined their objectives and direction of attack [and] also distances to objectives", made good time and were able to reach their objectives all along the line and begin digging in.[12] Communications between 4th Brigade headquarters and 15th Battalion headquarters had been cut almost immediately, and so, as with almost all of these operations around Pozières, brigade headquarters struggled to keep contact with the men of the 15th Battalion in the field. Brigade command could glean information from the noise of bombing and machine gun fire in the direction of the objective which seemed to be far enough in that direction to warrant the assumption that it had been reached, but for a number of hours that was all they knew. Finally enough information was pieced together by 1.45am on 9 August the 4th Division could report that the "15th Battalion commander ... has every reason to believe he has made good his objective

12   AWM: AWM 4/23/32/17: 8 August 1916, 15th Battalion War Diary.

but is concerned about his left".[13] Within hours of the launch of the attack the 15th Battalion had in fact taken all its objectives, albeit some with heavy casualties, and was waiting for support to arrive from the left.

As previously mentioned, a small operation was being conducted by the 7th Suffolks of the British 35th Brigade in support of the left flank of the 15th Battalion's operation. The Suffolks' orders were for a small assault on German positions incorporating one platoon moving up the north side of Ration Trench, one on the south, and one with bayonets at the ready rushing along the trench itself. There was no artillery barrage for this operation, which would be supported by a trench mortar bombardment alone. On the boundary between the two operations was a German strongpoint known by its coordinates – R.33.d.7.8, or Point 78. Once they captured this point, the Suffolks were to meet up with the Australians. But by the time the operation was to ordered, the Suffolks had become aware that 'Point 78' was in fact a triangle of trenches and a much more extensive defensive position than first thought. As a result, they ordered two platoons of their A Company to attack the other points of the triangle. The Suffolks began referring to Point 78 as 'Trench BCD', in order to reflect the fact that this position was much bigger than had been previously known. But although the threat from this stronghold was increasingly recognised, the Suffolks' attack never evolved into more than a strong bombing raid up a trench.

The Suffolks' flank operation, as with the Australians' main operation, was launched in good time. The Suffolks had also suffered from a lack of communication during the battle, and so it was not clear for some time that their attack had been seriously held up, a problem that endangered the successful part of the 15th Battalion's operation along several hundred metres of front. At 10.05pm, forty-five minutes after zero hour, the Battalion Grenade officer reported "no definite information so far but we seem to be progressing".[14] But three hours later it was apparent that this was not the case. The officer in charge of the right sector of the Suffolks' attack, Captain Norman Leith-Hay-Clark, reported just after 1am that he had:

> … no information of A Coy other than that they did not succeed in their attack … I am informed that Lt. Jenkins, Lt. Collins & Sgt. Myer Watts are wounded – I understand that the remainder of the Company are lying out in front of the old Anzac line on the "no man's land" in front of BCD trench which is strongly held by Germans.[15]

13   AWM: AWM 26/59/6: 4th Division to 1st Anzac Corps, 9 August 1916, 1.45am, Operations File Somme 1916, 4th Australian Division General Staff,.
14   TNA: WO 95/1852: G.H. Taylor (Bn Grenade Officer) to Adjutant, 8 August 1916, 10.05pm, 7 Battalion Suffolk Regiment War Diary.
15   TNA: WO 95/1852: Leith-Hay-Clark (OC Right Sector Suffolks) to OC 7th Suffolks, 9 August 1916, 1.07am, 7 Battalion Suffolk Regiment War Diary.

The Germans had been seen moving around openly on their parapet, and most of the men lying in the open in front of them were presumed to be dead or wounded. But whether alive or dead, these troops lying out in the open prevented the Suffolks from using their trench mortars. With no solid information as to the position of his men, Leith-Hay-Clark could not, or would not, order the use of his trench mortars at all, and the attack was conducted almost entirely without heavier fire support. The battalion's operation report read:

> … the assault was well carried out, but the bombardment had been insufficient, and all three waves were destroyed by machine gun fire, only one Officer, 1 NCO and 12 unwounded men came back. The Officer and men concerned deserve credit for the correctness of their assault from a narrow crowded Trench after a very severe 24 hours' previous shelling.[16]

After a promising departure from the jumping-off trench, the attack was a disaster. The Suffolks got to within 60 yards of Point 78 but could go no further.

The consequence of this situation was that the left Australian flank was dangerously unsupported and threatened from Point 78. Captain Leith-Hay-Clark came across two officers of the 15th Battalion just after 3am and reported that they:

> … appear to be misinformed of my position … [the] two officers … stated that they received information from our brigade headquarters that "A" and "D" Companies Suffolks had made good their objective – I fortunately met them before any error could take place.[17]

As a result of this chance meeting, the 4th Brigade sent an officer and 20 men of the 16th Battalion to support the British and to try to re-establish appropriate lines of communication. But the situation simply could not be cleared up. By 5am definite information was received that the Suffolks had not and could not make good their objectives. Any time the Australians tried to link up with the Suffolks they met with uninterrupted machine gun fire from Point 78, which was able to enfilade their line for a considerable distance. In the early hours of the morning they reported:

> … owing to Suffolks not being able to take [Point] 78, left Company 15th Battalion suffered heavily in taking their objectives [Points] 89 and 99 [in Park Lane] and position became untenable so withdrew to original line.[18]

16   TNA: WO 95/1852: '7th (Service) Bn The Suffolk Regiment Operations 8th and 9th August 1916', 7 Battalion Suffolk Regiment War Diary.

17   TNA: WO 95/1852: Leith-Hay-Clark to OC 7th Suffolks, 9 August 1916, 3.10am, 7 Battalion Suffolk Regiment War Diary.

18   AWM: AWM 26/59/6: 4th Division to 1st Anzac Corps, 9 August, 5.25am, Operations File Somme 1916, 4th Australian Division General Staff.

Lieutenant-Colonel Cannan had been forced to withdraw his men on the left from this position and consolidate the remaining line as best he could. News of this situation finally filtered through to the British 35th Brigade by means of little more than gossip coming through the Suffolks battalion. A telephone call was put through to the 4th Australian Brigade to strongly object to their action, and a liaison officer sent from the Suffolks to Cannan to "point out the folly of this" withdrawal.[19] Lieutenant-Colonel A.H. Wilson, commanding the 7th Suffolks agreed, reporting that "with the holding of Point 89 [by the Australians] and the capture of Ration Trench the enemy were caught in a trap, the taking of Point 78 only locked in the jaws of the trap".[20] Given the machine guns in Point 78 could pour an inordinate amount of fire into either side of the jaws of this 'trap' at will and had so far proven impregnable, this assessment was ludicrous. Fortunately, all objections either arrived too late or were ignored and the withdrawal of the 15th Battalion on its left flank was successful. At dawn the battalion held around two thirds of their final objective line, but on the left the Australian and the Suffolk infantry were in their original trenches, blaming each other for the failure on the boundary between them.

This failure of the Suffolk battalion on the night of 8/9 August cannot and should not be attributed to any sort of generic inability in the field. Theirs was a very small-scale assault, with just a few platoons of infantry and one squadron of bombers ordered to work their way up Ration Trench towards Point 78. Because of the size of the operation and the fact that they were enfilading their target, they did not have an artillery barrage to follow, rather a small, somewhat haphazard lifting barrage fired by trench mortars. This was simply not enough firepower for the job at hand, and did not eventuate in the end anyway. Trench mortar fire was ineffective against the strong German defensive emplacement, and the planned barrage itself would probably have proven much too short. The Australians had outrun much of the deeply established German wire defences in their various advances by this stage, but there was still heavy barbed-wire emplacements facing the Suffolks. The trench mortar barrage, where it was fired, had little to no effect on the wire, making the infantry's job almost impossible. None of this could be rectified for the simple reason that they were fighting along a trench with no effective heavy fire support. The threat from Point 78 was not reduced, and the German machine guns there made short work of the attacking Suffolk infantry. The Australian and British brigades had shared their preparation plans with each other, and were overtly ordered to conduct a joint operation, their actual methods of attack were entirely different. This was not one operation across two divisions, but more closely resembled two simultaneous but distinct attacks. The failure to closely connect these two operations, or to provide enough firepower to reduce the threat from Point 78 and adequately support the infantry of the 7th Suffolks as they advanced, was the primary cause of failure.

19   TNA: WO 95/1847: 6.00am 9 August 1916, 35th Brigade War Diary.
20   TNA: WO 95/1852: '7th (Service) Battalion The Suffolk Regiment Operations 8th and 9th August 1916', 7 Battalion Suffolk Regiment War Diary.

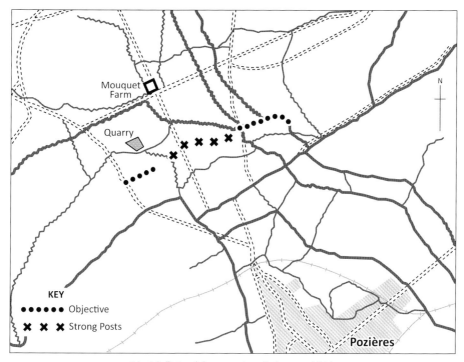

16 4th Brigade's operation, 9 August 1916.

Another attack

Point 78, then, was the most obvious problem with this operation. But although a strong German position, it was not a major threat to the general security of the line in 1st Anzac Corps' sector, although it certainly could cause a large number of casualties among working parties in the new advanced line if they exposed themselves, and seriously hindered completion of the new line. Once the men in this advanced position had been withdrawn to a safe distance, and the men holding it were generally out of reach of the German machine guns in the strongpoint, the threat was dramatically reduced. The only reason to make a second attempt to capture this point would be no more than to reach the previous night's objective. It should be remembered that this operation had been ordered as a diversionary operation in support of Fourth Army's efforts at Guillemont, which had, in any case, completely failed. A second attempt at the capture of Park Lane was not necessary in the sense of the wider campaign. A charitable observation might be that any attempt to recapture Point 78 would bring a more solid connection between the 4th Brigade on the right and the British 35th Brigade on the left, but this was not of great concern at the time as the line was solidly joined further to the rear. A less charitable observation would be that it would be a better reflection on corps or divisional command if all of the objectives of the previous night's operation had been achieved. But regardless of motivation, during the day of 9 August Birdwood hastily arranged another attack to correct the shortfalls of the night before. There could have been any number of reasons behind this renewed operation's implementation: a need to report that all objectives were captured; an attempt to straighten the line; a knee-jerk reaction to an obvious threat; or a simple failure to re-evaluate the strategic importance of another (potentially costly) operation. It is impossible to say at this remove which, or how many, of these reasons were behind Birdwood's decision to order a second operation to capture Point 78 and the failed left of the Australian line. But it is possible to say that this operation was borne of no pressing strategic or tactical requirement.

Wedged as it was between the two sectors of operation, Point 78 could not have been the true focus of either battalion in the previous operation, but had to be a flank attack for one or the other. Some adjustment to the boundary and traffic areas for the left flank of the operation would be necessary for the new operation. The 4th Australian Brigade and the 35th Brigade on their right appealed to their divisional commanders to rectify the issue. In the divisional commanders were given leeway to resettle the boundary between themselves, and they decided to put the strong-point in the Australian sector for the next assault on the line. The 4th Brigade put in the 16th Battalion under command of Lieutenant-Colonel Edmund Alfred Drake-Brockman for this follow-up attack. As before preparation for the attack was fairly straightforward because the German artillery fire, although continuing to be heavy, was still not targeting the area from which the attack would be launched and the damage it caused was minimal. Once again the 7th Suffolks would provide support by bombing up Ration Trench, but as the northerly part of this trench was now in the Australian sector, they would not be required to advance as far as they had, rather they would simply have to establish a firm flank connection with the Australians when the German strongpoint was captured.

This operation was not markedly different to the one before, but suffered from a lack of time to prepare both the artillery and the infantry for the assault. There was not sufficient time to organise much of an artillery barrage at all. A quick bombardment onto (or very near to) the objective, would be all that time allowed, although a sort of lifting barrage would be provided by trench mortars. Similarly the infantry of the 16th Battalion were wedged in between the 7th Suffolks and the line still held by the remnants of the 15th Battalion and did not have the space to form up in more than one wave. Quite simply the plan was that at midnight:

> … the intense bombardment of the objective will be commenced. Prior to the barrage lifting the first wave will move forward as close to the barrage as possible and rush the trench the moment it lifts. As soon as the line has been secured it will be consolidated and held as lightly as possible.[21]

21   AWM: AWM 26/60/6: '4th Australian Infantry Brigade Order No. 31,' 9 August 1916,

There was to be no finesse to this operation, which was again little more than a large-scale raid. The 16th Battalion was in place and ready for the operation to begin at midnight. All of its officers and senior non-commissioned officers had had the opportunity to make personal reconnaissances of the front line during the day of the 9th in preparation for the attack, as per the 4th Brigade's usual practice. The units of the 16th managed to leave their jumping-off trench in good time and within three hours could report most of the objective had been captured. An hour later the battalion adjutant, Captain Edward Joseph Parks, confirmed "everything successful. Have joined up with 15th Battalion on my right flank and Suffolks on my left flank. Am consolidating positions".[22] The 16th Battalion was responsible for the capture of as many as 70 prisoners and a number of German machine guns. A link between the Australians and the Suffolks was established and, once the 7th Suffolks removed a block at the end of their most easterly trench, for the first time a solid connection was made between the 1st Anzac Corps and II Corps in the forward lines.

With all objectives captured, this operation was ostensibly a success. It also fulfilled the brief to "think out and suggest enterprises" instead of waiting for instruction from above. But what this operation did not do was meet any major strategic requirement, nor did it meet or advance any particular tactical need. This operation to take Point 78 was little more than a raid. But importantly for the 4th Brigade, it cemented in the headquarters of the 4th Australian Division the idea that these smaller, close-range operations could be successful. Suddenly, a rush was on to conduct more of these small attacks. At 4.30am on 10 August 1916, even as the 16th Battalion's operation was ending, the 4th Brigade sent a message to the 13th Battalion to arrange an operation for the following night against a very small portion of trench slightly forward of the Australian front line. Brand told 13th Battalion headquarters was that their own battalion had so far "only [had] 70 casualties and though doing all the carrying of rations etc. for the Brigade is practically fresh". He went on to take matters out of the hands of the commander of the 13th Battalion, Lieutenant-Colonel Leslie Edward Tilney, by adding, "am arranging for 13th Battalion officers to reconnoitre ground today".[23] At the same time another operation was being planned to be undertaken by the 16th Battalion against a similarly small series of objectives. It would appear both of these attacks were simply to be conducted for the sake of continuing the small advance of the night before. Neither objective was wider than 300 yards, nor was either against a particular landmark or strongpoint. In fact the 16th was not even attacking in order to establish a new front line, but instead a series of blocks and strong posts. This battalion had already suffered a number of casualties in the attack

    Operations File Somme 1916, 4th Infantry Brigade.
22 AWM: AWM 26/60/6: 16th Bn to 4th Bde, 10 August 1916, Operations File Somme 1916, 4th Infantry Brigade.
23 AWM: AWM 26/60/6: 4th Bde to 13th Bn, 10 August 1916, 4.28am, Operations File Somme 1916, 4th Infantry Brigade.

against Point 78, although perhaps not as many as other recent operations simply as a result of the smaller scope of their attack. The 13th Battalion had not yet moved into the front line and was still preparing to relieve the 15th Battalion. The 15th had been pushed to the right to facilitate operations of the 16th Battalion against Point 78. All of the battalions of the 4th Brigade were scrambling to establish their new position. Neither the 16th nor the 13th Battalion was particularly prepared to push on with an assault on the German line, no matter on what scale, but had to scramble during the early evening to prepare for one anyway.

These smaller operations were emphatically different to anything conducted by 1st Anzac Corps since its first major operation on the Somme at Pozières weeks before. They were small, limited in scope and only a battalion or smaller in strength. Even the pre-planned attack of 8 August was on this small-scale, although the 4th Brigade had had enough preparation time to incorporate other arms. The hurriedly-planned operations of the 16th and 13th Battalions that followed were organised with such little preparation that it was not possible to have machine guns and trench mortars in place with enough time to be useful to the infantry in the field. At least there continued to be a marked reluctance to send the infantry forward for even a simple raid without artillery support wherever possible in the 4th Australian Division. But 4th Division's two planned operations for 10 August were not even connected. The two battalions conducting them were not obliged to synchronise their operations, and were openly advised that each would operate independently of the other.[24] There is little or no evidence of any influence from the experience of the 1st or 2nd Australian Division in this little series of operations – either in the planned attack of 8 August or in the follow-up operations of succeeding days.

The attack – 10 August 1916

On the night of 10/11 August the operations of the 13th and 16th Battalions went ahead as arranged and both battalions successfully gained their objectives. The 13th Battalion had attacked with two Companies in the front line (A and D Companies), and a third in close support (B Company). At 1am on 11 August, the battalion reported:

> … the bombardment commenced and [the] first wave moved into no man's land. At 1.03am the Barrage lifted and A and D Companies advanced. Word [was] received at 2am that we were in our objective and consolidating. Operations [were] seriously impeded by a dense fog. Enemy replied with a Heavy counter bombardment at 3.04am. Soon after about forty Germans made a bomb attack … but were driven off leaving about twelve killed.[25]

24   AWM: AWM 26/59/6: '4th Australian Divisional Order No. 13,' 10 August 1916, Operations File Somme 1916, 4th Australian Division General Staff.
25   AWM: AWM 26/60/6: entry for 13th Battalion 11 August 1916, 4th Brigade War Diary.

The 16th Battalion, too, launched their operation at 1am, and at 2.50 reported that they had taken their objectives and were constructing the strong posts and links they had been ordered to establish. The battalion had established some strongpoints in advance of their front, but struggled to maintain a constant garrison of them as a result of the ongoing heavy shellfire. As the sun came up they withdrew from one of these advanced posts, but maintained control of the position by constantly patrolling it during daylight, and re-occupying it during the night.

These reports of success belie a serious situation in the front lines. These ongoing operations had resulted in a relatively high casualty rate, which was taking its toll on the 4th Brigade. Artillery fire was still extremely heavy from both sides and exacted a toll, and meant that shellshock was becoming a common occurrence. The 16th Battalion was in a worse condition, having conducted two attacks in two days. But even the 13th Battalion, fresh to the front line, struggled with its circumstances and was quickly in a parlous state. This battalion had spent the three or four days before moving in to the front line providing working and carrying parties, and although the seventy casualties the battalion suffered in the process was not at all high by recent standards, the men were worn out. After a serious fight to take their objectives, they had to defend their newly-advanced line against the German bombing attack and heavy counter bombardment. Over the following day the battalion continued to come under heavy and increasingly accurate artillery fire. But instead of simply holding their new front line, companies of the battalion actively sought opportunities to push ahead in the spirit of Reserve Army's memorandum for 'rapidity, energy and offensive action'. This constant action took another toll for no gain. One such company of the 13th Battalion, D Company on the left, advanced a small distance to establish a new strongpoint, but found themselves confronted with an enemy bombing party. Although they managed to take 15 prisoners, the advance proved untenable and they withdrew. These small back-and-forth movements set the front line into a constant state of flux and left the men exhausted.

Within days any coherence in fighting to a strategic vision was gone. One operation was suggested by brigade command while another arose with divisional headquarters. At other times battalion commanders like Tilney ordered small-scale operations to advance small portions of their own front line. Tilney described the situation on 12 August 1916:

> Owing to all my front works being new and only partially dug the troops are practically unable to obtain sleep during day, and incessant digging operations go on throughout night. Tonight's operation will prevent any rest being obtained. The result is that the men and officers are becoming very fagged. I am of opinion that, for safety sake, it is necessary to relieve the Battalion tomorrow at latest.[26]

26   AWM: AWM 26/60/6: Tilney, (OC 13th Bn) to 4th Bde, 12 August 1916, Operations File Somme 1916, 4th Infantry Brigade.

The constant shellfire and movement of the line also caused serious problems with the supply of rations and ammunition. A battalion or company designated as ration or ammunition carriers might suddenly be called forward to reinforce the line, resulting in front line units receiving blunt messages such as the one Tilney received on 13 August: "It will be necessary for you to make your own arrangements for your rations tonight. The Battalion which carried this morning is going up to the line and is not available".[27] But the day before, 12 August, supplies for the 13th Battalion had not been received because the company assigned ration carrying duties had been required to act as reserve to the 16th Battalion.[28] The men of the 13th Battalion went more than 36 hours in the front line without food or water. Other materials were also in short supply. Tilney requested "wire, corkscrews,[29] picks, shovels, chloride of lime, Lewis Guns and extra magazines" at 5pm on 12 August. Other companies reported "practically no picks or shovels" and could not borrow any from neighbouring units, who were similarly undersupplied.[30]

Not only was keeping up supply challenging in the face of the constant movement and readjustment of the line, but it was difficult for battalion headquarters to know where these front-line companies were at any given time. Tilney reported in the late afternoon of 12 August "my available strength for Front Line is not more than 500 including C Company which has not yet arrived nor can I get in touch with it".[31] The situation in the front line, too, was confused and the men under great stress. Captain Hugh Douglas Pulling, the officer commanding D Company on the left of 13th Battalion's sector, struggled both to maintain a working relationship with his fellow company commanders and also to maintain a cohesive line across the battalion's front. During August 12, while in the front line, he took it upon himself to take command of all units at the front, sending the message:

> I don't know whether I am right [to take over], but I am trying to supervise the three Companies for two reasons. One that Chook[32] doesn't know much about where he his – and two Murray won't keep still and moves about everywhere.[33]

27   AWM: AWM 26/60/6: 4th Bde to OC 13th Bn, 13 August 1916, 2.10pm, Operations File Somme 1916, 4th Infantry Brigade.
28   AWM: AWM 26/60/6: 13th Bn to 4th Bde, 12 August, 7.00am, Operations File Somme 1916, 4th Infantry Brigade.
29   Iron posts for holding up barbed wire.
30   AWM: AWM: EXDOC20: Pulling (OC D Coy, 13th Bn) to OC 13th Bn, 12 August 1916, 9.35pm.
31   AWM: AWM 26/60/6: Message ST.264 from Tilney, (OC 13th Bn) to 4th Bde, 12 August 1916, 5.00pm, Operations File Somme 1916, 4th Infantry Brigade.
32   Probably Captain John Keith Henderson, KIA 14 August 1916. Pulling refers to him as "Bob" Henderson in a message sent to the CO 13th Bn, at 9am on an unspecified date, AWM: AWM 26/60/6.
33   AWM: AWM: EXDOC019: Pulling, Hugh Douglas (Major), MC.

Captain Hugh Pulling was the officer commanding D Company of the 13th Battalion. A steady and reliable officer, he often found himself the primary conduit of information into and out of 13th Battalion's sector of the front line.

Little could be done about the problems with his fellow company commanders in the field at that time and it took a great deal of effort on the part of Pulling and a few other officers working with him to establish and maintain a cohesive line. Pulling became not only an important conduit of information into and out of the front line like Captain Ferdinand Medcalf on 23 July, but made important decisions as to how the attack would go ahead, such as when he and Captain Francis Maxwell Barton "conferred … and … decided to reduce the distances the 1st and 2nd waves [of A Company] are to go out before the barrage by about half".[34] Pulling was equally energetic in establishing and maintaining a strong defensive line, and was later awarded a Military Cross for his work in the front line from 10 to 15 August 1916. Not only did he command the first wave of three attacks during the 13th Battalion's time at the front, but he went on to take command of the whole of the line in his sector "without rest or relief", and it was noted that "his presence always inspired the men, who kept cheerfully to their work under the frightful shelling and most trying conditions for six days".[35] With this the situation in the freshest of 4th Brigade's battalions, it was clear that the brigade would have to be relieved. Its battalions began to be revolved out of the line on 12 August.

The 4th Brigade's small operations had to date extended the salient to the point that they could now fit three battalions in the front line and one in close support. For support during the relief period, and to prevent gaps in this extended line, the brigade

---

34   AWM: AWM: EXDOC021: Message from Capt. F.W. Barton, OC A Coy, 10 August 1916.
35   AWM: AWM 28/2/81: Recommendation File for Honours and Awards, 4th Australian Division.

was given the services of the 50th Battalion. The 50th Battalion belonged to the 13th Brigade, also of the 4th Australian Division, which would soon take over the front line. Before the 13th Brigade could do so, however, the 50th Battalion came under the orders of Brigadier-General Brand and 4th Brigade headquarters to supply the extra manpower required to hold the line. The 50th battalion was handed over to the 4th Brigade for service from 11 August and began to relieve the 16th Battalion within 24 hours. Under cover of a heavy fog, most of the 50th were able to get through to the front line, although violent and continuous enemy shellfire held up part of the relief. They were placed into the far left of the line against the boundary with II Corps. Not only did the 50th Battalion have to move into the front line under heavy shellfire, the battalion also had to contend with embarking on a new operation immediately. At this time Reserve Army had been planning a general operation for three or four days, timing it to begin on the evening of 12 August. For reasons which remain obscure, the 4th Brigade chose to employ the 50th Battalion for this assault together with the 13th Battalion, regardless of the fact that as the attack began the 50th had only been in the front line for two hours, had already suffered what had been termed "fairly heavy" casualties from the German barrage on the way into the front line,[36] (in fact it was around 10 percent of its nominal strength) and was being asked to work under the command of another brigade which operated quite differently from its own.

The 13th Infantry Brigade, commanded by Lieutenant-Colonel Thomas William Glasgow and to which the 50th Battalion belonged, was somewhat different in its approach to training and preparation to Brand's 4th Brigade. It was considered by some the least experienced group in the 1st Anzac Corps and had yet to conduct so much as a trench raid. Like the 4th Brigade, the 13th had participated in a number of large-scale training operations under a live artillery barrage prior to entering the front line at Pozières. But the vast majority of its training focussed on route marching and bayonet fighting instead of paying closer attention to the roles of specialists in these sorts of operations. In fact the training of specialists seems to have been kept separate from the larger group exercises altogether, and no significant combined drills such as that conducted by the 14th Brigade seem to have been carried out in the 13th. And while each battalion in the brigade experienced one full-scale exercise before entering the front line, attack practices were usually undertaken by groups no larger than a company, ostensibly because suitable ground was generally not regularly available for training by larger units. In direct opposition to the training doctrine of the 4th Brigade, the function of the infantry within a large, integrated, mechanised battle-field was considered of no more than average importance in the training of the 13th Brigade, on a par with route marches and rifle training. This difference in training between the two brigades would soon become a source of tension between the 50th Battalion and battalions of the 4th Brigade.

36   AWM: AWM 26/61/15: entry for 50th Bn, 12 August 1916, Operations File Somme 1916, 13th Infantry Brigade.

The attack – 12 August 1916

For this new operation, Reserve Army's focus was on the left of 1st Anzac Corps, where two brigades of the British 12th Division were ordered to conduct an assault to straighten their line. Initially designed to be a broad-fronted attack, at the last minute the attack by the British 37th Brigade on the left of this attack was modified by Gough to involve no more than the capture of a small portion of trench through a small number of "minor attacks … with a view to keeping the enemy busy on this front".[37] This shifted the focus of the operation to the right, where the most important part of the action would be conducted by the British 35th Brigade in the centre of the operation, and the 50th and 13th Battalions of 1st Anzac Corps on the right. These two battalions were to conduct an assault on their objective line that synchronised with the attack of the 35th Brigade on their left, but orders issued by 4th Division and the 4th Brigade the day before the attack say that "as much ground as possible will be made good towards [tomorrow night's] objective" *before the operation went ahead*,[38] indicating that "if it is possible to reach any of these objectives by bombing [alone] it should be done".[39] This would remove the infantry from both their protective barrages and cooperation from their flanks, isolating them in the technology-driven battlefield and meaning that the entire burden of the operation was on their shoulders alone. Even given a chance to pause and prepare to cooperate in a broader-fronted operation, both Cox and Brand showed a clear preference for ad hoc, small-scale operations to try to take their objectives.

Bombing parties were pushed forward, but to little effect. Certainly it did not prove possible to reach any of the objectives by bombing alone. But because these parties were now operating between the established jumping-off trench and the objective line, they were in danger from their own artillery barrage which was supposed to be helping them in their attack. Orders now had to allow for the 4th Brigade to "ascertain the exact position these parties will be in when the attack takes place, so that the Artillery may be informed and the attacking troops notified".[40] The barrage itself was the same as others organised for the 4th Division. It once again landed on the objective line before carefully lifting away, providing a very minimal cover for the infantry. It is not possible to say from extant records whether or not the artillery were successfully notified of the exact position of the advanced infantry parties, but given the nature of the barrage itself, they were in little danger from anything other than misfired and stray shells for most of the barrage timetable. And so, at 10.30pm on

37 TNA: WO 95/1823: 13 August 1916, 12th Division War Diary.
38 AWM: AWM 26/60/6 '4th Australian Infantry Brigade Order No. 33,' 11 August 1916, Operations File Somme 1916, 4th Infantry Brigade.
39 AWM: AWM 26/59/6: 4th Division to 4th Brigade, 11 August 1916, Operations File Somme 1916, 4th Australian Division General Staff.
40 AWM: AWM 26/59/6: '4th Australian Divisional Order No. 14,' 12 August 1916, Operations File Somme 1916, 4th Australian Division General Staff.

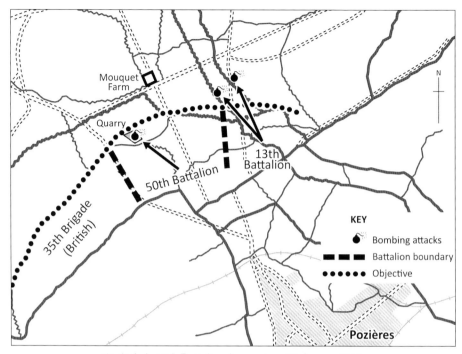

17 50th & 13th Battalions' operation, 12 August 1916.

12 August, the operation went ahead as planned. The British operation was partially successful; importantly for 1st Anzac Corps' story the greatest gains were made in 35th Brigade's sector on the right against the corps boundary. Both the 50th and 13th Battalions were also able to advance to their objectives, with the 50th successfully capturing 750 yards of trench and the 13th making similar gains along with securing a large supply of enemy shells and two large German dugouts.

As a result of this operation both the 50th and 13th Battalions advanced their line a small distance. But within a very short time the 50th Battalion ran out of critical supplies. A lack of supplies had affected various units in the front time at different times for some weeks, but there was a new, more ominous reason for the shortages experienced by the 50th Battalion. At last the Germans had the measure of the change in direction of 1st Anzac Corps' operations. Their artillery had been slow to notice that the new operations were not advancing in an easterly direction from the OG Lines towards Courcelette and Bapaume, but were now headed towards Thiepval to the north-west. But as the experience of the 50th Battalion during the relief demonstrated, the German artillery was now concentrating on the new area of operations and was hampering work in a way it had not done since the 4th Australian Division entered the line. The constant heavy bombardment meant that parties carrying food and water forward to the 50th Battalion found it almost impossible to get through.

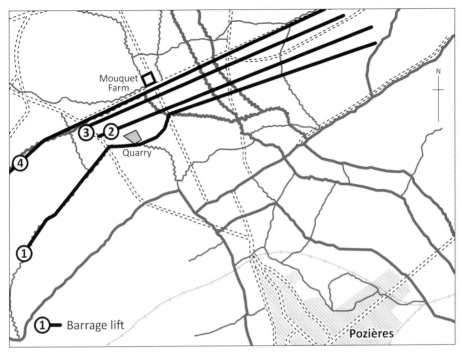

18 Artillery barrage for the 4th Division's operation, 12 August 1916.

Despite what was described as "numerous fatigues doing their utmost to provide those necessities," only seven tins of water had arrived for the entire battalion by the morning of 13 August.[41] The battalion continued to sustain reasonably heavy casualties as a result of the artillery bombardment, and work was slowed by a lack of tools. The 50th Battalion was in a similar position to that faced by the 13th Battalion just a few days earlier, and with 4th Infantry Brigade headquarters demonstrating little or no ability (or indeed desire) to ameliorate their conditions.

Following the withdrawal of his men, the officer commanding the 4th Infantry Brigade, Brigadier-General Brand, submitted some notes on his recent successes to the 4th Division. He made many important points about his successes coming from a reliance on things like receiving early information of the task at hand so it could be disseminated to all concerned in good time, "resolute patrolling of no man's land" and personal reconnaissance by every officer, and being aware of the enemy's habits before launching an operation. One of his particularly interesting tactics was to have his first infantry wave thicker than succeeding waves. He observed:

41   AWM: AWM 26/61/15: entry for 50th Bn, 12 August 1916, Operations File Somme 1916, 13th Infantry Brigade.

The first wave must get its objective; if it hesitates chaos follows in the rear. Men want to feel that their mates are on their left and right. The necessary cohesion is secured [with enough men. It is] only human nature for men to hesitate when alone and ignorant of what is taking place.

"Good leaders," he added, "are essential in [the] front line. A few calm words from them stop men from pushing forward into our own barrage."[42] But while Brand noted that 'confidence in the artillery was an important factor' in the successes of the 4th Brigade, he made no comment on the nature of the barrages fired as a part of his operations. To date they had been inappropriately fired – landing first on the only objective of the attack before carefully moving away in a series of timed lifts. The timed lifts were completely pointless without having infantry to follow them, and the artillery might as well have stopped making them after the first movement off of the objective line. Experience had increasingly demonstrated that the more closely the infantry and artillery worked together, the greater the potential for success, particularly in large-scale operations such as that at Pozières on 23 July. There was only so much Brand's confident, cohesive first wave of infantry could achieve in the face of unhindered German machine guns – and that was very little indeed without sustaining very high casualties. Morale without firepower was all but redundant on the Western Front. But Brand was not alone in failing to understand the importance of firmly connecting the plans for the lifting artillery barrage with the infantry in the field, as became apparent when the 4th Division renewed its operations after the relief of the 4th Brigade.

The story of the 4th Brigade's first period in the front line at Pozières is complicated and busy. This short period of time set an alarming precedent for future action by the 1st Anzac Corps. From 9 to 12 August, any perceived opportunity to keep up forward momentum was seized at a number of different levels – Army, corps, brigade and even battalion. This was a direct result of the directive from Reserve Army for 'relentless pressure' everywhere and subordinates commanders putting forward operations of their own. 1st Anzac Corps' series of operations from 9 to 12 August 1916, no matter at which level they arose, were all narrow-fronted, small-scale attacks against very close objectives. There was little finesse to these attacks. The artillery bludgeoned the objective and then carefully lifted a short distance away to protect the infantry rushing it. Where these attacks were not successful, they were generally poorly supported by artillery, such as the Suffolks' operation which relied on lighter fire from trench mortars instead. But this was not the norm. The 4th Australian Division established that this method could work – all of their smaller operations were more or less entirely successful in capturing their objectives. But while the division was celebrating 'success' on a regular basis, it was extremely limited in scope. Their advances were tiny. They never encompassed their entire front, rarely if ever taking in more than 500 yards of

42   AWM: AWM 26/60/6: 'Notes on successes of 4th Australian Brigade,' 16 August 1916, Operations File Somme 1916, 4th Infantry Brigade.

the front line. They advanced these short portions of the line only around 150-200 yards and no more. Yes, the threat from one or two German strongpoints was reduced, but these did not threaten the line as it stood and could have been dealt with either in conjunction with, or in preparation for, another large-scale operation. Apart from a more solid point of contact with the 7th Suffolk Battalion on the left, nothing that happened while the 4th Brigade were in the front line advanced the general strategy of northward movement in any meaningful way, or materially benefited the position of the 1st Anzac Corps.

In the meantime, the 4th Brigade had exhausted itself through this constant jockeying for position. The 15th and 16th Battalions were depleted through the conduct of one or more of these small assaults on the German line, and the 14th Battalion had suffered from a series of strong German counter-attacks not dealt with here. The 13th Battalion, as has been demonstrated, was in a similarly depleted state through supply problems and battle casualties, and within hours of its arrival in the line as reinforcement, the 50th Battalion, too, was suffering heavily. By 12 August 1916, the 4th Brigade had suffered 1,283 casualties. Small-scale success came at a cost and a very serious cost at that when compared to the limitations of the achievement. But nevertheless it meant that regular reports could be made of objectives achieved and lines advanced, and the example of this period would prove dangerously seductive in the future.

4

"He will not move forward tonight":
The 13th Brigade Demonstrates the Danger of Ongoing Operations and Low Morale

The 4th Australian Division did not change its tactical approach in the second half of its first spell in the front line, and continued to prosecute small-scale operations in a north to north-westerly direction. If these operations were not ordered at Army and corps level, operations were created by the division itself. The loose correlation of operations on the ground to Reserve Army's overall plan for northward movement was slipping away ever faster, and attacks were being conducted on such a small-scale that had they not been so costly in lives they would be inconsequential. And yet the seduction of being able to report a 'success' meant that the second part of the 4th Division's spell in the front line firmly established the idea that small-scale attacks were a useful approach to operations on the Somme even more firmly both within the division and indeed at 1st Anzac Corps headquarters. And yet, this short period of time would be another very costly period for 1st Anzac Corps not only in terms of both of men and materiel, but also, in a very serious way, morale.

On 13 August 1916 the 4th Brigade was replaced by the 13th Brigade. Two battalions remained in the line following the departure of the 4th Infantry Brigade. One was the 50th Battalion, which reverted to its usual brigade, and the other the 13th Battalion of the 4th Brigade, which was temporarily transferred to command of the 13th Brigade. Once the relief was complete, the north west part of 1st Anzac Corps' line was held by the 50th Battalion on the left, next to the boundary with II Corps; the 13th Battalion in the centre; and then the 51st Battalion on the right and at the apex of the salient. The remainder of the line, comprising the OG Lines facing the village of Courcelette, was held by the 49th Battalion in a predominantly defensive role. But although a new brigade was in charge of the front line, the approach to battle changed very little.

The 50th, 13th and 51st Battalions would soon be called on to continue the series of small operations to the north west. The 4th Division's ongoing insistence on these small attacks to inch the line forward caused a great deal of difficulty for the battalions in the front line which had had little or no rest. Both the 50th and especially

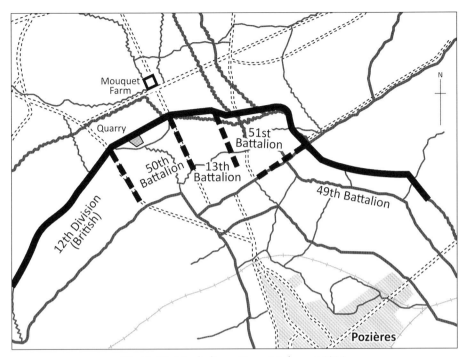

19 4th Division's dispositions, 13 August 1916.

the 13th Battalion were feeling the effects of front line exposure and exhaustion. The 50th had suffered some 100 casualties on its way into the front line, and was finding it very difficult to take food and water up to its men. The 13th Battalion was no better. Lieutenant-Colonel Tilney had already requested relief of his men. On 12 August he wrote to 4th Brigade headquarters to say:

> I find that C Company has been working almost continuously for the last two days and nights. The rest of the Battalion has done the same. Tonight and tomorrow will make 72 hours without sleep. I think this is approaching the limit of human endurance. Of course if it is absolutely necessary to hang on another night we will do so.[1]

His plea fell on deaf ears, and his battalion would be called on to do much more than just hang on for another night. The two most worn out battalions in the line would be a major component of the next operation of the 4th Australian Division.

1   AWM: AWM 26/60/6: Tilney (OC 13th Bn) to 4th Bde, 12 August 1916 (untimed), Operations File Somme 1916, 4th Infantry Brigade.

Preparation

Even as operations were going ahead on 12 August, 1st Anzac Corps was preparing a memorandum to the 4th Division to spell out its future plans. The document went as far as to identify objectives for the next attack, and would form the basis for planning for the next few days. It also gives an indication of the mindset in 1st Anzac Corps headquarters in regards to the limited vision being applied to operations. Birdwood considered the amount of front his corps had been allotted to hold "considerable for the troops available",[2] and sent a request to Army Headquarters to have the boundaries of his sector of operations brought closer together. Birdwood's suggested solution was for Gough to extend II Corps to the right to take over more of the line from 1st Anzac Corps. It should be noted that at this time II Corps was holding at least five times the amount of front line that 1st Anzac Corps was, although it was not attacking along the full length of its front. But according to Birdwood, a reduced line would make operations easier. The main problem, this document outlines, was that part of the objective was 400 yards from the jumping-off trench and so "even with a reduced line … the arrangements for attack will not be simple". But more than once in the recent past narrow-fronted attacks had either put the flank advance in serious danger or caused it to fail. Furthermore, operations at Pozières had comfortably dealt with an advance over 400 yards, and demonstrated that it could be done in the face of serious opposition and well-established defences. 1st Anzac Corps headquarters was becoming more and more short-sighted, and did not demonstrate any tendency to seek out and apply lessons from the past few days and weeks.

So from 12 August, directed 1st Anzac Corps, the energies of the corps would be "limited to the occupation of a line in the vicinity of Mouquet Farm".[3] Even the major objectives of the entire corps had come down to arbitrarily-drawn positions on a no further than 200 yards away. It is significant that the portion of the line Birdwood wanted to pass off to II Corps in order to shorten his front contained Mouquet Farm, the most significant obstacle in his area of operations. However, perhaps sensing it was not realistic for II Corps to take over yet more of the front and that his request would be turned down (which it was), Birdwood also put in place contingency plans just in case "the present boundary between us and the adjoining Corps is to be adhered to". In that case "then our attack must be extended to the left".[4] Surely now Mouquet Farm would have to be taken.

---

2   AWM: AWM 26/50/16: Brudenell White to 4th Division (S. 637), 12 August 1916, Operations File Somme 1916, 1st Anzac Corps General Staff.
3   AWM: AWM 26/50/16: Brudenell White to 4th Division (S. 637), 12 August 1916, Operations File Somme 1916, 1st Anzac Corps General Staff.
4   Ibid.

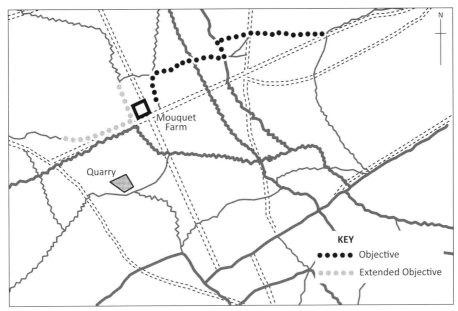

20 Birdwood's future plans explained, 12 August 1916.

Developing plans

Despite Birdwood's bluster on 7 August about advancing far beyond the farm, there had been no concerted attempt to take it, prepare to take it, or include it in the objectives of any of the small operations that had been going on in the interim period. As the plans from 12 August were modified for action, Mouquet Farm was included – although it should be said its inclusion was tentative at best. The ruined farm buildings of Mouquet Farm itself were only encompassed by the 'extended' attack which would take place only if the present boundary between 1st Anzac Corps and II Corps was to be maintained. In other words, only if Birdwood could not wriggle out of having to do it. Unfortunately for Birdwood, with his requests to shorten his front denied, Mouquet Farm would have to be dealt with in the next major operation. This came when Reserve Army ordered a wider operation for the night of 14 August 1916 which crossed the boundary between II Corps and 1st Anzac Corps as the operation of 8 August had. Once again the cooperation across the boundary line was minimal for II Corps. While 1st Anzac Corps was to push forward to a line as far as 400 yards away in some cases, II Corps would support them by pushing forward "a strong bombing attack … with a view to joining up with the left of the [1st Anzac Corps] attack".[5]

5   TNA: WO 95/518: 'Reserve Army Operation Order No. 19', 13 August 1916, Headquarters Branches and Services General Staff.

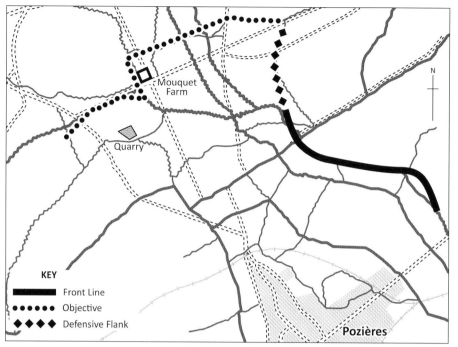

21 Reserve Army's objectives, 14 August 1916.

Their bombing attack was to be pushed up an existing but as yet uncaptured trench 400 yards to the north west of Skyline Trench, roughly parallel to Ration Trench.

If this plan sounds familiar, it is because it is almost exactly the same as previous recent operations devised by Reserve Army. The objective line was different, but the method of a stronger attack by 1st Anzac Corps with a weak supporting attack on the left flank by II Corps was exactly the same tactic that had caused problems on 8 August. In that particular operation the 7th Suffolks had suffered from the lack of an artillery barrage to protect their advance, causing heavy casualties and preventing the battalion from reaching its objective. This plan differed only in that the corps further to the left of Reserve Army's line was to cooperate to discharge gas and smoke in the direction of the German trenches if the weather permitted. Not only that, but the orders given by Reserve Army extended the marked salient that 1st Anzac Corps' line formed. The new plans for 1st Anzac Corps had the centre right advance in a way which would add some 450 yards to the front line in their sector. There is no evidence in official papers that there was any recognition that this would stretch 1st Anzac Corps further, despite complaints that at 1,200 yards the line was already 'considerable for the troops available'.

But the plans for this attack would be modified still further. Orders passed from Reserve Army on to 1st Anzac Corps on their way to the 4th Division. Birdwood did not modify the line further as it passed orders down to division. But he did open the door for Reserve Army's objective line to be modified, leaving it to Major-General Cox to decide whether or not the new operation should include the capture of Mouquet Farm. In orders which set the date for renewed operations towards the farm for the night of 14 August 1916, Birdwood also left it up to unit commanders to "determine the best forming up places for the attack [and] the best approaches and lines of defence".[6] Aside from, ordering troops to advance under the bombardment, to consolidate with specially told off parties and to issue troops moving forward with green flares to communicate with aircraft, Corps orders are empty. They do little more than pass on information from Reserve Army, issue very generic infantry plans, and leave it up to other commanders to provide any form of specific planning. And in the end Cox decided to exclude Mouquet Farm. Although this did not agree with Reserve Army's objective, there appears to have been no repercussions for doing so.

So yet another operation conducted by 1st Anzac Corps omitted the most significant defensive feature of the immediate vicinity. The main part of the advance was to be made by the 51st Battalion at the apex of the salient. The advance here as laid down by Reserve Army did not change, and the 51st Battalion continued to make the biggest forward leap of the operation with an objective as much as 400-450 yards away. The end result of all this was that if the plan succeeded, the line would continue to form a sharper salient than ever before – Birdwood's original objection to the position of his corps. Birdwood apparently remained silent. The left sector of this operation made even less sense than the continued advance at the apex. Here the 13th Battalion, instead of taking Mouquet Farm as it had originally been designed to do, would now, if successful, end up skirting around the south side of the farm. And not from a safe distance – they would be so close that they could almost put their hand over the parapet and touch it. But further modifications to the left of the 13th Battalion can only be described as bizarre. On the boundary with II Corps, where the 50th Battalion held the line, the plan was for the men in the jumping-off trench to leave their position and move back 250 yards to facilitate a close barrage. The battalion's objective then became *their own original front line positions*. The 50th Battalion formed a link between the bombing attack of the 145th British Brigade to their left and the advance of the 13th Battalion on their right, but there was simply no need for them to move. The plan to attack such reduced objectives made no sense at all.

The reason for the reduction in the objective on the left appears to have been a series of concerted German counter-attacks against the 145th Brigade in the area of the

6   AWM: AWM 4/1/48/5 Pt. 2: '1st A. & N.Z.A. Corps Order No. 24 by Lieut.-General Sir W.R. Birdwood,' 14 August 1916, 4th Australian Division General Staff War Diary.

corps boundary between II Corps and the 1st Anzac Corps. Most of these counter-attacks were unsuccessful. A more serious assault on the night of 13 August pushed the British out of Skyline Trench and the adjacent Sixth Avenue for a period of time. The Germans then retained control of two points on the junction of the Australian and British line. The 12th British Division had been relieved earlier that day, and as a result of the counter-attacks and ongoing heavy German artillery fire, plans for them to coordinate with the Australian operation did not come to fruition. And, as had happened so often in the past, there was ongoing uncertainty over just how well the line was established on the left of 1st Anzac Corps' line. On the morning of 13 August Lieutenant-Colonel Tilney had reported that it was "impossible to define [my] exact position owing to obliteration of landmark and trenches".[7] This was the area in which the objective was most modified. But while the reduction in the objective on the left may have dealt with uncertainty felt about the situation in this sector, it did nothing to flatten the salient, or deal with 1st Anzac Corps headquarters' concern about the extension of its front line. II Corps' participation was reduced further to pushing forward strong offensive patrols; it would only occupy trenches found to be empty, instead of actively joining the larger operation. As always, although some significant problems were thrown up with the planned attack for 14 August, Gough, in his impetuosity, much preferred to push on rather than reassess or rewrite (and therefore delay) his plans.

The final plan consisted of an operation that was reduced to a degree that defied operational logic at all. The main thrust of the attack advanced the line 400 yards in a direction that was only vaguely related to the encirclement of Thiepval as envisaged by Reserve Army's earlier statement of intent. It also extended 1st Anzac Corps' line, despite Birdwood and his staff considering their troops thinly stretched as it was. The most serious concern, however, was that the areas of greatest resistance received the least attention. On the left of the line the Germans were resolutely and repeatedly conducting counter-attacks, and seriously destabilising the British line in II Corps' sector of operations. Mouquet Farm was also a significant threat that had been repeatedly demonstrated to be a considerable obstacle full of Germans with machine guns and troops. These would not be dealt with by the reduced objective line, and would in fact be left behind the advance of the 51st Battalion should all go to plan. The newly-advanced line would then be threatened with enfilade fire from German strongpoints. None of this was taken into account, nor was it raised as either a potential problem before the operation went ahead, or a factor that had been of concern in after-action reports. The weaknesses in not pushing the attack on the left or simply in advancing too far on the right went unnoticed.

This situation is particularly noticeable in relation to Mouquet Farm. Mouquet Farm is a familiar name to Australians interested in the history of the First World

---

7   AWM: AWM 26/60/6: Tilney (OC 13th Bn) to 4th Bde, 13 August 1916, 9.15am, Operations File Somme 1916, 4th Infantry Brigade.

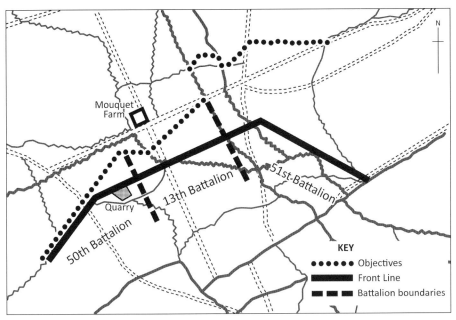

22 4th Division's final objectives, 14 August 1916.

War even today, and has a sort of iconic presence in many later studies as 'Moo-Cow Farm' or 'Mucky Farm',[8] a place of great significance to Australian soldiers of the Great War. It was certainly a significant feature of the battlefield, particularly once the village of Pozières was secured. But Mouquet Farm was simply never a significant feature of operational orders. Even three or four weeks after the Australians began operations along Pozières Ridge Mouquet Farm was not an objective, and those who may have thought they were attacking the farm were simply attacking in the direction of it. Mouquet Farm remained outside all objective lines and therefore strictly out of reach. It was simply not accorded the particular attention it required as a threat to the projected advance. Bizarrely, the German stronghold at Mouquet Farm seems to have been almost wilfully ignored by 1st Anzac Corps.

8   So often it is stated with confidence that Mouquet Farm was always known to the Australians as 'Moo-cow Farm' or 'Mucky Farm', but neither term is present in any orders, reports, messages or any other official documents relating to operations in the area. Soldiers were more likely to render the name of the farm "Mokay," "Mouquette" or "Mouque", and even then these spelling errors decrease as the soldiers became more familiar with the name. They do, however, indicate probable pronunciation. More persisted in using the French name *Ferme du Mouquet*. 'Moo-cow Farm' or 'Mucky Farm' should not be considered the usual Australian term for the place at all.

And yet the farm was well known to be a hub of German infantry activity, with large numbers of soldiers repeatedly seen moving towards it. In early August a sketch had been drawn of the farm using information from an old French woman who was a refugee from the area, but that information had yet to be widely disseminated.[9] Counter-attacks, some of considerable size, were reported to have been launched from the rubble of the farm compound on more than one occasion. On 11 August a strong German counter-attack against the 16th Battalion issued from the destroyed buildings, with observers reporting the "enemy leaving Mouquet Farm in large numbers … leaving the farm and spreading fanwise [to form] a thick line".[10] This defensive network was a serious problem to any future advance – much more than Point 78 had ever been – and yet its capture was simply not a priority. It was photographed from the air on a number of occasions, and every now and then had some mortar rounds aimed at it. The Heavy Artillery also used it as a kind of practice target and scored a number of direct hits. But no special measures to attack it had ever been incorporated into infantry orders, and on the occasions the farm dropped out of the objective line, no particular procedures seem to have been taken to maintain a safe distance until it could be dealt with. Should the 13th Battalion's operation succeed, their front line would be less than 10 yards from the ruined walls of Mouquet Farm's buildings.

The attack on 14 August with its reduced objective line was, as always, planned to be conducted under an artillery barrage. The barrage for the operation would take place in three lifts. It would begin on the road running along the southern face of the farm buildings at 10pm. After three minutes it would lift 100 yards to just beyond the farm buildings for two minutes, then another 100 lift for another two minutes, and finally, seven minutes into the attack, it would fall on a line about 200-250 yards to the north of the farm buildings, or as much as 300 yards from the objective line. Mouquet Farm itself would receive one bombardment by heavy trench mortars at an unspecified time, but otherwise received no special attention from the artillery, the barrage lifts of which were mostly directed beyond it. This was entirely inadequate, particularly given the persistent failures of the trench mortars in recent operations. But worse than this, the artillery plans bore almost no resemblance to those of the infantry. The closest point of correlation between the two was the 51st Battalion. In most places the 51st Battalion had the benefit of their objective being under the second lift of the barrage, giving them the cover of one lift as they crossed no man's land. That first fall of the barrage was almost 300 yards from their jumping-off trench, however, and so even this small 'benefit' was of very little use. The 13th Battalion's objective was mostly around 80–100 yards short of even the first fall of the barrage, and so they would not

9   AWM: AWM 26/52/4: '1st Anzac Corps Summary (Intelligence) No. 14. From 6pm on 6th to 6pm on 7th August, 1916, Part I,', Operations File Somme 1916, 1st Anzac Corps Intelligence.

10   AWM: AWM 26/60/6: 'Report on Enemy Attack on 16th Bn 11-8-16,' 12 August 1916, Operations File Somme 1916, 4th Infantry Brigade.

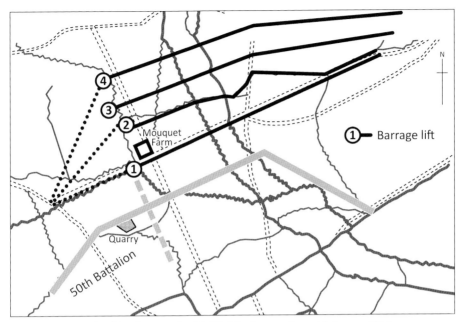

23   Artillery barrage for 4th Division's operations, 14 August 1916.

be able to closely work with the artillery plan at any point in the operation. As for the 50th Battalion's sector, in which the infantry was being withdrawn in order to facilitate a close-falling barrage, there were actually no concrete orders given for the barrage. Worryingly, however, the barrage indicates through some dotted lines that it was unlikely to fall anywhere near the infantry at all.

Reserve Army had ordered that at "Zero [hour] an intense fire of 18-pounders at the highest possible rate consistent with accuracy will open on the whole front of attack" but that the "details as regards the actual distance behind the objectives of assault to which the barrage is to be lifted finally will be mutually settled by the GOC's RA[11] of the Corps concerned".[12] This demonstrates that this inadequately applied artillery barrage was the work of 1st Anzac Corps. But worse came when the barrage was then further weakened the commander of the 4th Division, Major-General Cox. To deal with German advanced posts that had been breaking up infantry attacks, Reserve Army had arranged for an advanced barrage on the night of 14 August to add to the firepower of the attack. There had been no chance to bombard the objective for any period of time before the operation simply because it was so rushed, although

11   General Officers Commanding the Royal Artillery.
12   TNA: WO 95/518 'Artillery Instructions No. 21. Reference Reserve Army Operation Order No. 19,' 13 August 1916, Headquarters Branches & Services: General Staff.

strongpoints like Mouquet Farm and the Quarry had been bombarded on at least four occasions before 12 August. But Cox determined that he would prefer the German front line to receive as much of the main barrage as possible, and specifically requested that this arrangement be altered. The number of guns firing this advanced barrage was therefore reduced from forty-eight to sixteen. This left few guns to deal with any advanced posts established by the Germans until the infantry stumbled upon them as they crossed no man's land.

The infantry plan was quite straightforward. The men were deployed in two waves, but there was only one objective, so again the only role the second wave of infantry had left to play was close support to the first wave. Once again, it should be remembered that aside from a small portion of the line at the far right of the attack, every lift of the artillery barrage would take place beyond the infantry operation. The division continued to apply firepower, but failed to integrate it with its infantry plan beyond a shared 'zero hour' between the artillery and the infantry. Instead of protection from German machine guns and rifles, the best the infantry could hope for was that the inadequate barrage would prevent German reinforcements reaching the front line, but, given 1st Anzac Corps Intelligence was not yet aware that Mouquet Farm could provide reinforcements for the German line via an extended system of tunnels, they could not know that even this slim hope was in vain.

The attack – 14 August 1916

The infantry were in place and ready to go on time, and so at 10pm on the night of 14 August the operation commenced. Almost immediately it was evident that on the right of the line, where the 51st Battalion was making the longest advance, the barrage had been almost completely ineffective. This was the sector in which the barrage started more than 300 yards from the jumping-off trench. D Company of the 51st, in reserve, recorded that four enemy machine guns were still firing as they watched the other three companies move forward. Unsurprisingly, A Company on the farthest right of the advance failed completely. B Company on the left and C Company in the centre made an advance to within 60 yards of a previously uncharted German trench, probably near their objective, and attempted to dig in on a front of 300 yards. With them were some Lewis gunners, but even this extra firepower could not protect the group from the deadly rifle and machine gun fire that had not been suppressed at all by the inadequate barrage. Lieutenant-Colonel Arthur Murray Ross, commanding the 51st Battalion, could only make the assessment that there was little chance of the line being held as the sun came up. The final straw came when the officer commanding B Company realised that he was no longer in touch with the 13th Battalion on his left, and so retired. As the post operation report states, the lack of touch:

> … this exposed the whole line and a general retirement was ordered – lack of support on the left and the weak numbers at the objective decided [the officer commanding B Company] to come away. Several detachments however dug in at

various points and held on; these had to come away by daybreak on the morning of the 15th.[13]

The 51st Battalion's operation had failed completely, simply the result of an artillery barrage that was too distant from the jumping-off trench to provide any protection for the infantry in the field at all.

In the centre Tilney, commanding the 13th Battalion had, as ordered, attacked in two waves. Three companies attacked side by side, with two platoons of each company in each attacking wave. Although they, too, got away in good time, as they advanced the first wave of infantry came across an unexpected trench about seventy five yards from the jumping-off trench, which delayed their advance. Another trench 150 yards further on was captured by A Company, who found it to be full of Germans. Around the same time Captain Pulling reported from the front of the advance that he had "eleven Fritzes here, a machine gun [has also been] captured and destroyed".[14] Captain Hugh Pulling was still acting as the main focus of the messages and plans of the 13th Battalion. His continued cheerfulness and reliability both in sending and receiving messages and in organising men of both his and neighbouring companies were an important factor in the cohesion of the 13th Battalion both during the operation itself and during the period of consolidation that followed. A message from 13th Battalion headquarters in reply to him stated "[f]rom all accounts we have done excellently ... The boys must have done wonders".[15]

However, it was becoming clear that some of the battalions of the 13th Brigade had neglected some of their reconnaissance duties. When it became apparent to brigade staff that their unit was about be sent into the line, they had sent a number of officers forward to reconnoitre the road to Pozières Cemetery through Mash Valley. Knowledge of this route was clearly important for any unit entering the battlefield, but there is no evidence of widespread reconnaissance any further forward, or of potential objectives or German strongpoints, or indeed of a broad dissemination of any of this sort of information to subordinate officers. Specialist units made a point of reconnoitring prior to the attack; for example the 13th Australian Machine Gun Company made sure all officers saw the position of guns to be taken over and the officer commanding the 4th Australian Machine Gun Company consulted about his experience in the line. But it cannot be assumed that this higher level of preparation also occurred in the infantry units. During the battle this became increasingly apparent, with the 51st Battalion digging in along a line they could not locate in relation to the original objective, and the 13th Battalion coming across unexpected

13   AWM: AWM 26/61/15: '51st Battalion Operation Report August 13th -17th 1916,' 15 August 1916, Operations File Somme 1916, 13th Infantry Brigade.

14   AWM: AWM 26/60/6: Pulling, (OC D Coy 13th Bn) to OC 13th Bn, 14 August 1916, 11.15pm, Operations File Somme 1916, 4th Infantry Brigade.

15   AWM: AWM 26/60/6: 13th Bn to Pulling (OC D Coy 13th Bn), 14 August 1916, 11.55pm, Operations File Somme 1916, 4th Infantry Brigade.

trenches and obstacles on their way. This was particularly frustrating for the 13th Battalion who were operating in a different brigade to their home unit. Whereas the 4th Brigade was particularly diligent in its preparation and reconnaissance, the 13th Brigade was proving that it was much less so.

Having managed to advance through several unexpected obstacles, the 13th Battalion found itself increasingly isolated. The congratulatory message to Captain Pulling about having 'done wonders' carried the added warning, "[b]e careful old chap as 51st and 50th don't seem to have met with same success".[16] Shortly afterwards, around midnight, it was confirmed:

> … neither [of] the two flank Battalions had come up, and that in consequence our right and left flanks were exposed. [At] 12.45am [we were] heavily counter-attacked from front and flanks compelled to retire onto our original lines.[17]

Pulling proved to be the only hope the battalion command had of fixing the situation. He had been the most reliable in maintaining lines of communication and getting regular situation reports back to battalion headquarters, and therefore was given the responsibility of steadying the rest of the battalion. He was advised to "try and get word to front to consolidate what they take, and if flanks (50th and 51st) do not come up to build strongpoints on flanks with Lewis Guns".[18] Pulling reported around midnight that "reports [have] come in from [the] 51st Battalion who don't seem to be advancing at all and rather disorganised", and at the same time that the "enemy seems quiet".[19] The reason for the quietness soon became apparent when within minutes the Germans counter-attacked in force. Pulling's next situation report sent just fifteen minutes after the last one read:

> I have to report that all our men have had to return to our original trenches owing to the fact that there was no one on either flank and a counter-attack in force drove our men out … the stunt has eventuated into a very successful raid on our part as we killed a lot – captured a number of men and one machine gun but owing to flanks we have gained no ground. We are ready for any eventuality now and awaiting further orders from you.[20]

16   AWM: AWM 26/60/6: 13th Bn to Pulling (OC D Coy 13th Bn), 14 August 1916, 11.55pm, Operations File Somme 1916, 4th Infantry Brigade.
17   AWM: AWM 26/60/6: 13th Bn to 13th Bde, 15 August 1916, 1.14am, Operations File Somme 1916, 4th Infantry Brigade.
18   AWM: AWM 26/60/6: 13th Bn to Pulling, 14 August 1916, 11.55pm, Operations File Somme 1916, 4th Infantry Brigade.
19   AWM: AWM 26/60/6: Pulling to OC 13th Bn, 14th August 1916, midnight (error on message: should read 15 August 1916), Operations File Somme 1916, 4th Infantry Brigade.
20   AWM: AWM 26/60/6: Pulling (OC D Coy 13th Bn) to OC 13th Bn, dated 14th August

Isolated and under pressure, there was little else Pulling and the men of the 13th Battalion could do. Tilney reported "[a]m further strengthening original position as far as possible owing to exhausted condition of battalion. Our strength now well under 400".[21] Neither flank of the 13th Battalion was connected to its neighbours of the 13th Brigade. Tilney had no other option but to complete his battalion's withdrawal.

What had happened on the left of the 13th Battalion? On 14 August the 50th Battalion had had the hardest time of the three – and they were simply attacking and retaking a position they already held. But events before the operation went ahead would have very serious consequences for the morale and the actions of the 50th Battalion. They had been on the receiving end of a German counter-attack during the day preceding the assault which resulted in heavy machine gun fire being brought to bear on them from the left. Their position from the outset of the operation was badly enfiladed and was repeatedly subjected to heavy German shelling. Some of the men had to be evacuated from the left of the line before the main operation went ahead. A "terrific bombardment" was kept up on their lines all day with "enemy guns blowing trenches and saps to pieces".[22] This resulted in 45 men being killed and another 105 wounded before midday. The barrage also wreaked havoc on the battalion's ability to keep up the supply of food, water and ammunition to the front line. Out of a party of sixteen men sent to get water and food to the front line in the afternoon, fifteen became casualties before they could complete their task. Water became particularly scarce in all parts of the 50th Battalion's line, and messages regularly mentioned the desperate thirst of the men in the front line.

50th Battalion headquarters was heavily shelled throughout the afternoon and into the evening of 14 August. The battalion received a further blow in the form of the evacuation of their commanding officer, Lieutenant-Colonel Frederick William Hurcombe, with shellshock around 6pm. Hurcombe was an experienced soldier who had been commissioned in the South Australian Garrison Artillery in 1894, served as a major in the Boer War and was the original second in command of the 10th Battalion on its formation. He served in this capacity with the 10th Battalion throughout the Gallipoli campaign, following which he was appointed commander of the 50th Battalion. However, after thirty six hours of shellfire at Mouquet Farm his nerves gave out and the 49-year-old officer was evacuated, never to return to the front line. The situation of the 50th Battalion was desperate before the operation even began.

Command of the 50th Battalion was taken over by Major Ross Blyth Jacob. He inherited a situation in which one of his companies was completely isolated and

21   AWM: AWM 26/60/6: 13th Bn to 13th Bde, 15 August 1916, 1.14am, Operations File Somme 1916, 4th Infantry Brigade..
22   AWM: AWM 26/61/15: entry for 50th Bn, 14 August 1916, Operations File Somme 1916, 13th Infantry Brigade.

another contained only thirty-five men by the time the attack began. They were hungry, thirsty and shellshocked, but despite this the men of the 50th Battalion were able to move backwards into their makeshift jumping-off trench on time and then moved forward as ordered. They were also largely able to reach their objective in good time. However, the artillery barrage continued to fall too close to their 'new' position. As a result, almost as soon as they left their trench the men of the 50th ran into heavy rifle and machine gun fire which had not been subdued by the artillery barrage. Having lost touch with the 13th Battalion and therefore having dangerously unsupported flanks, the 50th Battalion, too, was forced to retire.

Tension between the 13th Battalion and the 50th that had been simmering since their first operation together steadily worsened. During that first attack, the 50th Battalion had reported that their objective had been gained but the 13th Battalion staff were sure that the 50th had not reached their objective. Captain Pulling had been advised to "do all you can to push the 50th along"[23] despite the fact that the 50th Battalion staff stubbornly maintained that they were in the right place. Both battalions had proven more than willing to blame the other for any problems they encountered, and regularly sniped at each other in messages to brigade headquarters. The relationship between the 13th and the 50th Battalions had become so bad that the two could not communicate effectively before the operation of 14 August even began. The process of preparing for this renewed operation saw relations between the two deteriorate further. The front line had been reorganised on 13 August, in part to give the 13th Battalion more room. But the 13th Battalion's front trenches had become seriously congested when their line shortened to only 200 yards as the 50th and 51st Battalions spread out. Tilney reported:

> Find now that owing to congestion in trenches my frontage is only about 200 yards. Am squeezed in on both flanks by 50th & 51st Battalions. 51st Battalion is also congested with three Companies in front [24]

Note that this message excuses the situation of the 51st Battalion by stating that their trenches too were overcrowded. Although the 50th Battalion's trenches were similarly packed full, the entire situation, in Tilney's eyes, was their fault. He complained that the "50th Battalion were unable to hand over more than 200 yards of frontage last night and as a result we are hopelessly jammed between 50th and 51st Battalions with all communications choked".[25] Pulling, who had long since become

23   AWM: AWM 26/60/6: 13th Bn to Pulling (OC D Coy 13th Bn), 13 August 1916 (untimed), Operations File Somme 1916, 4th Infantry Brigade..

24   AWM: AWM 26/60/6: 13th Bn to 13th Bde, 14 August 1916, 10.55am, Operations File Somme 1916, 4th Infantry Brigade.

25   AWM: AWM 26/60/6: 13th Bn to 13th Bde, 14 August 1916, 11.05am, Operations File Somme 1916, 4th Infantry Brigade.

the primary conduit of information into and out of the 13th Battalion's sector was contacted to say:

> … the Colonel wants you to squeeze in as much as you can to the left of hopping out trench … We will get in touch with 50th and try and make them move, but in meantime see what "Chook"[26] can do by talking to the company commander on his left.[27]

The disorganised 50th Battalion only reluctantly moved its companies to the left after brigade intervention, earning them no friends on their right. The battalion was showing significant signs of demoralisation, and would deteriorate further before the battle began.

During the counter-attack on the morning of 14 August, before this new operation began, the 13th Battalion had been ordered to assist 50th Battalion if required. Given the already exhausted and over-extended condition of the 13th Battalion troops, this was trying news indeed. The 50th Battalion seems to have been in some danger of crumbling altogether, and were exhorted on a number of occasions as they were enduring the attack to 'hang on' by 13th Brigade headquarters. On at least one occasion the 50th Battalion headquarters sent the 13th Battalion a message encoded according to the 13th Brigade code book – a brigade the 13th Battalion did not belong to, and could not be expected to hold the codes for. The 13th Battalion sent a snippy reply to the effect that "we have not a copy of your code but were able to get a glimpse of that of [the] 51st Battalion".[28] The 50th was suffering the most from shellfire and due to being the closest to the German artillery batteries at Thiepval which could enfilade their lines. Men were being killed and wounded, and more were being affected by shellshock. The battalion's left flank was further threatened by a loss of contact with the British division on the left, which, it was felt, was "not keeping touch as well as they may".[29] Some officers of the 50th, both at headquarters and in the field, were seriously shaken by their situation and increasingly began to use the word 'anxiety' in their messages in reference to various situations. The loss of Hurcombe only worsened the situation, and the staff work at headquarters began to suffer.

At around this time the morale of the 50th Battalion reached a critically low level, and would result in perhaps the most serious incident in the field in 1st Anzac Corps' time at Pozières. Just prior to the operation on 14 August, headquarters of the 13th Battalion received a worrying report, which they passed on to 50th Battalion headquarters. They wrote:

---

26 Probably Captain John Keith Henderson, OC C Coy, 13th Bn.
27 AWM: AWM: EXDOC022: 13th Bn to Pulling (OC D Coy 13th Bn), 14 August 1916.
28 AWM: AWM 26/60/6: 13th Bn to 13th Bde, 14 August 1916, 3.30pm, Operations File Somme 1916, 4th Infantry Brigade.
29 AWM: AWM 26/61/15: 50th Bn to 13th Bde, 14 August 1916, 6.22am, Operations File Somme 1916, 13th Infantry Brigade.

... we hear from [our] front Company that Major Herbert of 50th Bn states that he will not move forward to-night. Can you confirm as this action would jeopardise the whole operation. Please treat as very urgent.[30]

Mervyn Herbert: Major (then Captain) Mervyn Herbert, officer commanding B Company who, on 14 August 1916 reportedly refused to move forward in conjunction with a wider operation. (Image courtesy of the National Library of Australia)

Major Mervyn James Herbert was in command of B Company with Lieutenant Victor Gillard Driden as second in command, and Lieutenant Randall Lance Rhodes. They were situated on the right flank of the 50th Battalion's sector on the boundary with the 13th Battalion. At about 8.30pm on 14 August Dridan's arm was shot off and he was forced to lie in a shell hole in the front line for some thirty-six hours before he could be evacuated for help.[31] Dridan was hit at around the same time B Company received word of Hurcombe's evacuation due to shellshock. Lance Rhodes had been buried and unburied by shellfire four times that night, displaying "great bravery and coolness under heavy fire" before having to be evacuated with a serious wound to his shoulder.[32] He had remained remarkably cheerful and even sent an optimistic message to Herbert to say "[e]verything going well. Have stopped three different pieces of shell with great success,"[33] but he became badly shellshocked and had to be evacuated. Rhodes later recalled walking out of the front line surprised to find himself "crying to myself as if my heart would break; the tears were running down my face and you would have thought I was a kid of two that had lost a lollie".[34] These were serious blows which, combined with a lack of supplies and the severe

---

30   AWM: AWM 26/60/6: 13th Bn to OC 50th Bn, 14 August 1916, 9.10pm, Operations File Somme 1916, 4th Infantry Brigade.

31   AWM: AWM 1DRL/0428: Australian Red Cross Society Wounded and Missing Enquiry Bureau files, Lieutenant Victor Gillard Dridan, 50th Bn. Dridan was later stretchered out but a shell struck his party, killing both stretcher bearers. Although Dridan ran the rest of the way to the casualty clearing station, he died of his wounds shortly afterwards.

32   AWM: AWM 28/1/180: Recommendation File for Honours and Awards, 4th Australian Division.

33   Message from Rhodes to Herbert, 14 August 1916, 4pm. Private collection courtesy of Ashley Ekins.

34   Captain [sic] Lance Rhodes in Freeman, *Hurcombe's Hungry Half Hundred,* p.64.

shellfire contributed to a rising sense of panic in B Company, ultimately leading to the situation in which Herbert apparently said he (and by extension, his company) was going to refuse to advance.

Although a great deal of time and effort was spent in gauging morale during the First World War, it was not often that a situation this desperate arose in the BEF – particularly not immediately preceding an operation. Tilney, in receipt of the news, wrote to Hurcombe, not realising he was no longer in command:

Lieutenant Victor Dridan was Major Mervyn Herbert's second in command in B Company, 50th Battalion. He was severely wounded in the arm near Mouquet Farm in mid-August, and later died of his wounds. The two stretcher bearers who carried him in from the field were fatally hit by a shell on the way back. (Image courtesy of the National Library of Australia)

> Dear Colonel Hurcombe,
> One of my Company Commanders on my left flank has reported that one of your Company Commanders (Major Herbert) states he will not advance tonight. If this happens it will jeopardise the whole operation. Colonel Ross suggested my writing you a private note re the matter. Could you take steps to ensure that the Company advances. I understand it is the Company on your Right flank.
> Yours, L.E. Tilney[35]

And so the situation seems to have been dealt with privately, if at all. Certainly the event was not made public, and no reports of it exist at a higher level of command. Not that it worked. There is no evidence that anything was done in the confusion of last-minute preparations and the change of command at 50th Battalion headquarters.

It is difficult to say for certain whether or not Herbert went ahead with his determination to deliberately hold back the advance. There is, however, enough evidence to say that Herbert's company did not do well if they went ahead at all, which perhaps

35   AWM: AWM 26/60/6: Tilney (OC 13th Bn) to Hurcombe (OC 50th Bn), August 1916, 8.14pm, Operations File Somme 1916, 4th Infantry Brigade.

suggests they lacked strong leadership. Captain Harold Edwin Salisbury Armitage, the officer commanding C Company, later reported:

> Major Herbert must have become a casualty early in the shelling for a block ensued at [the] head of [his] company – in fact it almost amounted to a panic. I ran forward to find out what was wrong and found men running in all directions. I steadied them and tried to find D Company but was unsuccessful. I found the quarry and started with great difficulty to form the line up. We were under severe fire from artillery (not barrage) and a machine gun on the left was causing trouble – result many casualties. We stayed about twenty or thirty minutes trying to get in … considering the casualties, the fire, and the fact that I was not connected to any flank, and also the slow progress made – I decided to return to our original position. This I did and consolidated especially the left … Are we likely to be relieved today – the men are deplorably knocked about.[36]

In Armitage's own words, the "stunt was very disastrous". But even with the extensive problems with shellshock and catastrophically low morale in the 50th Battalion, some exemplary company commanders were able to work hard in the field to stop the 'disastrous stunt' from turning into a rout. Armitage took control of the panic resulting from Major Herbert's disappearance and reorganised the line with Captain Murray Fowler. The two were able to consolidate a line a little short of the objective, and give their precise location back to brigade headquarters. However, the animosity between the 50th Battalion and the 13th continued, with Armitage complaining that the 13th had "instead of inkling left last night – went straight out to the front" and were therefore to blame for any problems in keeping touch.[37]

What had happened to Major Herbert and his company? Herbert had previously been active in the line, organising his men and keeping them busy to maintain their morale. He had become a career soldier in Australia after what has been described as "an adventurous career in Asia Minor and other countries".[38] He had served with the Colonial Auxiliary Forces, originally as a private, but for the three years before the war as a commissioned officer, and was posted as area officer at Prospect in South Australia. He had written a number of technical articles on machine gun tactics and entrenchments which were a feature of many Australian military libraries. In 1914 he was immediately commissioned into the Australian Imperial Force on the outbreak of war, receiving the rank of captain. He served with distinction at the landing at Anzac Cove in April 1915 with the 10th Battalion, and was mentioned in Army Corps

---

36   AWM: AWM 26/61/15: Armitage (OC C Coy 50th Bn) to 50th Bn, 15 August 1916 (untimed), Operations File Somme 1916, 13th Infantry Brigade.
37   Ibid.
38   "For Meritorious Service: Major Herbert of Moorook", Murray Pioneer & Australian River Record, 7 November 1924, p.17.

Routine Orders of 19 June 1916 with other men of the 10th Battalion for "having performed various acts of conspicuous gallantry or valuable service".[39] This was an experienced and educated soldier, and his behaviour on 14 and 15 August was completely out of character. Shellshock was probably a factor in this uncharacteristic behaviour; it was certainly a result of the strain of the 50th Battalion's last few days in the line. This situation was kept very quiet, and no reports in relation to Herbert or his actions are present in the formal written record of the battle. But Captain Pat Auld later recalled seeing Herbert in a dugout at the quarry, "sitting at a table surrounded by a gloomy selection of officers and men belonging to technical units, sitting disconsolately in silence".[40] Captain Armitage's report listed Herbert among the missing of the battle, but his name has been crossed off the list with a note by Armitage's lieutenant, Noel Loutit, who amended the message to say that Herbert was "all right".[41] He had arrived back just in time to be struck off the missing list.

Captain Harold Armitage, officer commanding C Company, 50th Battalion, who worked to stop the gap caused by Major Herbert's failure to advance his company on 14 August 1916. He was killed in action at Noreuil on 2 April 1917. (AWM P09291.100)

There was only so much a company commander could do in the front line to turn a disastrous situation into a successful operation. Neither Armitage with the 50th Battalion, nor Pulling with the 13th, could change the course of an operation with fatal flaws inherent from the start. Two problems condemned the attack of 14 August. The first was that the artillery barrage was not strong enough, nor correctly placed, to subdue enemy rifle and machine gun fire. From their first attack on 7 August, the 4th Division had been rushed, bullied and propelled into a series of operations with hastily-organised, inappropriately applied barrages. These barrages were not necessarily particularly weak, but they were swift-moving and almost always fully beyond

39   NAA: B2455/HERBERT M J MAJOR.
40   Captain Pat Auld in Freeman, *Hurcombe's Hungry Half Hundred*, p.68.
41   Report in message from Armitage (OC C Coy 50th Bn) to 50th Bn, 15 August 1916 (untimed), AWM: AWM 26/61/15.

the objective line every time, providing only a bare minimum of effective protection to the infantry in the field. The other major problem was that this operation suffered badly from the three battalions in the line failing to keep touch with each other. Some of this was due to the animosity between the 13th and 50th Battalions, but in many cases can be attributed to the simple fact that the centre battalion came from a different brigade and did not share code books or systems with the others. However, given that in most of these operations the infantry could not get ahead due to unsub-dued German fire, the greater part of responsibility lies with those plotting the inad-equate artillery barrages.

The entire situation – rushed attacks, high casualties, heavy shellfire, poor supply lines and confusion in the field – had a terrible effect on the battalions conducting the operation. Casualty figures were extremely high. The 13th Battalion had already been approaching the limit of human endurance according to its commanding officer, and many of its surviving men had been several days without any sleep before the operation even went ahead. Their front line was mixed up and had been for a number of days. The 50th Battalion had suffered 341 casualties, including its commanding officer and another six officers, one of whom would later die of his wounds. The 51st Battalion had lost at least six officers and nearly 300 men dead, wounded, shellshocked or miss-ing.[42] Men of all battalions were exhausted, hungry, 'shocky', and without sleep. The 13th Infantry Brigade was finished, and needed immediate relief.

The commanding officer of the 51st Battalion, Lieutenant-Colonel Arthur Murray Ross, submitted a tactical appreciation of his battalion's recent fighting. In it he wrote:

> … it is a gross mistake to keep on a series of small offensives without prop-erly consolidating and fixing communication trenches first [his emphasis]. The upkeep of communication trenches requires much attention … I did not see one single good communication trench within one mile of the firing line.

The result of this, according to Ross, was:

> … many lives are thrown away in approaching the firing line and to suffer casu-alties before going into action is very demoralising. Also ration and water parties suffered severely and consequently had to drop much of their supplies … unless such trenches in the firing line are built, it is very difficult to deploy squarely and I consider that loss of direction in attack is only to be expected when troops have no time to cut saps and improve communication solidly before a further advance.[43]

---

42   AWM: AWM 4/23/13/7: '13th Australian Infantry Brigade Amended Casualty Return,' 21 August 1916, 13th Infantry Brigade War Diary.

43   AWM: AWM 26/61/15: '51st Battalion Operation Report August 13th -17th 1916', 15 August 1916, Operations File Somme 1916, 13th Infantry Brigade.

This report confirmed that solid preparation was needed before an attack for the sake of the infantry who had to operate under heavy fire. He also suggested that for the sake of infantry cooperation with the artillery he should have a forward observation officer from the artillery with him during ranging and also during the battle. One of his more startling assertions was that "[i]t is sound and quite easy to gradually advance the firing line by means of patrols and strongpoints put out at night". In some ways, gradually advancing the firing line was actually a reasonable alternative to the series of small offensives that the 4th Division had been conducting. But these small advances were of no use to Reserve Army's stated plan of encircling Thiepval. At this rate it would simply take months to reach it. Nor was a policy of strong patrols going to be able to deal with the threat from major obstacles like Mouquet Farm. Indeed, Pozières village and the OG Lines had just proven major obstacles to attack that had needed significantly more than active patrolling and quick construction of strongpoints. So while patrolling and night raids might more effectively achieve 1st Anzac Corps' objectives, the objectives themselves were the problem and should have been seriously revised to bring them in line with Reserve Army's aims of northward movement.

As the state of the casualty lists from 1st Anzac Corps was demonstrating, these small attacks were very costly indeed. The unceasing flow of operational orders for small-scale attacks was simply destroying the 4th Division. The consequence of constant raids, patrols and small-scale operations was a force that was as exhausted and demoralised as the 13th Brigade was when the 4th Division was withdrawn. Their supply lines could not be firmly established through the shellfire, the constant need for working parties and the persistently shifting front line, and so they were hungry, thirsty and lacking other vital requirements for their work. There was a constant flow of wounded men coming out of the front line even when the battalions were not attacking anything. The 50th Battalion's experience of shellshock, disorganisation and potential mutiny demonstrated the real dangers of low morale in the field. Units that failed to advance, even a single company, seriously undermined the potential for success of any operation.

Other problems with the approach of the 4th Australian Division went unheeded or misunderstood as well. Although the division appeared to rely heavily on firepower to get its infantry ahead, in fact, the modifications made by Major-General Cox to the basic artillery structure supplied from Reserve Army demonstrably weakened the barrage fired for the assault on 14 August, and was a direct contributing factor to the failure of the operation. As Reserve Army pointed out, the infantry of 1st Anzac Corps:

… had failed on only two occasions. On both those occasions the artillery programme has been altered almost at the last minute, at the request of the

Divisional Commanders, and in each case fundamental principles have been disregarded.[44]

The first of these occasions was the first attack of the 2nd Division against the OG Lines when Legge almost succeeded in launching an attack without artillery cover at all. This, the second occasion where artillery was particularly noted to be responsible for a failed operation, was less the result of a last-minute alteration to part of the plan and more a complete misapplication of it. The barrage was not only too weak and swift-moving, but it completed all of its movements outside of the infantry's area of operations. And the 4th Division had been applying artillery in this manner unnoticed from its first operation. Nevertheless, this warning from Reserve Army was a clear lesson to be taken forward by the divisions of 1st Anzac Corps. They would have to return to the 'fundamental principles' of artillery application.

But paradoxically the other problem with these small-scale operations was success. But it was success of a very misleading kind. Certainly the line was always in motion, sometimes 100 yards forward, at other times backwards and then forward again to its original position. But none of the operations conducted by the 4th Australian Division had the potential to advance the line in a significant manner. They did not even deal with Mouquet Farm, now the major German defensive work in their way, much less advance to any meaningful objective in terms of the wider campaign. The idea that these attacks were a viable tactical alternative to determinedly advancing the line was short-sighted at best, but it was one that would stay. Still, many of the small-scale attacks made by the 4th Division managed to succeed. This was particularly true if they were conducted by the very organised 4th Brigade, who had units which had managed to reach their objective for five successive attacks. That these successes were on an almost inconsequential scale and came at a high cost in casualties seems to have been an almost trivial factor in assessing one against the other. The 4th Division's period in the front line set an extremely dangerous precedent for the 1st Anzac Corps and its ongoing operations.

Reserve Army decided not to renew operations in 1st Anzac Corps' sector until 18 August 1916 to give the 1st Division a chance to relieve the exhausted 4th Australian Division and for the 48th Division to clear up the situation in their sector. But the ongoing failure to achieve any form of meaningful movement towards Thiepval from this direction was encouraging Gough to look for other ideas. A conference at II Corps headquarters on 15 August threw up some new concepts for future operations. Some of these included concentrations of mortar fire on the points to be attacked and the use of smoke. It was felt that the Germans might be more easily surprised with a daytime attack, given that recent operations had almost invariably been conducted at night. This was a concept that had been tried a number of times by both the British

---

44   AWM: AWM 26/42/4: Malcolm to 1st Anzac Corps, 16 August 1916, Operations File Somme 1916, Reserve Army General Staff.

and French armies, generally with disastrous results. In the desperate scratch for new ideas, it was also suggested that there was a possibility of combining an attack over the open from west and south.[45] This idea seems to have been originally applied to the situation on the boundary of II Corps and 1st Anzac Corps. It would soon be applied to operations against Thiepval. But once Gough's attention had more fully turned to attacking Thiepval from a different direction, the efforts of 1st Anzac Corps would soon be entirely in vain.

45   AWM: AWM 26/42/3: 'Notes of Conference at II Corps Headquarters, 15/8/16,' 15 August 1916, Operations File Somme 1916, Reserve Army General Staff.

5

"Our artillery barrage has not lifted sufficiently": The Ever Diminishing Objective Line

With the 4th and 13th Brigades of the 4th Division exhausted, the division could not continue. It was relieved by the 1st Division, which had seen success a long four weeks earlier when they had captured the village of Pozières. The 1st Division would be called upon to push the line northwards in connection with Reserve Army's articulated plans of 28 July. It will be remembered that these plans focused on the 12th Division on the left of 1st Anzac Corps being the primary source of movement, with the Anzacs on the right protecting the flank and generally moving 'methodically northwards'.[1] In accordance with this idea, Reserve Army headquarters ordered an attack to be conducted simultaneously by II Corps and 1st Anzac Corps. Gough ordered that this should take place on 18 August 1916, the same day as an attack by Fourth Army. There was potential for this new operation to either advance the agenda of the Reserve Army by adhering closely to the plan of 28 July, in which the II Corps would spearhead an attack that would encircle Thiepval and assault it from the north. Or equally the operation could closely adhere to the attack being conducted by Fourth Army on the same day and act as a support by advancing on the right. While Fourth Army's operation did not extend to the boundary between it and Reserve Army, it included the German intermediate line south of Martinpuich, a village a little over four kilometres to the east and north of Pozières. A synchronised operation by Reserve Army could have had some material benefit in tying up German reserves, or taking advantage of a broader front of operations than had previously been available.

This new operation did neither. Reserve Army's plan made no attempt to coordinate its operation to that of Fourth Army. Although on the same day, there was nearly six hours between the jumping-off time for Fourth Army at 2.45pm and 1st Anzac Corps at 8pm. But neither can this operation be said to be a serious attempt by Reserve Army to advance to the northwest as per their own strategic plan. II Corps, which had been envisaged as advancing "methodically northwards past Farm du Mouquet

---

1   See Chapter 2.

towards the Crucifix … ultimately to attack Thiepval from the east and north"[2] was ordered to make no more than an extremely limited advance from one trench system to another. Their objective line in fact did not even bring them as far north as the salient still held by 1st Anzac Corps on their right. While these limited advances could certainly be deemed 'methodical', using them to effect an encirclement of Thiepval would take weeks, if not months, if continued on this scale, and would use up an enormous amount of manpower. And yet the new operation was once again on an extremely limited scale. Not only that, but it was split in half, and so the first Division would attack in two unconnected areas. The first of these split operations, known as 'Operation A,' was a small advance in front of Mouquet Farm that was designed to rectify the shortfall of the failed 14 August attacks and bring the Australian line up to the road that ran in front of Mouquet Farm. On the right, 'Operation B' was against a series of trenches from the junction of Munster Alley to a point north of the Bapaume Road, an advance of no more than 150 yards.

These two operations are a major departure from the previous operations conducted by 1st Australian Division. In its first spell in the line the division had advanced more than 500 yards and successfully captured an entire village. Now even the German strong post at Mouquet Farm was not a feature of their objectives. Although formidable, this was hardly on the scale of the fortified village of Pozières. Their new pair of operations, although bigger, were much more akin to the hurried, raid-like attacks of the 4th Australian Division. The northerly movement once again did little more than extend an already marked salient and hardly advanced the line at all. On the right, where Operation B could have been coordinated with Fourth Army's operations against Martinpuich, it was not. This operation was occurring on a very small front four kilometres away from the far left flank of the main operation which would be carried out six hours earlier. Operation B had nothing to do with Fourth Army's attack at all. These two separate operations planned for the 1st Australian Division were tentative movements at best, and would gain no more than simply the next trench line. They made very little sense in the context of the wider situation on the Somme.

On receiving orders from 1st Anzac Corps, Walker immediately recognised that Operation A, or the attack towards Mouquet Farm was "on a different front and is not necessarily part of the same operation" as Operation B, the assault on Munster Alley and the sunken road.[3] He sensibly suggested that the second operation should be synchronised with that of Fourth Army, and that the attack against Mouquet Farm should be treated as an entirely separate operation. These suggestions were ignored by Birdwood and his staff. Walker also raised concerns with the objective line in front of Mouquet Farm which, he pointed out, "constitutes a wedge driven along the main

---

2   TNA: WO 158/334: 'Outline of Plan of Attack on Thiepval,' 28 July 1916, Scheme "F".
3   AWM: AWM 26/51/30: Walker (OC 1st Div.) to 1st Anzac Corps HQ, 17 August 1916, Operations File Somme 1916, 1st Australian Division General Staff.

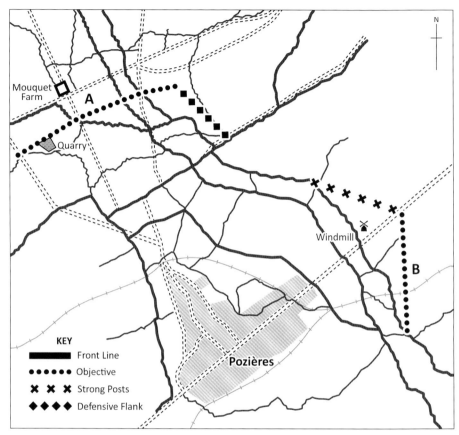

24 Operations "A" and "B", 18 August 1916.

ridge and as it advances is susceptible to enfilade fire from both flanks".[4] This attack was in danger of forming another salient on one side of an already established salient and creating too many corners in the front line. These corners invited German fire from a number of different directions. Yet once again his objection was disregarded.

But although able openly to express sensible observations without fear of reprisal (even if those suggestions went unheard), Walker did not do much more than hint to Birdwood that his division was not in a fit state to undertake either operation. The battlefield was by now a muddle of shell holes and damaged trenches. The Germans were aware of the change in attacking direction towards Thiepval, and had extended their artillery coverage of the area to regularly take in both sides of the salient. The

---

4   AWM: AWM 26/51/30: Walker (OC 1st Div.) to 1st Anzac Corps HQ, 17 August 1916, Operations File Somme 1916, 1st Australian Division General Staff.

Australian front line trench was completely destroyed in parts leaving gaps in the line, and many previously established communication trenches had ceased to exist in the interminable shellfire. The line was not clearly mapped, and Lieutenant-Colonel Thomas Blamey, Chief of Staff for the 1st Division, admitted to suffering from "vagueness … both as to our own and hostile positions" which he was trying to rectify through increased activity of battalion and brigade Intelligence Officers.[5] Even those at 1st Anzac Corps headquarters were forced to acknowledge that "some doubt existed as to [the] exact position of our trenches", although this uncertainty did nothing to delay either operation. Walker wrote to 1st Anzac Corps headquarters on the 17th to say that "if due preparedness is to be permitted, the main operation should now be postponed till or after the 20th".[6] But 'due preparedness' was clearly not to be permitted, despite so many reports to say that it was an absolute prerequisite for any successful operation. Reserve Army itself had more than once issued notes to the effect that all preparation should be complete before an operation launched. Yet Walker was absolutely not allowed the time he considered necessary. Even though he had been successful in obtaining a delay in July against Pozières on the grounds of being unprepared, this time Walker and his division was obliged to advance entirely on Reserve Army's terms simply because it was considered too late to alter artillery arrangements. This was a specious argument at best, given that 24 hours had proven more than enough time to postpone or cancel artillery orders in the past. But Walker did not insist on having his suggestions and requests followed, and the operation went ahead.

Operation A – 18 August 1916

The assault towards Mouquet Farm, 'Operation A', was allocated to the 1st Infantry Brigade, which had held the left of the line at Pozières. This time they held the area the 50th, 13th and 51st Battalions had just vacated. The 4th Battalion was on the far left of their sector, directly opposite Mouquet Farm on a thousand-yard front facing north-north-west, and in touch with the 145th British Brigade on its left. Next to them came the 3rd Battalion in the middle of 1st Brigade's sector and the most northerly formation, holding 500 yards of line facing north. Finally the 1st Battalion formed a 750-yard-long defensive flank on a line turned back towards the OG Lines, at roughly 90° to the rest of 1st Brigade's line and facing north east. The attack towards Mouquet Farm would be conducted by the 3rd and 4th Battalions pushing to the north and north west. Each battalion was assigned German trenches to seize and hold. It must be stressed that these objectives were very close to their own line, some 50 yards ahead, others no more than 100 yards. Not a single position constituted a

5   AWM: AWM 26/51/30: Blamey (1st Australian Division) to 1st, 2nd & 3rd Bdes. 17 August 1916, Operations File Somme 1916, 1st Australian Division General Staff.
6   AWM: AWM 26/51/30: Walker (OC 1st Division) to 1st Anzac Corps HQ, 17 August 1916, Operations File Somme 1916, 1st Australian Division General Staff.

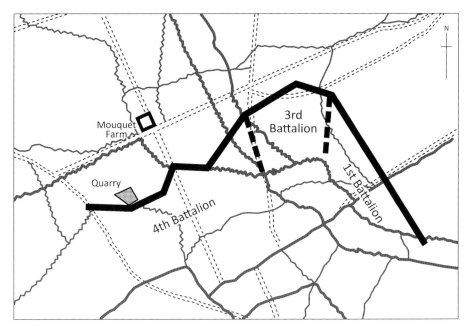

25 1st Brigade dispositions for Operation "A".

major landmark, and instead were no more than coordinates, dugouts, two strong-points and a few small trenches or trench junctions. The objective once again failed to encompass the primary German defensive position at Mouquet Farm.

The operation was preceded by an hour-long bombardment of the German posi-tions with heavy guns, following which a lifting barrage was fired using the familiar three-lift pattern. But this was to be the briefest barrage yet. Most batteries firing this barrage were instructed to employ the quickest rate of fire possible, but each lift lasted only a single minute before lifting 50 yards further on. A standing barrage was then to last until further notice, depending on the outcome of the operation. The barrage was to begin 50 yards forward of the jumping-off line. This meant that in some cases the barrage began on the objective itself, where it was just 50 yards on from the starting positions. In other cases, where the objective was slightly further away, the barrage reached it on the second lift. As with recent operations conducted by the 4th Australian Division, the artillery plan was not going to assist the infantry operation in any meaningful way.

The most concerning aspect of this barrage plan was that it was not consistent with the capability of the artillery. At this stage of the war, the artillery simply did not have the ability to fire accurately at a target at almost any distance. A variety of factors affected the flight of an artillery shell once it left the gun, from weather conditions to inconsistently produced or poor-quality ammunition to barrel wear. Artillerymen were not so much aiming for a particular point as an area around the particular point.

This meant that the infantry were obliged to keep a certain distance from the artillery's particular objective to avoid an expected amount of variation in the fall of shell during a barrage. The safety distance at this stage of fighting on the Somme was 200 yards. This means that where the barrage started on an objective 50 yards from the front line the infantry were well within its zone of fire and were in danger of being hit by their own artillery. They would have to move 150 yards back to be clear of the danger zone. While this made little sense, instead of lifting objectives and barrages to a more appropriate distance, corps and divisional command increasingly turned to withdrawing their front line for the barrage before sending the men forward over their original positions as it lifted. But even this tactic had not yet become common practice, although it had been employed by the 4th Division on occasion. It was not applied here, and so the men in the front line for this operation were under fire from their own guns from the moment the barrage began to fall.

The 1st Brigade commander, Lieutenant-Colonel Smyth, ordered a very different attack from the one that he had conducted on 23 July. It is probable that this was the result of this operation being on a small-scale against such a close target, particularly in comparison to his previous experience weeks earlier. Instead of organising his infantry into waves as he had before, Smyth deployed his infantry in strong patrols with bombers. They were ordered to push forward and occupy various points in the objective which would form the basis of the new line to be consolidated by parties following the initial patrols. Because the artillery barrage was radically different to the one with which Smyth had worked previously, he diminished the strength of his infantry plan to fit. He clearly saw this operation much more as akin to a large-scale raid than anything like his original series of operations, and so he organised his infantry accordingly, relying on patrols and groups to work their way forward instead deploying bold waves of infantry behind a curtain of artillery shells.

There had been some problems with the initial orders. A little over half of the objective line given in Reserve Army orders – that on the right – was already in Australian hands, and in some cases comfortably behind their front line. This went unnoticed, or at least unedited, by 1st Anzac Corps staff. It took either Walker at divisional level or Smyth at brigade to modify the orders for the 1st Brigade to put the objective some distance ahead of any part the current position. This was the only way the Australians could try to make an advance, as insignificant as it was, and would bring the brigade almost up to Mouquet Farm. It is hard to identify where this modification of the objective took place. Most orders were the result of face-to-face meetings between commanders in conferences or meetings to discuss the future. Written orders, especially at higher levels, were usually in confirmation of what had been decided in these meetings, and it is quite likely that Walker and Smyth had personally discussed this matter together before the change was made.

Regardless of how this shift in objective was generated, the move demonstrates that the geographical objective was not the important thing here. The objective line could have been arbitrarily scrawled across the for all the attention paid to the actual situation on the ground. Instead, there was an impulse to advance with the Reserve

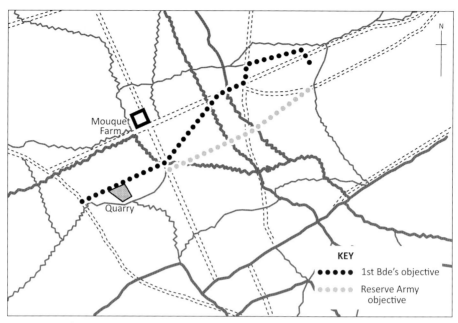

26 Objectives compared – Reserve Army and 1st Brigade, 18 August 1916.

Army and 1st Anzac Corps that was so strong that it disregarded overall strategy, ignored the poor preparation of the attacking troops and the lack of any coordination or breadth to the attack and the state of the weakened infantry division. Clearly what was important to Army, and therefore to corps, was that the division make a move forward, no matter the size of the movement, or exactly to where it went.

Operation A was timed to begin at 9pm on the evening of 18 August 1916 following an hour-long preliminary bombardment. The battalions of the 1st Brigade had been in the line since 16 August, and so were at least prepared by being in position. On the left, the 4th Battalion was subjected to a heavy bombardment from the German artillery about an hour before the assault went ahead which caused a number of casualties and quickly began to "interfere with [the] supply of bombs and preparations".[7] To ameliorate the 4th Battalion's position, reinforcements were sent forward, including Major Rowlands, 102 other ranks and a Lewis Gun from the 2nd Battalion. Fifty more men and a Vickers gun were later sent forward to join them. Although their exact time of departure from the jumping-off trench was not documented, records indicate that the 4th Battalion was somewhat delayed in starting the attack because of the heavy shellfire. But by 9.15pm A Company of the 4th, on the far left of their

7   AWM: AWM 26/53/24: entry for 4th Bn, 18 August 1916, Operations File Somme 1916, 1st Infantry Brigade.

sector, had advanced their line and established a strongpoint in the prescribed area. But, under a weak, swift-moving and distant barrage, they had suffered considerable casualties in capturing their line as the result of German sniping and a heavy barrage.

In the centre of the 4th Battalion's line, C Company made some territorial gains before stopping and consolidating a trench that was probably just short of their objective. However, the barrage supporting the assault of the 4th Battalion had completely failed to reduce the threat from two enemy strongpoints towards the right of their objective, which were strongly garrisoned and protected by a number of machine guns and wire. These two German positions were largely responsible for breaking up the attack in several places. Here on the right, D Company had been heavily reinforced with new recruits. Together with the bombing platoon, they had advanced to a German barricade in a trench shared by the two sides. Here a bomb fight ensued during the course of which the 4th Battalion's bombing platoon suffered from a lack of support. The new recruits in the company, rather than providing covering fire for their bombers, withdrew to the jumping-off trench. Nor did the inexperienced reinforcements ensure a constant supply of bombs got forward to the advanced party, who quickly ran short. The Germans, who had been almost driven off by the attack, returned to the barricade and the Australian bombing platoon was forced to withdraw. The efforts of two lieutenants, Isaacs and Boileau, who "endeavoured by personal effort to rally the men", could not induce the new, inexperienced infantry to leave the relative safety of their trench, and the attack in this sector failed.[8]

The problems on the right flank of the 4th Battalion advance were made worse by the fact that the 3rd Battalion was seriously delayed. This particularly enabled the Germans to focus the attention of all of their bombers in the area on the bomb fight with D Company and the 4th Battalion's bombing platoon. It seems the 3rd Battalion's advance had been hindered by friendly fire. During the afternoon and evening of 18 August the battalion had apparently been repeatedly subjected to fire from their own heavy artillery. The problem of shells falling short in that sector had been reported a number of times and was investigated by staff of the Anzac Heavy Artillery. Earlier that day they had registered their guns on the target using an aircraft to observe the fall of shell and ensure that each gun was ranged accurately. Their response, after "a most careful check" was to say that "it appears these must be enemy shells".[9] Without specific information as to time and location of incidents, or without verification of the types of shells falling, it was difficult for the artillery to do more, and despite repeated reports of shells falling short, the problem was treated as improbable throughout the battle. However, the commander of the 3rd Battalion, Lieutenant-Colonel Owen

8   AWM: AWM 26/53/24: 'Report from Lieutenant-Colonel Iven Mackay, Officer commanding 4th Battalion to 1st Infantry Brigade,' 19 August 1916, Operations File Somme 1916, 1st Infantry Brigade.
9   AWM: AWM 26/51/30: 'Operations of 1st, and 2nd, Aust. Inf. Brigades towards Mouquet Farm & Martinpuich respectively,' Operations File Somme 1916, 1st Australian Division General Staff.

Lieutenant-Colonel Owen Howell-Price, officer commanding 3rd Battalion who, through his successful partnership with 1st Battalion commander Lieutenant-Colonel James Heane, led his battalion in the greatest advance on 23 July 1916. He died of wounds on 4 November 1916 near Flers. (AWM P00267.003)

Glendower Howell-Price, was convinced it was his own shells falling short, and sent a number of messages during the afternoon requesting that the range of the heavy guns being lifted. Some Anzac guns must have been involved in the problem because when, just before the preliminary barrage began at 8pm, heavy shells again fell on a large proportion of the front trenches, the number falling increased with the onset of the barrage itself. Much of that fire fell on the jumping-off position, breaching the front line in at least three places and causing a number of casualties. The situation was so serious that Howell-Price, an experienced and competent commander, reported again at 8.35pm that the "barrage is on my line which is now about demolished … I am doubtful whether we shall be able to carry out our stunt laid down tonight as a consequence".[10] The problem was exacerbated by there being no heavy artillery liaison officers at Brigade headquarters, so communication between brigade and the artillery was too slow to correctly identify the source of the problem. However, despite Howell-Price's regular reports of a serious problem, there was no question of stopping or delaying the operation. The infantry were forced to wait for the barrage to lift, reporting to 1st Brigade as late as 9.45pm that they were "unable to push ahead as our artillery barrage has not lifted sufficiently. The heavies continue to fall short."[11] The barrage finally lifted enough around 10pm, and twenty minutes later the infantry were reorganised enough to advance nearly an hour and a half late, leaving the 4th Battalion on their left without support.

10 AWM: AWM 26/53/24: Howell-Price (OC 3rd Bn) to Adjutant 1st Bn, 18 August 1916, 8.35pm, Operations File Somme 1916, 1st Infantry Brigade.
11 AWM: AWM 26/53/24: Howell-Price (OC 3rd Bn) to 1st Bde, 18 August 1916, 9.34pm, Operations File Somme 1916, 1st Infantry Brigade.

At the junction between the 3rd and 4th Battalions, the patrol assigned to conduct the attack left the jumping-off trench, but it, too, "was unable to push out sufficiently owing to the barrage not lifting enough".[12] Shells from the 1st Anzac Corps Heavy Artillery were falling no more than 100 yards from the firing line, which brought the barrage dangerously close to the advanced jumping-off position. As the patrol moved through the centre of the 3rd Battalion's sector, they did not encounter many Germans, but neither did they come across a German trench. Without an already-established trench line or strong post to capture and consolidate to their own advantage, this patrol could not build one able to withstand enemy fire in the time they had available, and so its commander made the decision to withdraw. Again, after a tentative start delayed by a poor artillery barrage, a solid enough gain could not be made and the assault failed.

The only unit of the 3rd Battalion to get well away was the patrol on the right. There the barrage lifted enough for the group to advance to their objective point and beyond. The patrol managed to push out a considerable distance, encountering the enemy in strength about two hundred yards from their line. They engaged this party of German infantry, but were outmanoeuvred when the Germans sent out "a strong flanking party of about thirty men", and so the Australian patrol was forced to withdraw to their own trenches.[13]

At the end of the night's fighting, some gains had been made by the 1st Infantry Brigade, mostly on the left where the 4th Battalion had achieved some of its objectives, but the cost had been enormous. The Brigade reported having lost more than 480 men by 9am on 20 August, most of them in this operation. Despite the fact that the operation was to have been conducted by no more than a series of strong patrols, the entirety of the 1st Brigade had been drawn into the line, leaving only one company to act as brigade reserve at 11pm. The 1st Brigade's strength had been seriously completely sapped by this action. The obvious failure came with the artillery barrage which almost completely failed to support the infantry in any way. Having begun on or very near the objective line, it swiftly lifted away, leaving the German defenders ample time to train their machine guns and bombing teams towards the small packets of soldiers approaching their line. As patrols failed, more men were sent forward in support and so many were drawn into the fight without forming one cohesive effort that systematically approached the objective. The result was a patchy attack in which those that gained ground did it in spite of the plan, and without support on their flanks. The overall plan as devised by upper levels of command had once again failed the men in the field.

12   AWM: AWM 26/53/24: entry for 3rd Bn, 18 August 1916, Operations File Somme 1916, 1st Infantry Brigade.
13   AWM: AWM 26/53/24: Howell-Price (OC 3rd Bn) to 1st Bde, 23 August 1916, Operations File Somme 1916, 1st Infantry Brigade.

Operation B – 18 August 1916

On the right of the 1st Australian Division's line, the smaller operation against the trenches around Munster Alley, "Operation B", was given to the 2nd Infantry Brigade. As with the 1st Brigade on their left, the 2nd Brigade was given the objective of capturing nothing more than a series of coordinates and suspected German strong posts. Simply put, they were to push the line straddling the Albert – Bapaume Road out to a point about 100 yards further along that route. This attack was also timed to begin at 9pm, synchronised with the 1st Infantry Brigade's disconnected operation on the left, despite Walker's conviction that Operation B would have been better coordinated with Fourth Army's operations some distance to the right. In this operation the 7th Battalion on the left and the 8th Battalion on the right would advance following a barrage timed to lift fifty yards a minute for three minutes after zero hour – similar to that of Operation A, but fired by fewer batteries. As with the other barrage, it would begin 50 yards from the jumping-off trench, before making each lift of 50 yards, meaning that somewhere between the preliminary barrage and the second lift; it would be completely clear of the infantry's area of operations and would complete its lift programme too far from the infantry's objective line.

The 2nd Brigade had been in reserve at Pozières, but many of its units had gradually been absorbed into the front line as the original attacking units weakened, and so much of the brigade had had some experience of front-line conditions. However, its commander, Lieutenant-Colonel Henry Gordon Bennett, had yet to lead his men in a set-piece attack. He took a different approach to that of Smyth and the 1st Brigade by choosing not to attack with infantry patrols. Instead he ordered waves of infantry to follow each other in a much more orthodox battle plan. The main attack was to take place south of the Albert–Bapaume Road, where the 7th and 8th Battalions formed the main attacking force, and the 6th Battalion formed a flank defence. Each battalion was organised into four waves of infantry and a reserve force. Two companies of each battalion would be in the forefront of the attack and supplying the waves, each wave being formed of half of a company. One company followed in close support and the final company of each battalion waited further back in reserve. These waves of infantry were ordered to follow the lift of the artillery barrage closely, while the support units would follow and consolidate any gains. Trench mortars were used to strengthen the artillery barrage, firing from the 44th Brigade's sector directly at a designated German strongpoint. Bombing parties strengthened the first infantry wave and further assisted with the assault on strongpoints. Finally, the left flank would be protected by the 6th Battalion who were to move forward and complete the line from the left of the 7th Battalion to the jumping-off trench. This method of attack is in fact very similar to that of the 1st Brigade on 23 July. It relied on a battle plan of waves of infantry following a barrage, but it did not make the previous mistake of overly-complicating the movement plans for infantry waves, nor did it overpopulate those waves. Bennett was taking his first operation very seriously.

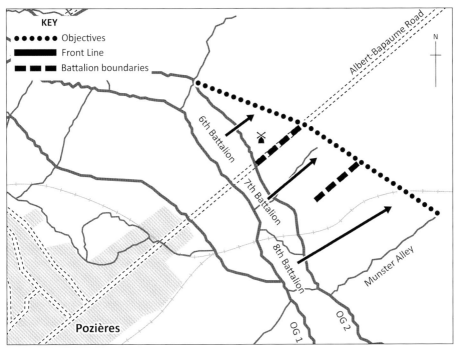

27 Dispositions for Operation "B".

Preparation for Operation B was reported to be "much restricted by the activity of the enemy's artillery and also by the urgency for rapid progress in our constructional work."[14] On 16 August, while repairing OG2 in order to gain touch with the 1st Brigade, men of the 2nd Brigade discovered an old and battered German trench that covered part of the area they were supposed to build strong posts as a part of Operation B. Bennett decided to have his men dig a line along this part of the objective before the attack went ahead. Extra Lewis guns were put into the front line to free as many men as possible to dig this new line. On the left and right flanks of the brigade sector the new trench was well made, deep and narrow but in the centre progress was very slow. At the same time, existing saps were extended and new ones pushed forward to advance the line as much as possible prior to the attack. And as the day of the operation drew near, work began on a new jumping-off trench across no man's land from the eastern end of Munster Alley to the Windmill.

Working parties on these preparatory works frequently had to take cover for extended periods, and found that during the night of 17 August, "the shelling and

14   AWM: AWM 26/54/7: 'Report on Operations POZIERES from 15th to 21st August 1916,' 25 August 1916, Operations File Somme 1916, 2nd Infantry Brigade.

machine gun fire was so severe that the working parties had to be withdrawn, with very little progress made."[15] Yet somehow the Brigade's working parties managed to construct the jumping-off trench from Munster Alley to the windmill during the daylight hours of the 18th. This trench, known as Dot Trench, had the added benefit of straightening the line and reclaiming some dead ground. In most positions this new trench was adequate for cover, although it was very shallow and there were gaps in places, and in the 7th Battalion sector it was only big enough for one man carrying a full pack at a time. Here, "to pass, one had to crouch in the bottom of the trench while the other clambered over," and so the infantry forming up into waves had to get out of the trench and move over open ground to get into the right order.[16] Again, against the odds the assaulting troops were reported to be in the correct position when the bombardment opened, and, according to divisional reports, they advanced closely behind the barrage as it lifted.

However, despite the employment of an infantry plan similar to those that had had demonstrable success in the recent past, and an apparently successful start to the operation, as the sun rose, daylight revealed the operation to have been an almost complete failure. While the 6th Battalion, in its role of flank support, had achieved all of its (very limited) objectives, the 7th Battalion had only managed to reach part of its objective line, and the 8th Battalion, despite having made three separate attacks, was back in its original lines, having suffered heavy casualties.

What had happened? Divisional reports that the assaulting troops followed the barrage closely were somewhat exaggerated. There had been a serious problem with the issue of the artillery timetable to both the 7th and 8th Battalion, and so throughout much of the process of forming up for the assault, they had no idea when it would actually begin, or at what speed and distance the artillery barrages would lift. Orders had been issued to the battalions without the time of attack included. This was normal practice to prevent the Germans from having advance warning of any impending operation in the case of documents being captured beforehand. The time of assault – "zero hour" – usually followed by message separately. However, in the case of 2nd Brigade's operation notification of zero hour did not come in time for any meaningful coordination, much less the timetable of the artillery barrage. The men in the front lines were in a desperate situation simply by being there. They were under heavy fire, and in places were unable to move without exposing themselves to the enemy. Worse, most were almost completely unprepared for action when the orders finally arrived, and the launch of the operation was a mad scramble to keep up.

Before the operation, the 7th Battalion was under heavy enemy shellfire in the jumping-off trench, and the men suffering from shellshock if not becoming casualties. B company in particular suffered considerably, with the fire only easing towards

---

15   AWM: AWM 26/54/7: '7th Battalion AIF Report on Operations 15th/21st August 1915 [*sic*],' 26 August 1916, Operations File Somme 1916, 2nd Infantry Brigade.
16   Ibid.

the evening. At 5.25pm platoon commander Lieutenant Eric Woodruff Hill sent a message to say "[s]helling eased off considerably. Jumping-off trench in fair order. About six [men of] B Company buried – remainder pretty shaken."[17] Hill's company commander, Captain Frederick James Hoad, reported around the same time that the "enemy [are] shelling our front trench we are being enfiladed on our left flank trench slightly damaged. About six men being [*sic*] buried. Men are shaken."[18] The front line troops had to be withdrawn to OG2 to avoid what was described as a "sheer waste of men".[19] Captain Hector Ernest Bastin reported on the implications this would have for the operation:

> URGENT Will require at least two hours' notice from operation unless troops are to be packed into forward trenches forthwith … it is necessary to hold forward line thinly to avoid casualties and majority of troops are well in rear and have to dribble into their place through battered communication trenches.[20]

But at around 8pm, more than two hours after the above message had been sent, and just one hour before the operation was to begin, neither the barrage timetable nor notification of zero hour had yet been received by the 7th Battalion. Its commander, Lieutenant-Colonel Care Herman Jess sent a further message to say the barrage time-table "has not been received. As it takes at least half an hour to communicate with Companies could durations and localities be phoned to me using [code]".[21] This was the bare minimum of time they could work with – half an hour gave them no more than a chance to briefly notify their troops and no more. Even so, the 7th Battalion was required to make do with even less time. The timetable did not reach battalion headquarters until 8.45pm, giving them no more than 15 minutes' notice of the artillery barrage's timetable – the one feature of the battle on which all other timings depended. They had no chance to communicate that time to their forward lines, and thanks to their messages, brigade command knew it.

The 8th Battalion found the jumping-off trench a more tenable position, but they, too, received the barrage time table far too late to communicate it to their attacking companies – just 10 minutes before the barrage was to commence. Again, this was a serious oversight. At this remove it is not possible to say why the delay in the

17   AWM: AWM 26/54/7: Hill (7th Bn) to 2nd Brigade, 5.25pm – undated but corresponds to 18 August 1916, Operations File Somme 1916, 2nd Infantry Brigade.
18   AWM: AWM 26/54/7: Hoad, (OC B Coy 7th Bn) to OC C Coy (7th Bn), 18 August 1916, 4.50pm, Operations File Somme 1916, 2nd Infantry Brigade.
19   AWM: AWM 26/54/7: '7th Battalion AIF Report on Operations 15th/21st August 1915 [*sic*], Operations File Somme 1916, 2nd Infantry Brigade.
20   AWM: AWM 26/54/7: Bastin (Adj, 7th Bn) to 2nd Brigade, 18 August 1916, 5.45pm, Operations File Somme 1916, 2nd Infantry Brigade.
21   AWM: AWM 26/54/7: '7th Battalion AIF Report on Operations 15th/21st August 1915 [*sic*],' Operations File Somme 1916, 2nd Infantry Brigade.

transmission of times occurred. It was the result of poor staff work at one level of command at least, if not more. What it meant was that all of the infantry involved in the attack, although somehow well-positioned and prepared prior to the assault, did not have time for a final coordination with the barrage timetable. Nor did they know when the attack would take place. Fortunately (or otherwise), in the event the moment the barrage lifted was unmistakeable to the infantry, and they left their jumping-off positions to advance under it, but with little confidence and no idea what was to come in the way of ongoing artillery support for their assault.

The German defenders in this sector were alert to the possibility of an imminent attack, probably because they could observe of the construction of the new jumping-off position, Dot Trench, that had taken place during daylight hours on the 18th. As soon as the attack began they put down an extremely heavy barrage on the area around Munster Alley. This was slightly misplaced, however, and caused particularly heavy casualties in the 44th British Brigade on the right instead of on the attacking Australian troops. But at the same time, the infantry in the front line were convinced that their own artillery was falling short as well. As with the 1st Brigade, a continuous stream of messages flowed back from the front line throughout the day of the 18th reporting short-falling shells. But while in 1st Brigade's sector the artillery vehemently denied the possibility that their guns were doing the damage, in this case an Artillery Liaison Officer was with the 2nd Brigade and corroborated the reports. As a result, in some places the bombardment was successfully lifted. In other areas, however, even after a lift had been requested by the infantry artillery fire was reported as falling in the same place hours later. While the artillery were working from an inadequate timetable supplied to them by higher levels of command, they were also failing to fire accurately enough to keep their infantry safe, much less to provide them with the cover they so desperately needed.

The pre-alerted German infantry had responded quickly to reports of an assault by moving forward clear of the barrage and using shell holes as emplacements for machine guns to defend against the attackers. This was a very early example of a 'chequerboard defence', part of the elastic defence-in-depth formally adopted by the German Army in late September 1916. Experiences such as those at Pozières and Mouquet Farm were, in August 1916, teaching the Germans that their defence had to rely on firepower and not large numbers of troops. These tactics were particularly effective when combined with the ineffectual barrage fired by the Allied artillery in these operations. Because the Germans were not concentrated in their trench lines, but instead scattered through random shell holes, their positions were very hard to hit, and the artillery found it almost impossible to even get them to keep their heads down and stop firing.

Ultimately, both the 7th Battalion and in particular the 8th Battalion ran into a 'most hellish machine gun fire … [and] were also heavily bombed and shelled'.[22] The 8th Battalion diary records a stark story of a failed operation:

22   AWM: AWM 26/54/7: 'Report from Lieutenant-Colonel Care Herman Jess, Officer

As the barrage lifted the attacking companies moved forward and the right of "A" Company immediately came under a heavy fire from Bombs and Machine Guns. The centre and the left also suffered severely from M[achine] Gun fire from the left. The fire was so heavy that the line withdrew and was reformed and again attacked, but, as enemy strongpoints and trenches had apparently not suffered from our Artillery fire, they had an immense superiority of fire and our attack was again beaten back. I then ordered "D" Company to reinforce "A" and made a further attempt but though the line reached the enemy position it could not gain a footing and returned to Dot Trench. Our left Company was under a galling fire from both flanks and could make no progress and also fell back on their original position.[23]

The 8th Battalion attempted to advance in the face of this fire three times during the night, each attack failing with heavy casualties. They gained no ground at all. The 7th Battalion were able to advance a little on the left, meeting up with the right of the 6th Battalion and digging in across the Bapaume Road. But for the gain of just tens of yards, the 7th Battalion suffered enormous casualties, worst of all in the already-weakened B Company. Of the 111 men of B Company who went forward for the assault, only 37 answered roll call the following morning. In the four days from 16-20 August the 1st Division suffered the loss of an estimated 57 officers and 1524 other ranks.

Consequences

Both Operation A and Operation B had failed miserably. A long list of casualties had resulted in only the most negligible of gains. The strength of two of the three brigades of the 1st Australian Division was seriously compromised. And yet the 1st Division was not to be relieved, nor was action in this sector stopped. The 1st Infantry Brigade was relieved at 3.30am on 20 August by the 3rd Brigade, a unit still depleted by casualties from the July operations. The 3rd Brigade arrived into a front line almost completely unprepared to stage another assault. Hostile shellfire had destroyed communication trenches and stores of ammunition; bombs, grenades, water and many other supplies were very low in the front line. There was nowhere for supports or reserves to form up, and the continuous passage of carrying parties trying to rectify the shortage of stores in the front line, not to mention the ongoing damage from the ever-present shell-fire, seriously hampered the work of working parties repairing the damage. Despite a great deal of hard digging throughout the day and night of the 20th, men were still

Commanding 7th Battalion, on actions of B Coy on the night of 18 August 1916,' 19 August 1916, Operations File Somme 1916, 2nd Infantry Brigade.

23   AWM: AWM 26/54/7: entry for 8th Bn, 19 August 1916, Operations File Somme 1916, 2nd Infantry Brigade.

regularly exposed to view as they moved about the battlefield. The exact position of the front line was still unclear on the morning of 21 August, when patrols reports of the location of the enemy line differed from aerial photographs. The situation was a shambles, and needed some serious attention to even identifying and correctly plotting locations, both of the Australian and the German lines.

Aerial photography had become increasingly important during the 1st Anzac Corps' occupation of the lines around Pozières. Photographs of German positions taken from the air were passed on to brigade and divisional artillery commanders, some even making it into company commander hands. By 20 August the 7th Squadron of the Royal Flying Corps was flying daily sorties to provide the most up-to-date photographs possible, and could supply images within four to five hours of demand. But commanders in the field were still inclined to rely most heavily on patrol reports, and had to scramble to assimilate information sent through from other sources. The positions of trenches, strongpoints and German troops seen on photographs were painstakingly confirmed by patrol, and reconnaissance parties made aware of what they should expect, where they should expect to find it, and whether or not the information on photographs was being corroborated by that provided by the patrol. As an example, Captain Leone Sextus Tollemache,[24] the Brigade Major of the 3rd Brigade sent a message regarding a patrol conducted on 21 August:

> Ref[erence] your patrol reports of this morning. You must see there is no mistake about the enemy line. He has two distinct lines of trench … THIS IS THE OBJECTIVE TO BE TAKEN AND HELD. He also has a good trench … which is probably that to be seen "lightly held" by patrol last night. Your first two waves will pass straight through the first trench (leaving the clearing parties of the second wave to clear it up) and push straight into the main objective. See that all ranks are carefully warned.[25]

More care was being taken than before to see that men were in the correct position and aware of their objectives and potential obstacles as much as possible during their time in the line and before the operation went ahead.

An attack date as early as 20 August had been considered, but had to be postponed because of the sheer impossibility of getting through pre-operation preparations and a major relief in time. So the attacking brigade was granted another 24 hours, during which time more patrols were pushed forward to try to ascertain the exact position of the line. But 24 hours was little more than a bandaid on a broken arm. The line

---

24 Thought to have one of the longest names in the British forces, his full name was Leone Sextus Denys Oswolf Fraudatifilius Tollemache-Tollemache de Orellana Plantaganet Tollemache-Tollemache. He enlisted as Leone Sextus Tollemache.

25 AWM: AWM 26/55/4: Tollemache (Bde Maj 3rd Bde) to 3rd Brigade, 21 August 1916, 10.30am, Operations File Somme 1916, 3rd Infantry Brigade & Battalions.

was still woefully unprepared to stage another assault. Once again this demonstrates that despite the fact that Gough clearly stated that 'preparation must be thorough and careful' in his memorandum of 3 August, preparation was always of secondary importance to the ever present imperative to push on with operations – wherever and however – as soon as possible, or sooner. Delays were always granted miserly and reluctantly.

Preparations

This new operation to be conducted by the 3rd Brigade on 21 August 1916 was to be a little earlier in the day that the previous two, at 6pm instead of 9. In the French summer, this was the difference between attacking in late afternoon daylight and the soft darkness of early evening. The objective was very similar to that of the 1st Brigade's attack, falling just short of Mouquet Farm once again and advancing no more than 100 yards from the jumping-off positions. In most places the objective made very little sense to the surrounding geography, but skirted in front of Mouquet Farm and very roughly followed the road to the north east. On the left the 12th Battalion would make the attack, in the centre a small force of the 11th Battalion would operate and on the right the 10th Battalion would once again make the largest advance. And so, once again 1st Anzac Corps' salient would be pushed further to the north, putting the 10th Battalion in particular into a very narrow bulge into the

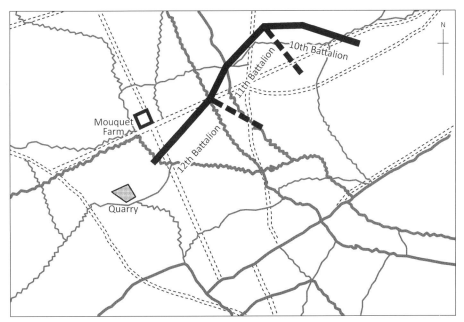

28 4th Division dispositions, 21 August 1916.

German lines. This was a remarkable plan given the serious problems with enfilade fire the 2nd Brigade had suffered from, and the regular reports that the salient was stretching the 1st Anzac Corps too far. Should this new operation succeed, both problems would be made worse.

Despite the fact that both brigades that had participated in the operations of two days before had repeatedly complained about ineffective artillery barrages, the artillery plan was weakened. In the recent operation, several messages had been sent that had specifically complained about the inadequacy of the barrage, and operational reports fingered it as the primary cause of failure. All of these messages and reports went ignored. This new operation was given a standing barrage of one hour falling just beyond the objective. There were no lifts across no-man's-land, and no barrage on the enemy trenches. At least the redundant artillery lifts beyond the objective had been removed in the plan for this next operation. But that was no more than a small consolation for the infantry conducting this attack. The standing barrage beyond the objective did protect the attacking infantry to some degree, but it did it by simply prevented the Germans from reinforcing their front line troops. The standing barrage did not keep the German machine gunners and riflemen in the front lines under cover. Without the initial bombardment of the objective followed by a lift away to the standing barrage at least, the German defenders could man their machine guns at will as the infantry crossed no man's land. None of the reports and recommendations made by brigade or battalion commanders on the use of artillery in recent operations was taken into consideration for the artillery plans for this renewed operation. If any lessons were taken from the immediate past, they are hard to find in the artillery orders given to the 3rd Brigade. Yet another variation of the basic artillery plan by Reserve Army and 1st Anzac Corps, this barrage was once again inadequate, if for a different reason than before.

Lieutenant-Colonel Sinclair-Maclagan at least did not underestimate the task at hand as Smyth had, and assigned it to the better part of three battalions. Nor did he make the overly-complicated plans for manoeuvre he had at Pozières, although this was probably as much the result of the extremely limited objectives as his particular choice. Like Bennett, Sinclair-Maclagan deployed his infantry in four waves. The 10th and 12th Battalions were on the flanks, and both attacked with all four companies – two forming the first two attacking waves, and the other two in the following waves.[26] The 11th Battalion in the centre was to attack with just two raiding parties of fifty each in the first two waves, with another two raiding parties in reserve. Because there was only one objective rather than a series, the main actors would be the infantry of the first and second waves. The first wave was to leave the jumping-off trench and attack the objective, while the second wave followed about fifty yards behind, helping to consolidate gains. The third wave was assigned a mobile support

---

26   The 10th Battalion's frontal attack was strengthened by an extra platoon from their rear companies.

role of assisting wherever an attack was held up, potentially carrying the first and second waves forward with it. The commander of this third wave was given leeway to decide on the spot whether to make a general deployment of his wave of infantry, or to send a portion of his line of infantry to areas that were bogged down. The waves of infantry were carefully coordinated to work with each other, and were strongly deployed without necessarily being overcrowded.

This was a carefully-crafted infantry plan which, had it been more integrated with available firepower, had the potential for success. But once again the Germans were aware of the imminent attack. Following a period of British domination of the skies, there had been an increasing number of German aircraft over the Somme in August 1916. On 21 August, the day of the attack, at least six enemy aircraft were reported to have crossed over the lines and had been seen flying over Sausage Valley with impunity. German prisoners captured during the battle later reported that these planes "saw the movement of troops getting into position and [so the Germans were] ready for the attack when it was launched".[27] The first indication to the Australians that their attack might have been discovered came when the German artillery put a notably severe bombardment onto the forward lines from 5pm. This caused so many casualties in the 10th Battalion on the right that their third and fourth waves had to move up and reinforce the front line before the operation began, leaving the battalion with only two platoons in reserve. The German artillery fire confused the front line and weakened the force going forward, endangering the entire operation.

The operation – 21 August 1916

Nevertheless, the operation went ahead at 6pm on 21 August 1916. Unsurprisingly, the planned artillery barrage was almost completely ineffective. The 10th Battalion again experienced the worst of the problem when the artillery barrage in its sector completely failed to negate German rifle and machine gun fire. The enemy fire did not pause in the slightest as the artillery barrage began. All of the officers of the 10th were hit on leaving the jumping-off trench except one – and he was hit the minute he reached the objective. On the left and in the centre of the 10th Battalion line some men somehow managed to make it to the objective, but then came under enfilade fire from the Germans to their right. In this direction a German strongpoint was untouched by the barrage, and was heavily manned by infantry and several machine guns both near the point and to the north east of it. These machine guns caused serious casualties among come parties of the 10th Battalion, including the bombing platoon and the company detailed to cover the right flank. Only three men out of two bombing teams remained alive and unwounded. On the left the advanced parties were losing

---

27   AWM: AWM 26/55/4: '3rd Australian Infantry Brigade Report on Operations about Mouquet Farm and Pozières. 19th to 23rd August 1916,' Operations File Somme 1916, 3rd Infantry Brigade & Battalions,

casualties steadily from the moment they advanced, and had become seriously weakened and under pressure on their flanks. Despite all of the battalion reserve coming forward to reinforce them, the remnants of the 10th Battalion had very little choice but to fall back. This battalion was already depleted from previous operations and had only been able to field about 620 men out of their nominal 1,000 from the start of the battle. In this operation they suffered 346 casualties, including 10 officers, in less than 24 hours. This was attributed to the heavy shellfire before the battle commenced, the enormously high rate of officer casualties, and the oblique and enfilade shellfire on the salient they were busy extending. The 10th Battalion had been almost entirely destroyed in just two short periods of time spent in the front line.

On the left the 12th Battalion had quite a different experience, reportedly having gone over the parapet as soon as artillery barrage started and managing to gain their objective with very little opposition. The battalion deployed in four waves of infantry, each comprising one company. Their first two infantry waves (A and D Companies respectively) left the jumping-off trench three minutes apart and secured their objectives, causing the Germans to fall back, men of the 12th noting "some of the enemy moving to the trenches on the flanks and some retiring over the open".[28] In fact, the Germans were so willing to withdraw and the battalion encountered so little opposition that "the left were carried away in pursuit of the flying enemy, entered the Mouquet Farm and bombed the dugouts, securing a few prisoners", although they were eventually called to fall back in line with the right.[29] A third wave of infantry, B Company, moved forward half an hour after the operation began and were directed to the right, where they filled a gap in the line and joined the rest of the 12th Battalion in consolidating their new position. The fourth and final wave of infantry, C Company, did not need to be used at all.

Mouquet Farm was once again strictly outside the objective here, and had in fact not been part of the objective of any operation that had gone ahead. That is not to say that Australians had not been in the farm. The Australian Official Historian Charles Bean credited Lieutenant William Paton Hoggarth of the 50th Battalion as being the first Australian to reach Mouquet Farm.[30] Hoggarth had entered the southern part of the ruined farm buildings in the operation of 12 August. Since then others had entered the ruined compound, albeit briefly, and now again men of the 12th Battalion were able to enter without too much difficulty. There is something strange about this. A major obstacle was repeatedly entered but no attempt was made to order its permanent capture. In fact, orders were always given to withdraw from Mouquet Farm,

---

28   AWM: AWM 4/23/29/18: '12th Battalion AIF, Report on Operations Near Mouquet Farm', 21 August 1916, 12th Infantry Battalion War Diary.
29   AWM: AWM 26/55/4: '3rd Australian Infantry Brigade Report on Operations about Mouquet Farm and Pozières. 19th to 23rd August 1916,' Operations File Somme 1916, 3rd Infantry Brigade & Battalions.
30   C.E.W. Bean, *The Official History of Australia in the War of 1914-1918. Volume IV: The AIF in France, 1917* (Sydney: Angus & Robertson (1933, 1936), p. 213.

Lieutenant William Hoggarth of the 50th Battalion was later credited by official historian Charles Bean as being the first Australian to enter Mouquet Farm. He was killed in action at Noreuil on 2 April 1917. (AWM P09291.126)

often well before the men there were repulsed by Germans. It is true that the farm would ultimately prove to be very difficult to capture because of the myriad tunnels and dugouts underneath it from which the Germans could rise and fire at attackers before sinking back down underground. But at this stage there was very little idea in 1st Anzac Corps that the defences beneath the farm were so extensive, and they did not know that the position could enable the Germans to do this. Birdwood's reluctance to advance and capture the farm is a marked contrast to his corps' frequent small-scale operations, and suggests that he did not have, or perhaps had lost, the confidence to assign the capture of a significant German defensive work. Attacks would continue to be on trenches and small strongpoints.

Although the 12th Battalion had made good their objectives, advancing further threatened their operation. It became increasingly obvious that the battalion's right flank was completely unconnected to the 11th Battalion in the centre. In fact, it was worse than they thought; the two raiding parties of the 11th, forming the link between the attacks of the 12th and 10th Battalions, were simply not there. This was not even a case of their operation failing. Through what was called a "concatenation of circumstances," the 11th Battalion had not even arrived in the line when the operation began at 6.00pm.[31] The commander of this battalion, Lieutenant-Colonel Stephen Harricks Roberts, had been informed on the evening of 20 August that his men were to take part in the attack roughly 24 hours later. But at this time the entire battalion, less some signallers, pioneers, regimental police, batmen and a few others were permanently on fatigues, most at the Chalk Pit acting as carrying parties trying

31   AWM: AWM 26/55/4: '3rd Australian Infantry Brigade Report on Operations about Mouquet Farm and Pozières. 19th to 23rd August 1916.' Operations File Somme 1916, 3rd Infantry Brigade & Battalions.

to improve the serious shortages of equipment in the front line. The 11th Battalion's parties were only relieved by the 2nd Battalion at 3pm on the 21st. Roberts felt, quite rightly, that the battalion would not be able to continue on until 3.00pm, depart for the front line, reorganise and conduct an attack by 6.00pm. Therefore he tried on a number of occasions to negotiate both with the commandant at the Chalk Pit and with various officers at Divisional headquarters for the relief to happen earlier. He wanted to stop the carrying parties by midday at the latest, if not in the morning. Those requests had resulted in a large party of men of the 11th Battalion, including its bombers and machine gun crews, being formed up at 11.30 that morning. But instead of being sent back to headquarters for deployment as they were supposed to be, a brigade officer ordered them forward to the front line with a load of bombs. The rest of the Battalion could not be found; Roberts could only presume they were "up in the line on similar duties."[32] This last party of men did not return until 3.30pm, at which point they were immediately turned around and sent back to the Chalk Pit to collect bombs and rifle grenades for their own attack, and then sent forward again. The situation was so confused and the need to supply the front line so desperate that the Brigade Officer at the Chalk Pit was not aware that he was sending men required for the attacking party up to the front. Nor was the brigadier in charge of the 3rd Division, Sinclair Maclagan, aware that any men of the attacking party were working on fatigues that day at all. While Roberts estimated that "if no hitch had occurred the attacking party would have got into position in time," the men were heavily shelled and had at least two of its officers buried on the way, one of them twice, and the men scattered by the heavy fire.[33] The 11th Battalion was unable to attack until 8.00pm, two hours after the operations on its flanks went forward.

This is probably the most serious example of the major problems facing by the 1st Division on their second spell in the line – the shortage of manpower. This was apparent even before the formation experienced heavy casualties from their renewed operations. The division had suffered a significant number of casualties following the capture of the village of Pozières, and despite a steady flow of reinforcements, most of the division's battalions were still under strength. Fatigue and carrying parties took up a bigger percentage of the reduced battalions than ever. More than once when a battalion, or part thereof, was called on it could not be found, or was reported to be still completing a task. Headquarters regularly lost track of how many men were available. So when, for example, the commander of A Company of the 7th Battalion, Captain James Frederick Bowtell-Harris, was rebuked by 7th Battalion headquarters for only sending "sixteen other ranks to [the] Brigade dump [to form a carrying party]

32   AWM: AWM 26/55/4: Roberts (OC 11th Bn) to 3rd Bde, 23 August 1916, Operations File Somme 1916, 3rd Infantry Brigade & Battalions.
33   AWM: AWM 26/55/4: Roberts to 3rd Bde, 23 August 1916, 23 August 1916, Operations File Somme 1916, 3rd Infantry Brigade & Battalions.

Brigadier-General Ewen Sinclair Maclagan, officer commanding 3rd Brigade during the Battle of Pozières Ridge. (AWM H12187)

when you were ordered to make available all the men in your company,"[34] he had to remind 7th Battalion headquarters that "all my men are still out on fatigue in accordance with your instructions … they are on their way to the firing line at present."[35] There were no more left. In this case a company of the 5th Battalion filled the role, but then they found "the advance was impracticable and neither officers nor NCOs were familiar with the ground", and so they could do little more than dig trenches.[36] In fact, at that time the 5th Battalion's company had just 32 men in or near the front line, with its remaining 100 men on divisional fatigue in Puchevillers. Units were constantly being borrowed or divided up like this, and could not reliably be called on when needed.

Once the absence of the 11th Battalion became apparent, the brigade tried to cover it by inserting two platoons of the 9th Battalion to hang on while the 11th was located and reorganised. The report of the officer commanding the 9th Battalion demonstrates how ineffective this was as a stop-gap measure, and just how chaotic and disorganised the front line was:

34   AWM: AWM 26/54/7: Bastin (Adj. 7th Bn) to Bowtell-Harris (OC A Coy 7th Bn), 18 August 1916, 3.50pm, Operations File Somme 1916, 2nd Infantry Brigade.
35   AWM: AWM 26/54/7: Bowtell-Harris (OC A Coy 7th Bn) to 7th Bn, 18 August 1916, 6.47pm, Operations File Somme 1916, 2nd Infantry Brigade.
36   AWM: AWM 26/54/7: Bowtell-Harris to 7th Bn, 18 August 1916, 6.47pm, Operations File Somme 1916, 2nd Infantry Brigade.

… at 1630 (4.30pm) … these platoons moved off but owing to the congested state of the trenches a delay occurred and the rendezvous was not reached until 1755 (5.55pm) five minutes before the attack was timed. On arrival great confusion existed and there was only one trench which was filled with 11th Battalion, Engineers, etc. Apparently no one was in charge and the Senior Officer in charge of the Platoons was told they would not be wanted. However he waited and sent an Officer to me informing me of the situation. I informed Brigade and asked for instruction. I received this message which was as follows: "OC two platoons sent to assist 11th Battalion has just returned. He states 11th Battalion had full complement. These platoons now in jumping-off position. Please advise what they had better do".[37]

The situation was farcical. The officer commanding the two platoons of the 9th somehow had been given the impression that there was a full complement of the 11th Battalion in the line, when there simply was not. Given that nobody appeared to be in charge, the information he acted on was surely false. The parties from the 9th Battalion returned from the front line and were later employed elsewhere, and nothing was done to fill the gap between the 10th and 12th Battalions.

The right flank of the Anzac sector, where the 2nd Brigade was holding the line was not untouched during this time either, and was gradually drained of manpower. The 7th Battalion in particular continued to conduct both small attacks and large raids on their objective for days following their initial failed assault. Depleted by casualties and requests from division for working parties, the reserve battalion of the 2nd Brigade was reduced to a force of very few men. Early in the morning of 21 August the 1st Division had ordered more carrying parties from the 2nd Brigade's reserve Battalion to assist the 3rd Brigade. Pushed to the limit, Lieutenant-Colonel Bennett sent the following message back:

[The] working party … referred to has been detailed. I beg to point out that when these men leave my Reserve Battalion there will only be approximately 137 rifles in reserve of very tired men who only came out of the line at 1.30am this morning [and] have been in since the 15th which has completely knocked them out. Should my Brigade still continue to hold the line at 12 noon I consider that it is not safe to deplete the reserve as proposed. Moreover the men are so tired that I would respectfully suggest that this working party be detailed from some other force especially in view of the Brigade having to march on [the] 22nd.

37   AWM: AWM 26/55/4: '3rd Australian Infantry Brigade Report on Operations about Mouquet Farm and Pozières. 19th to 23rd August 1916,' Operations File Somme 1916, 3rd Infantry Brigade & Battalions.

I wish the question of the depletion of reserve brought specially to the notice of the GOC of the Division.[38]

At no point was the aim of these attacks reappraised or reconsidered at upper levels. It would appear that simply because an objective had been given by 1st Anzac Corps, the 1st Division was determined to take it, no matter what the cost. The cost, in the end, was a very significant proportion of the division's fighting strength, for the partial attainment of what was simply a line on a map. While the 2nd Brigade's strength was sapped, the 3rd Brigade, too, was seriously reduced by casualties, making "further offensive operations on any but a small-scale … out of the question, especially as the men were short of sleep and shaken by shellfire".[39] This was an exhausted division. These small ad hoc operations of the 1st Anzac Corps were now threatening the very stability of their sector and their ability to continue to make attacks on the German line. There were simply not enough men to do all of the jobs required to be done by a division, and not enough time to do them, without the added pressure of continued offensive operations. This situation had been building for some time, with lower-level commanders always under pressure to prepare the front line and be in formation in time for an operation. A lack of resources meant they had finally failed to do so.

The brigade commanders of the 1st Division had each approached their tasks in a different manner. Smyth saw his first operation of this period in particular as a large raid, and deployed his infantry accordingly. Bennett acted in the completely opposite manner, choosing to deploy his infantry in standard wave formation, maintaining strength through the formation of his men, while avoiding overcrowding his infantry lines. Sinclair-Maclagan's operation was a mixture of the two – two operations using waves of infantry joined by a series of large raiding parties. No matter the formation adopted by brigade, however, no approach could work more effectively than the others. This was because the brigadiers had been hamstrung by a series of completely inappropriate artillery barrages from corps command. Somehow the logic behind lifting artillery barrages had been lost, and they were now being applied in a totally inappropriate manner. Each lift of the barrage had been originally designed to protect the infantry as they advanced between objectives. The barrage would first fall onto an objective before moving forward, keeping the Germans away from their machine guns and off of their parapets until the very last moment so that the attacking infantry could get across the ground as unhindered as possible. Now that the barrages were beginning on the only objective and making a series of lifts afterwards, the plans of

---

38   AWM: AWM 26/51/30: 2nd Bde to 1st Division, 21 August 1916, 9.24am in 'Operations of 1st, and 2nd, Aust. Inf. Brigades towards Mouquet Farm & MARTINPUICH respectively. Summary of Messages,' Operations File Somme 1916, 1st Australian Division General Staff.

39   AWM: AWM 26/55/4: '3rd Australian Infantry Brigade Report on Operations about Mouquet Farm and Pozières. 19th to 23rd August 1916,' Operations File Somme 1916, 3rd Infantry Brigade & Battalions.

the artillery and the infantry were completely disconnected. The infantry stood no chance against the unchallenged machine guns of the German defenders.

The fault of this situation lay with 1st Anzac Corps. While Reserve Army continued to have some input into the artillery barrages for operations ordered by Gough, the Army headquarters was convinced that 1st Anzac Corps would be advancing further than they actually did. On 20 August a memorandum from Army was issued with a "forecast of future operations … with a view to enabling Corps Commanders to arrange their minor undertakings and to adjust the reliefs of their troops." This memo stated that "all efforts of the Reserve Army will be directed towards the capture of Thiepval."[40] It was predicted that, with the 1st Anzac Corps pressing on with its "preliminary operations" it should have reached a line of trench running 800-1000 yards to the north of Mouquet Farm by 25 August. By the 26th the corps was expected to have shifted to the left in the line by taking over from the 48th British Division and be prepared shortly afterwards by putting in an attack upon Thiepval from the south-east. But 1st Anzac Corps was not in any way capable of participating in even the first part of Reserve Army's plan. Gough expected the corps to have advanced more than 800 yards in four days, when they had barely managed to advance that far since the initial capture of Pozières some four weeks earlier. Birdwood's operations were so reduced in scope by this stage that his men were almost always threatened by their own artillery fire because the barrages were so close to their jumping-off trench. The outlook of 1st Anzac Corps was increasingly limited in scope and it had reduced the ability of their infantry to succeed in the field to naught. Reserve Army's hope that the capture of Thiepval would be accomplished by 1 September by this means was simply fantasy.

The combination of Gough's insistence that units press forward as much as possible, and Birdwood's willingness to do so only in the most limited of ways was costing the Australian forces of the 1st Anzac Corps more than they could pay. The 1st Australian Division was, on its second tour to the front line, completely finished. Battalions like the 10th were now well below half of their establishment figure, and the men who had not been killed or evacuated wounded were shaky and exhausted. There was no possibility of leaving the 1st Division in the line, much less using it to conduct another operation now or in the near future. There were not enough men to provide carrying parties to even feed those holding the line. As a result, the division was withdrawn on 23 August 1916 and replaced by the 2nd Australian Division. By 28 August the men of the 1st Division were in billets in Hoograaf in Belgium and would not participate again in fighting on the Somme for some months. Between 5 and 23 August the division had suffered 2,654 casualties. They had advanced the line no more than 400 yards.

---

40   AWM: AWM 26/63/11: Reserve Army to II Corps, V Corps, I Anzac Corps, XIII Corps & 3rd Cavalry Division, 20 August 1916, Operations File Somme 1916, supplementary unbound records.

6

"Mouquet Farm is causing many casualties at present": The Danger of Ignoring the Obvious

By 9am on 23 August, Birdwood had Major-General Gordon Legge's 2nd Division was back in the line. From the first day the 2nd Division arrived in the line, Birdwood and his staff were aware that 1st Anzac Corps' time around Pozières was coming to an end, and they would be relieved by the Canadians. As a part of this process the 2nd Division would soon be relieved by the 4th Australian Division. In the period immediately before Legge's division moved back into the front line, Reserve Army had given no specific direction regarding operational objectives nor had it ordered any attacks. But despite the looming withdrawal – or perhaps because of it – and without a demonstrated understanding of the problems in recent operations, Birdwood continued to plan and conduct small-scale, costly operations.

It is clear that by this time Birdwood thought he had hit upon the answer to forward movement on the Somme. His operations had become more and more uniform, and shared two major characteristics. The first of these was the closeness of the objective. Typically the Australian infantry was now aiming to attack objectives at a distance of around 50-100 yards from their current position. This distance was sometimes further in some small areas of some operations, but never for the greater part of the section of front being attacked, if at all. While Birdwood had been made responsible for an important first phase of Reserve Army's master plan – to move his corps to the north as a preliminary manoeuvre in the capture of Thiepval – he was not following this order with any resolve. His advances were tentative at best, and pointless at worst. While the operations were focussed in the direction of Mouquet Farm, the short objectives meant that each one was not even a significant step towards clearing the German dugouts in and immediately beyond Mouquet Farm, much less in pressing on towards Thiepval. By late August there had simply been no purpose in 1st Anzac Corps' operations. There had not been for several weeks.

The other major characteristic of this series of battles has to do with artillery support. Birdwood and his staff continued to rely on artillery barrages as an integral part of each operation. However, these artillery barrages were quite different to those used in the Pozières battle of 23 July, or even in 2nd Division's operations against the OG Lines the following week. The danger was that superficially they looked the same. Both the earlier barrages and the later ones accompanying these small-scale operations lifted from objective to objective as the infantry advanced, and ostensibly were designed for the infantry to follow closely, gaining protection from the curtain of falling shells. The problem with the more recent artillery barrages were that they began *on* the objective, and so despite lifting slowly away, they could never be followed by the infantry. In a number of cases they actually began beyond the only objective of the attack, and the Germans could defend their positions within the Australian artillery barrage with impunity. And so although the barrages had the appearance of integrating with the infantry, there was a fundamental disconnect between the two. These barrages were always part of the orders handed to 1st Anzac Corps from Reserve Army. But the barrages that Corps then handed on to its divisions were almost always modified from the original orders to be shorter, weaker, and strangely disassociated from the task at hand. Nevertheless, the short objectives and the pointless artillery barrages were firmly ingrained in the tactical planning of the 1st Australian Corps by mid-August 1916, and would not be modified or regulated in any way until their withdrawal.

At the same time, there had been a number of notes disseminating 'lessons learned' in recent operations in early to mid-August. The most important of these had been summarised by Haig on 13 August 1916. This memorandum of general instructions contained some useful advice, such as the need to have sufficient depth in assaulting columns and to pay careful attention to lines of communication. Haig also stated that "isolated advances by detachments, pressing forward beyond the reach of support, should be avoided … the enemy can concentrate against these small bodies [and] the most gallant men are lost in vain." But in stark contrast to this instruction, 1st Anzac Corps regularly sent forward patrols of infantry and bombing platoons in advance of the leading wave of infantry during operations, if not hours before the operation ahead. These groups often established advanced posts in no man's land well ahead of the front line, in almost total isolation. This was in direct opposition to Haig's advice, but went unregulated.

One of the most emphasised points in Haig's memorandum was to do with flanks. While it was important to ensure that "flanks are sufficiently well protected", Haig observed:

> … the advance must not be delayed by large bodies of troops hanging back for those on their flanks, who may be checked, to come on. On the contrary, every effort must be made to turn the flanks of centres of resistance and surround them, and to continue the attack.[1]

---

1   AWM: AWM 26/40/4: O.B. 1782, 13 August 1916, Operations File Somme 1916, General Headquarters British Expeditionary Force General Staff.

This meant that an advancing line should push ahead where it could, bending around centres of resistance until they could be absorbed. What it meant in practice, particularly in areas of the line that were making small-scale, limited attacks, was that the advanced part of the line was very liable to become an isolated detached party without contact on either flank. So in fact what these general instructions, and others like them, did was effectively condone almost any approach. If a commander wanted to advance his line around centres of resistance, there was official sanction for his actions. Conversely, if his concern was the attack breaking down, he had been told not to allow isolated parties to get too far forward, and could rely on that instruction. Issues of general principles for attacks such as these in August 1916 almost always contained fundamental contradictions like this. Another example from this same memorandum comes when Haig wrote about "[t]he necessity of foreseeing and providing for defensive requirements on the flanks in all attacks, large or small. This includes arrangements to close gaps opening in advance."[2] There is an inherent assumption in this instruction that there would be enough men present and sufficiently unwounded to be able to effect this. And yet, even Haig was aware that the current battles were causing significant, if not catastrophic casualties. This memorandum clearly indicates a brigade or battalion due to be relieved "may have lost a large number of its effectives and is holding the position with very possibly half the strength of the relieving unit".[3] A battalion at half strength would surely struggle to provide sufficient defensive requirements. This memorandum, and others like it, provided only the most basic, and often contradictory, guidelines. Certainly Reserve Army and its component parts were able to act without any regard to this and other published directives with impunity.

Still facing the 1st Anzac Corps was the German stronghold of Mouquet Farm. Although they still could not be sure of exact numbers, 1st Anzac Corps headquarters was by now well aware that Mouquet Farm housed a sizeable German garrison. Australians soldiers had been in the farm compound itself and seen dugout entrances, and it had been noted that German machine guns could be withdrawn from the area around the farm and apparently vanish, giving further evidence of well-established and well-fortified underground shelters. And the numbers of enemy troops seen were not small. On 24 August the 24th Battalion reported that men in a bombing post within twelve yards of the farm saw "numbers of Boche ... Between 300 and 400 enemy passed ... along [a] low trench ... [and] ... disappeared into Mouquet Farm which must consist of a series of deep underground tunnels and dugouts."[4]

When the 2nd Division entered the line again, the men found much of the front remained the same as it had been the last time they were there – from Munster Alley along the OG Lines to the north there had been no change. This sector was given to the 5th Brigade, and it would only defend the line and not try to advance it. The biggest

2   Ibid.
3   Ibid.
4   AWM: AWM 4/23/41/12: 24 August 1916, 24th Battalion War Diary.

An Australian working party of the 7th Brigade carry empty sandbags past the old German strongpoint Gibraltar on their way to the front line.

change to the Anzac position came in the centre of the line, where recent efforts had managed to extend the salient northwards. Here there had been an advance of roughly 4-500 yards since 25 July. The line had also been extended to the left a short way, with Australian troops taking over control of some of the more northerly parts of Skyline Trench from the division next door. This northern area of 1st Anzac Corps' sector continued to be the focus of their future operations from the time the 2nd Division came into the line on 23 August, until the time the 4th Division was relieved in early September and the corps as a whole retired to Belgium. The 6th Brigade, under Brigadier-General John Gellibrand, held the line in this sector for the 2nd Division, and had found that the salient had extended the line so much they were obliged to put three battalions into the front line instead of the two proposed by Legge. The 7th Brigade formed the divisional reserve, and was distributed through Tara Hill, Sausage Valley and the brickfields.

The 2nd Division had been seriously depleted by its first experience of major operations on the Somme and had been incompletely reinforced or resupplied since. It surely could not have gone unrecognised at 1st Anzac Corps headquarters that the 2nd Division was in danger of ending up in the same state the 1st Division was currently in – massively understrength and withdrawn from active operations having gained very little. On entering the front line, the 2nd Division immediately commenced the by-now usual activity of construction or consolidation and improvement of front and communication lines on taking over the sector. The entire sector was repeatedly and considerably damaged by shellfire and deepening and strengthening of the trenches was an ongoing requirement. Work, too, was constantly hampered by shellfire; not only were trenches badly damaged, but when men of the 2nd Division arrived to man them, they found that many were shallow and unfinished. The situation was so fluid that there was an ongoing need to continually confirm the position of both Australian and German trenches on the map. The ground had become so churned up that aerial photographs were of little assistance. It was reported that it was only "with the utmost difficulty that [a] line of trenches can be picked up and marked on [the] with any degree of certainty".[5] The 6th Brigade commander, Brigadier-General John Gellibrand found on assuming command that that he had:

> … taken over an incompletely consolidated position without any communications worth speaking of, and that means terribly slow work in getting about and [getting] information. Many places can only be reached by going round three parts of a circle.[6]

The situation was worst in the forward lines – the area from which any new operation would launch, and which was the area least mapped or understood. Gellibrand reported:

> I am not at present in a position to report definitely on the actual line held by this Brigade or on the amount of work required to complete consolidation and provide some form of communication trenches.[7]

In fact, the exact position of the apex of the line could not be definitely marked on a until the afternoon of 23 August. Gellibrand wrote to Bridges at 1st Anzac Headquarters to say he hoped "that the 24th will not be the date of any push from here before essential preparation and reconnaissances are satisfactory".[8] As he noted, and Haig had before him, "communications are the whole business – nothing must be attempted till this is put straight".[9] This required well-established trench systems for

---

5   AWM: AWM 26/58/3: Savige (6th Bde) to HQ 2nd Australian Division, 23 August 1916, Operations File Somme 1916, 6th Infantry Brigade.
6   AWM: AWM 26/58/3: Gellibrand (OC 6th Bde) to Bridges, 23 August 1916, Operations File Somme 1916, 6th Infantry Brigade.
7   AWM: AWM 26/58/3: Gellibrand (OC 6th Bde) to HQ 2nd Division, 23 August 1916, Operations File Somme 1916, 6th Infantry Brigade.
8   AWM: AWM 26/58/3: Letter from Gellibrand to Bridges, 23 August 1916, Operations File Somme 1916, 6th Infantry Brigade.
9   AWM: AWM 26/58/3: 'Notes for Col. Bridges', 23 August 1916, Operations File Somme 1916, 6th Infantry Brigade.

messengers to be able to move around the battlefield under cover. With most trenches in a partially-destroyed condition, messages would take around an hour and a half to be run from the front line to brigade headquarters, which had no telephone communication to speak of to the forward lines. It should be noted that the 1st Australian Division cannot be blamed for the state of the front lines, either. The shellfire had invariably been heavy, consistent and accurate for weeks, and destroyed any works undertaken within days or even hours. The 1st Division had struggled with exactly the same problems during their period in possession of the front line too.

Preparation

It was into this situation that Birdwood introduced new plans to attack the German lines, under Gough's invitation for subordinate commanders to 'think out and suggest new enterprises'. Birdwood's original plan was for the 2nd Division to capture two objectives just two days after entering the front line. These objectives were a small triangle of German trenches to the left of Mouquet Farm, and a short piece of trench to the right of it. Unsurprisingly, these two objectives were very close to the existing Australian position. In fact, once again, such was their insignificance in terms of the overall situation, it is not possible to describe them without the use of coordinates. The small triangle of German trenches was known as Points 27–77–54,[10] and the points on the right were a trench between points 36 and 95, hereafter referred to as Trench 95–36. None of the objectives in this projected operation could be said to be causing any more than the usual threat to the current position. They were no more than strongpoints in the German line – heavily defended to be sure, but nothing on the scale of defences in Pozières village or the OG Lines, and not even anything on the scale of the fortified compound of Mouquet Farm. This new plan did not particularly contribute to a safer defence of the line. And given that this sort of minor objective had been attacked with extremely heavy casualties four or five times previously, there is absolutely no evidence of any process of weighing the benefit of the objective against a potential cost in lives or materiel at any level. Once again Mouquet Farm itself was not an objective of either operation. The operation against the triangular trench 27-77-54 on the left brought the line to the south-west corner of the farm buildings but no further. There would be no attempt to connect the two objectives by taking the farm compound which lay between them. Nor does there appear to have been any consideration whatsoever of the implications of having such a potentially formidable position in the middle of a disconnected Anzac line. This lack of foresight and acknowledgement of wider operational implications is quite simply remarkable.

10   At this time numbered points on maps were invariably read from right to left, so Point 54 was in fact the most westerly point and Point 27 closest to Mouquet Farm.

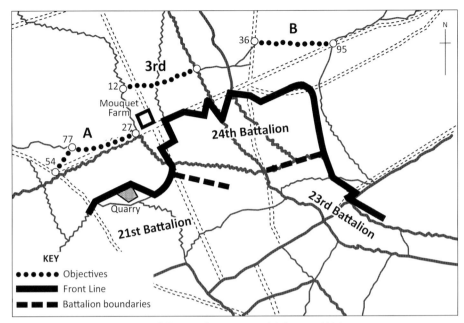

29 2nd Division's operation, 26 August 1916.

These plans were initially for two large raids on the points. The bulk of the plan, including the objectives and artillery cooperation, were provided by corps and grew over the space of some days from a strong raid to a small attack. The hope was to take the points by having the infantry probe forward through advancing posts or "by bombing alone, if no other course is open".[11] But gradually the idea developed over time into the by-now familiar format of small operations. Crucially, the day before the attack it was finally realised that the two operations would suffer from being separated. 1st Anzac Corps staff saw at last the serious danger the right flank of the operation against Points 27–77–54 was in. The objective was actually on the corner of the Mouquet Farm compound, and would expose most of the operation to fire from the German stronghold. Unfortunately, the 'remedy' to this problem was another large raid in front of the farm to provide protection for the flank of the operation and no more. But despite growing out of what was felt to be an operational necessity to protect the operation against Points 27–77–54 on the left, this raid was planned to be an entirely separate operation. This comprised more or less the strong patrol advances envisaged in early plans. No arrangements were made to maintain contact between the two forces conducting the attack, either when the attack was launched, or when

11 AWM: AWM 26/56/9: White to 1st, 2nd and 4th Aust. Divs., (undated – Appendix 1), Operations File Somme 1916, 2nd Australian Division General Staff.

it had achieved its objectives. Nor was this raid to have part of the artillery barrage modified to meet its needs. It was a last-minute, roughly planned, unsupported raid that was in no way a match for the force in Mouquet Farm.

The developing plans drew criticism from Gellibrand. The plan called for strong posts to be constructed at points 12 and 27 by isolated groups of infantry ahead of the main line, despite Haig's directive. Point 27 was roughly on the south west corner of the Mouquet Farm building compound and the most easterly point of the German triangular trench, and Point 12, about 100 yards to the north of it. It was not proposed to join these two points, but rather to push them out as strongpoints ahead of the main line, which would skirt Mouquet Farm's boundaries to the south. Gellibrand considered the capture of these points and the construction of strongpoints there would simply not be possible, explaining that:

> … the establishment of a post near 12 or even 27 is likely to prove costly at present. The position of my present left flank at the quarry is by no means satisfactory as it is said to consist of 300 yards of obliterated and unoccupied trench. I do not consider an attack on 27–77–54 to be feasible with the means at my disposal.[12]

Once again a brigade commander had been handed a plan he could do very little with.

The response to Gellibrand's criticisms was bizarre. On 25 August 1916 the 1st Anzac Corps issued orders that made the main purpose of this operation to capture the German trench at Points 27–77–54, for which an artillery barrage was ordered. The operation in the middle to capture three strong posts between the two attacks was arranged to be carried out by "specially organised and equipped parties" but this and Operation B against Trench 95–36 on the right were thereafter dealt with through "separate instructions … issued to the G[eneral] O[fficer] C[ommanding] 2nd Australian Division" by 1st Anzac Corps staff.[13] Birdwood left further arrangements for these operations up to Legge, having Brudenell White ask him:

> … to scrutinise particularly the arrangements for the establishment of posts at 73, 42 and 12. Barrages will be arranged to aid you in this to the utmost while protecting the right flank of your attack to the utmost at the same time. The posts named being on higher ground will be an important protection to the right of your line at 27. Such posts will however be somewhat exposed, particularly

---

12   AWM: AWM 26/58/3: Gellibrand (OC 6th Bde) to HQ 2nd Division, 23 August 1916, Operations File Somme 1916, 6th Infantry Brigade.
13   AWM: AWM 26/50/18: '1st A.&.N.Z.A.C. Order No. 35', 25 August 1916, Operations File Somme 1916, 1st Anzac Corps General Staff.

that at 73, and this is an added reason for effecting early the capture of the line 95 – 36.[14]

But these instructions had already informed Legge that "you will not, in all probability, be able to operate against … Trench 95–36 concurrently with your action on the left." Although Birdwood considered that Legge "should have ready complete preparations to advance the right of your northern flank to the line 95–36 as soon as possible after the completion of your first operation",[15] the time it took to organise and complete this advance would leave the right dangerously unsupported in the meantime. In the event, Legge placed considerable importance on the capture of the strong posts in the middle, but did little to effect the capture of Trench 36–95. But in reality, all three attacks would be desperately in danger from the German stronghold beneath Mouquet Farm, sitting in the middle of the objective without any plans to capture it.

The artillery barrage for this attack was once again light, although it did begin in front of the target. It was planned to be fast-paced, with just three lifts (one per minute) of roughly 50 yards on the left flank, after which the artillery was to make an enormous lift of some 200 yards to beyond Mouquet Farm, onto the line of Points 12, 42 and 73. Heavy artillery would initially bombard this same distant line from three minutes before the attack commenced to two minutes after 'zero', and from then would lift to a line even further away, between 200 and 500 yards from the objective. On the right there were no lifts at all, but the artillery would remain firing on the trench at Points 36–95 for the entire duration of the operation. This was the objective line for the infantry on the right, and so if their operation was fit to go ahead, they would have to wait for the barrage to lift and rush the trench. After a period in which 1st Anzac Corps had been ordering its artillery to fire its barrages first onto the objective and then made a series of lifts carefully beyond the infantry's area of operations – and thereby helping them not at all – most of the lifts for this operation were finally planned to fall in front of the objective and lead the infantry up to it.

Despite having areas where the barrage fell in ostensibly the right places, however, it was still of very little use to the infantry. The lifts up to the objective were so close together it would be possible for the entire program to have been fired and moved onto the standing barrage far beyond the farm before fire even moved beyond the 'safe zone' that allowed the infantry to operate without coming under their own fire. Artillery in 1916 was dangerously unreliable, and could only hit a rough area rather than a specific target. As a result, the safe zone for infantry was considered to be 200 yards from the barrage line. The objectives for the operation planned for 26 August

14   AWM: AWM 26/50/18: White to 2nd Division, 25 August 1916, Operations File Somme 1916, 1st Anzac Corps General Staff.
15   AWM: AWM 26/50/18: White to 2nd Division, 25 August 1916, Operations File Somme 1916, 1st Anzac Corps General Staff.

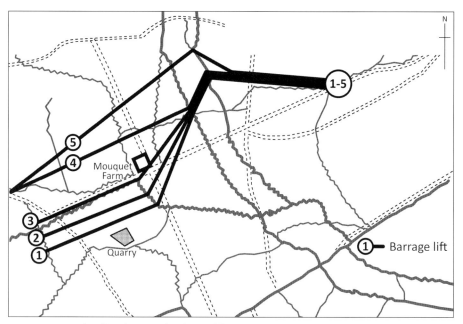

30 Artillery barrage for the 2nd Division's operation, 26 August 1916.

were uncomfortably close to that, or well within it, all along the line. Again, some of the infantry in positions opposite Mouquet Farm were so close to the first objective of the barrage that they would be forced to temporarily withdraw from the front line to avoid being killed themselves. When combined with such close objectives, this kind of barrage prevented the infantry from employing leapfrogging techniques as used on 23 July, and instead could only encourage them to attack a single objective *en masse*. This tactical degeneration had been evident in most of the 4th Division's small-scale operations, when the objectives were too close to the assembly trenches to safely fire a bombardment, and although perhaps ostensibly improved here, the plan was still largely detrimental to the infantry.

Legge and his staff considered that the artillery plan was heavy enough to win them the day with little effort. Legge's Chief of Staff, Lieutenant-Colonel A.H. Bridges, wrote that "in view of the barrages arranged the capture [of points 73, 42 and 12] will probably not be so difficult as it appeared at first."[16] But this was hardly the kind of barrage that would gain Legge's division automatic victory. On the left it was far too close to the infantry's area of operation, too fast-lifting, and then stood at too great a

16   AWM: AWM 26/56/8: Bridges to CRA 2nd Division, CRA Lahore Arty & CRE 6th Bde, 25 August 1916, Operations File Somme 1916, 2nd Australian Division General Staff.

distance from the final objective. But once again 2nd Division's plan crowded a large number of infantry into dense waves for the attack. Two lines of infantry (each nearly half a battalion in strength) on a 4-500 yard front were assigned to the attack on the left. Even with the battalions depleted by their first tour of the front line, this was at least one man per one and a half to two yards of trench, giving the Germans plenty of targets at which to aim their machine guns. It was only once the objective was occupied that the troops were to be thinned out, leaving parties of Lewis gunners and bombers sent forward to advanced positions in shell holes as a first defence. Legge's comment on the barrages at least demonstrates a more welcoming attitude towards the use of artillery than he had exhibited previously, but his overall plan demonstrates a failure to recognise the inadequacy of the artillery schedule to the planned infantry operation, and the danger of the infantry plan itself.

The 21st Battalion was given the main task of attacking the triangle of strongpoints formed by Points 27–77–54. This attack would be largely unsupported on either flank because the British division on the left did not propose to participate in the operation by attacking from Skyline Trench, and the operation against Points 12, 42 and 73, was 200 yards to the far side of Mouquet Farm. In the early stages of planning for these operations, Brudenell White noted that "the operation … will be greatly affected by the [action of the] division on the left", but in the event no cooperation was organised, and no contingency was put in place beyond the construction of a defensive flank.[17] The 21st Battalion was out of place before the operation, and had to swap places with the 24th Battalion to conduct the attack. The 24th Battalion would then provide the parties to capture the different points to the north of Mouquet Farm. If the attack on the right, against Trench 36–95 went ahead, it would be done by the 23rd Battalion.

The time set for zero hour was 4.45am. This time was carefully fixed for a number of reasons – the first was simply to try to throw the Germans off guard given that previous operations had all been held either at night or at sunset. But it also was intended to give the assaulting troops a chance to assemble under cover of darkness, and then make their advance with the half-light of dawn. The half-light, it was hoped, would also mask the activity of consolidation, giving the men the best of both the concealment of darkness and light to see by. Wires were run out along the ground on both flanks of the assembly trenches to ensure the men attacked in the right direction, which was of critical importance in the darkened, featureless battlefield. 2nd Division had already ordered the improvement and construction of a trench to serve as an assembly point for assaulting troops for the impending operation. And, at the same time the 6th Brigade were constructing this trench, they were improving communication trenches, mapping and identifying locations in the salient, preparing for full use of machine guns and Stokes Mortars, and making arrangements for the special protection of the left flank, which would be unsupported.

---

17   Memorandum from Brudenell White, General Staff 1st A&NZAC to 1st, 2nd and 4th Aust. Divs., 22 August 1916, AWM: AWM 26/56/9.

The attack – 26 August 1916

The attack against points 27–77–54 left the trenches precisely on time at 4.45am on 26 August 1916. The 21st Battalion deployed A and B Companies in the front line followed by two platoons of C and D Companies in a loose wave formation. It was a disaster. In all areas the light, swift artillery barrage failed to keep the German defenders in their trenches, and rifle and machine gun fire fragmented the organised lines of Australian infantry as they advanced. The men clumped into groups, and a number of parties were forced to withdraw. Others managed to push through to the final objective, but then promptly overran it and followed the barrage to its final distant position instead of staying behind to consolidate their objective. In the rear, reserve companies from the 22nd Battalion supporting the operation lost their way and went on with the leading waves of the attack, meaning that there were no close reserves available to make anything of the furthest advances. Thanks to their active defensive fire, the German defenders were able to keep most of the attacking waves of infantry at bay. Despite promising early reports, by 7.30am the 21st Battalion was finally obliged to report that they had "been stopped and driven back at places. Front line being heavily shelled. Enemy appear to be advancing in strength".[18] German machine guns in Point 54 in particular were causing heavy casualties, and holding up the advance. Apart from a small gain around Point 77 and scattered, disorganised advanced parties, the entire attack was floundering.

To the right of the 21st Battalion, the 24th Battalion pushed forward raiding parties and strong patrols to take points 12, 42 and 73. But between Corps-issued orders and battalion orders, the objectives had been modified. Their objectives as they advanced were to assist the 21st Battalion in attacking Point 27, to cooperate against Mouquet Farm and Point 31, and to push strong patrols forward from a number of points to the right. Crucially, a working party was to link the points 27 and 59 along the southern edge of the destroyed buildings of Mouquet Farm. At the same time, two bombing parties made a diversionary attack on Mouquet Farm. While Mouquet Farm was apparently easy to dismiss from a high level of command, it formed an unavoidable hazard for the men in the field. Without strong artillery support or a better plan, the best Gellibrand and his battalion commanders could do to try to negate the immediate threat from the farm was to assault it with small parties of infantry and box it off, even though it did not form an officially designated objective of the operation in any way. This time the proximity of the farm to the objective demanded that the farm be attacked, simply because the strong German garrison there threatened the operations both to the left and the south of the position. Officers of the 24th Battalion reported that the "Heavy Artillery had failed in making any impression on the farm", and that

---

18   AWM: AWM 26/56/8: Operations File Somme 1916, 2nd Australian Division.

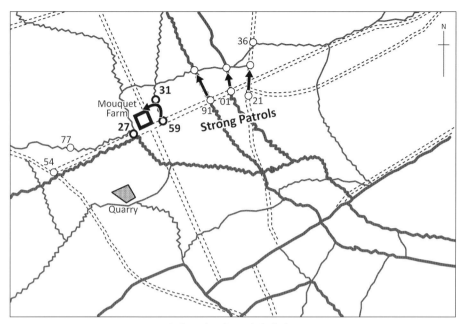

31   24th Battalion's modified objectives.

it was "exceedingly strong [and] holds a garrison of 400 men".[19] Mouquet Farm made the 24th Battalion's task almost impossible.

Before the operation began the 24th Battalion had been forced to leave their jumping-off trench and move back to accommodate the artillery barrage, and only managed to reoccupy their original positions three minutes after zero hour. The working party sent to link Points 27 and 59 went forward under command of Lieutenant John Austin Mahony shortly afterwards. As they began to work on the road in front of Mouquet Farm, Mahony became aware that the two parties sent into Mouquet Farm as a diversion had been held up by a heavy fusillade of 'Potato Masher' Bombs. "Evidently," 24th Battalion reports added drily, "the Boche had come to the surface in Mouquet Farm."[20] The enemy had indeed come to the surface, and, it appeared, in numbers. The raiding party in the farm was running dangerously low of bombs, and Mahony's working party were drawn into the action. The sergeant who had given him the report led Mahony and his party into the farm but could not find an officer. Lieutenant Mahony later reported:

19   AWM: AWM 26/58/3: Nicholas (OC 24th Bn), Untitled document begins 'night 22 …', Operations File Somme 1916, 6th Infantry Brigade.
20   AWM: AWM 4/23/41/12: 24th Battalion War Diary.

Captain (then Lieutenant) John Austin Mahony, 24th Battalion (far right) with Captain John Fletcher and Lieutenant Joseph Scales. Mahony took a working party forward into Mouquet Farm around 22 August 1916, fighting to maintain his position before being forced to withdraw. He was awarded the Military Cross in October 1916, but died of wounds in October 1918. (AWM P03668.006)

> … [he] went direct to where brisk bombing was going on on his right and we found three deep German dugouts full of Germans who were snipers. We settled these by throwing bombs down the dugouts and by opening rifle fire.[21]

Mahony then saw that a party of the 21st was being seriously held up by the resistance from Mouquet Farm but that to their left the line had advanced 300 yards beyond their objective. He left to sort the situation out, leaving a small party to try to consolidate the situation before the farm. In his absence the bombing fight ended, but rifle fire seriously hampered the work of digging a sap towards Point 27.

At 10.20 in the morning Major Eric Clive Plant, Brigade Major of the 6th Brigade sent a message to the 24th Battalion to say:

---

21   AWM: AWM 26/58/3: Nicholas (OC 24th Bn), Untitled document begins 'night 22 …', Operations File Somme 1916, 6th Infantry Brigade.

The situation now demands that an energetic bombing attack be directed against Mouquet Farm which is causing many casualties at present. Two teams of selected men each under an officer will attack it from the south and south east sides as soon as possible. The importance of silencing the post is a matter of urgency.[22]

Finally, for the first time a formal order to enter Mouquet Farm and negate the threat from within had been given. Unfortunately it came in the middle of an operation as a last-minute solution to a major problem. After making enquiries, 24th Battalion Headquarters received the disheartening news:

… [that] the Brigadier is unable to give you artillery preparation and coordination you asked for. The only thing that you can get is the assistance the T[rench] M[ortar] Battery can give you.[23]

Smythe tried to contact trench mortar officers, but found they had all gone to Sausage Valley to try to find ammunition for their mortars. Nevertheless, he replied:

Believe I can effect an entrance to Mouquet Farm but it is essential to provide reinforcements of men and bombs … D and B Companies are too weak to provide reinforcements or carriers. I will be unable to hold out long unless this is arranged for.[24]

Smythe was still preparing his pathetically small party of twelve to go when the battalion was relieved. In the meantime an emergency artillery barrage had been called down on a massing German counter-attack to the north of the Farm. The artillery behind the lines opened up about 2.30pm with indifferent results. Reports suggested that one in three rounds did hit German positions, but of the other two rounds one went wild, and one hit Australian positions. Once again repeated messages were sent in a desperate attempt to stop the short fire, with no results. The battalion suffered heavy casualties as a result.

Others managed to follow Mahony's example and get parties of men into Mouquet Farm during the early hours of the morning in spite of the lack of support from either artillery or trench mortars. Sergeant Robertson of the 24th Battalion led a bombing party into it but could not stay long. His party managed to throw bombs into the German dugouts during the operation to keep the defenders undercover. Running out of bombs, he and his party went back to collect more, but found they "could not

22   AWM: AWM 26/58/3: Plant (Brigade Major, 6th Bde) to 24th Bn, 26 August 1916, 10.20pm, Operations File Somme 1916, 6th Infantry Brigade.
23   AWM: AWM 26/58/3: 6th Bde to Smythe (24th Bn), 26 August 1916 (untimed), Operations File Somme 1916, 6th Infantry Brigade.
24   AWM: AWM: EXDOC026: Smythe (24th Bn) to OC 24th Bn, undated, Operations File Somme 1916, 6th Infantry Brigade.

regain entry into Mouquet Farm owing to M[achine] Guns which now opened up for [the] first time [and] from the German bombing parties".[25] Other parties were finding much the same. Eight men of the 24th under 2/Lt George David Pollington advanced into the farm but had to retire. Pollington was later awarded the Military Medal:

> … for gallant and skilful conduct of a patrol at Mouquet Farm and his gallant efforts to establish a point [there] … when [his position] had to be given up under heavy fire on the 26th August, he … engaged the enemy at Mouquet Farm with bombs contributing materially to relieve the pressure of the German bomb attacks.'[26]

These small parties, approaching from either side of the farm used all the bombs at their disposal, and were close enough to throw them at Germans above ground and pour rifle fire down the entrances of the German dugouts. All was to no avail. German troops in the farm continued to hold up the 24th Battalion advance on Point 27 on the left, and both the 21st Battalion's attack on Point 77 and the men of that battalion who had overrun their objective and were near Point 12 on the right.[27] All of these groups were ultimately forced out, however, because it was impossible to dig under the machine gun fire and bombs were directed against them from Mouquet Farm. The resistance given by the German defenders in the farm proved so strong that ground could not be held anywhere near it.

By 11am the only troops available to Gellibrand as brigade commander were two very depleted companies of the 22nd Battalion, about a fifth of their normal strength, and a similar number in the 21st. Gellibrand write "in view of the numbers of the enemy in front and the strength of posts 54 and 27, no less than the condition of the troops at hand I decided to restrict our action maintaining the line … at [Point] 77 and to the Eastward."[28] The main operation had more or less entirely failed. Although not required to attack on the right, Major William Brazenor of the 23rd Battalion sent a message at 8.30pm on 26 August to say "I am sending out a patrol to establish a post as far forward as possible towards Point 95".[29] Thirty men were then sent to sap out towards the patrol. 2/Lieutenant Robert Lloyd Tremain, one non-commissioned officer and five other ranks worked their way out into no man's land. At 11.30pm

25   AWM: AWM 26/58/3: 'Operations of 24 Bn while in Poziers Trenches from night Aug 23rd to Aug 27th 1916,', Operations File Somme 1916, 6th Infantry Brigade.
26   AWM: AWM 28/1/72: Recommendation File for Honours & Awards, 2nd Australian Division.
27   AWM: AWM 26/58/3: 'Operations of 24 Bn while in Poziers Trenches from night Aug 23rd to Aug 27th 1916,' Operations File Somme 1916, 6th Infantry Brigade.
28   AWM: AWM 26/58/3: 'Report on Operations, 22/3rd to 26/7th August 1916,' 28 August 1916, Operations File Somme 1916, 6th Infantry Brigade.
29   AWM: AWM 26/58/3: OC 23rd Bn to 6th Bde, 26 August 1916, 8.30pm, Operations File Somme 1916, 6th Infantry Brigade.

Lieutenant Tremain was reported missing, never to be seen again. The flank support provided by this effort was not nearly enough to prevent a costly failure.

1st Anzac Corps reported this shambles to be 'partially successful' – but it was considerably less than that. Certainly Australian troops occupied point 77 on the left of Mouquet Farm, but Point 27 at the southwest corner of the farm remained in German hands, as did the farm itself, Point 54, and almost all of the rest of the objective. Parties that had rushed ahead of the objective had been forced to fall back to a position on the west side of the farm and managed to hold on for some time, but were under constant, heavy fire from rifles, machine guns and bombs that came from Germans inside the farm itself. Parts of the 2nd Division front line had been so destroyed they amounted to no more than a line of shell holes. The failures of the 2nd Division were attributed to the enemy's superiority of numbers and machine gun fire, neither of which had been subdued at all by the inadequate artillery barrage. This operation gave the clearest picture of the threat Mouquet Farm posed to date. What is interesting to note is that the farm had been, and remained, approachable. Men like Mahony, Robertson and Pollington could lead their parties into or very near to Mouquet Farm and return alive. What they could not do was remove it from German possession, or remain there for any period of time. Birdwood and 1st Anzac Corps' headquarters could now be absolutely without doubt that there were dugouts of a considerable size under the farm. The 24th Battalion reported that the farm held a garrison of four hundred men, using the farm for protection during the day and actively manning the trenches at night. Not all of the Germans present in the farm were needed to protect the dugouts, either, given that a number of reports were made of the appearance of apparently recently-arrived troops such as those who met Sergeant Robertson. There were enough German reserves in and around the Farm to keep the defence strong against a considerable attack.

Nicholas, the 24th Battalion commander, and wrote that by the end of the day he doubted "if the men were physically fit to withstand a determined counter-attack or to make a desperate sally on an impregnable post garrisoned heavily and containing many M[achine] G[uns] there" – that is, Mouquet Farm.[30] What cannot be ignored is the cost of this operation in manpower. After the operation the men of the 6th Brigade were exhausted. Nicholas reported:

> … the five nights and four days in the trenches was a very severe test … the men were not physically fit to hold off a determined counter-attack or to make a [last] desperate attempt on a place that had withstood the attack that Mouquet Farm has done. [31]

---

30 AWM: AWM 26/58/3: 'Operations of 24 Bn while in Poziers Trenches from night Aug 23rd to Aug 27th 1916,' Operations File Somme 1916, 6th Infantry Brigade.
31 AWM: AWM 26/58/3: Nicholas (OC 24th Bn), Untitled document begins 'night 22 …', Operations File Somme 1916, 6th Infantry Brigade.

The 24th Battalion marched out with 200 men.

Even had every line of objective been taken, the result of this operation would have been less than negligible as far as the broader context of the operation was concerned. Within one month the actions of the 1st Anzac Corps had deteriorated from a purposeful, broad-scale attack which succeeded in taking an entire village of strategic significance, to piecemeal, extremely costly and ultimately pointless operations of very limited, if any, value. The 2nd Australian Division was finished, and was sent to Belgium to join the 1st Division, having suffered as many as 5,000 casualties in the fighting at Pozières, around 1,300 of which came from this small set of operations. This should have been a clear indication that there was something lacking in the approach to taking Mouquet Farm at some level – Army or Corps at the very least. 1st Anzac Corps was bludgeoning the front line with its infantry to a very great cost. Yet somehow the almost total failure of this operation was glossed over, despite reports that the 6th Brigade lost a total of 27 officers and 869 other ranks out of a fighting strength of 99 officers and 2,952 other ranks in four days of fighting. That represented nearly 30 percent of their total strength. At that rate the brigade would have been obliterated in less than two weeks. The toll could have been even greater had not the Germans stopped firing on parties of stretcher bearers in no man's land or indeed if larger attacks had been ordered for the 24th and 23rd Battalions. The only positive factor from all of this, woefully inadequate as it is, was that some men had been able to enter the farm for a short period of time before being driven back. Nevertheless, even faced with such blunt figures and such minimal success, the general consensus in 1st Anzac Corps still seems to have been to do very much the same, but *more*. This would have serious consequences for the 4th Australian Division, which began relieving the broken 2nd Division on 27 August 1916.

7

"The heroes they are":
The End of the 1st Anzac Corps at Pozières

The 4th Australian Division relieved the 2nd Division on 28 August 1916, General Cox taking over command of the front line once his brigades were in place at noon. One of his brigades, the 4th, had relieved the broken 6th Brigade at noon the day before as part of the relief of the 2nd Division. Within eight hours of Cox assuming command, the 4th Brigade had attacked two of the points around Mouquet Farm that the 2nd Division had failed to secure, 27 and 54, using one and a half companies and a bombing section. These were two points in the German triangular trench on the left that the 2nd Division had held briefly. Although the 4th Brigade report tried to put a positive spin on the result – "much valuable information re enemy positions was obtained"[1] – unsurprisingly, this small-scale, ad hoc operation failed thanks to a consolidated enemy counter-attack using superior numbers. But it was a concerning sign of what was to come.

Preparation

On 28 August Birdwood issued another order to the effect that "the 4th Australian Infantry Brigade will tomorrow attack the enemy" – another attack planned on his own initiative. It was left to the GOC of the 4th Brigade to "take special measures for the capture and consolidation of the position" given as the objective.[2] But this time the objectives were less tentative than before. The infantry were to take a continuous line of trench stretching roughly 1,200 yards across the apex of 1st Anzac Corps' sector, with Mouquet Farm about one third of the way from the left boundary of the attack. And finally the farm was within the objective line from the beginning of planning. Point 29 was to be taken, which was on the north western corner from the

---

1   AWM: AWM 26/60/9: Operations File Somme 1916, 4th Infantry Brigade.
2   AWM: AWM 4/1/48/5 Pt. 3: '4th Australian Divisional Order No. 20,' 28 August 1916, General Staff Headquarters 4th Australian Division War Diary.

compound, and from there the objective stretched northward to Point 12, about 200 yards to the north. But while a much more confident hand had drawn the continuous objective line across the map, it was still very close to the current position – 300 yards at the furthest – and so once again the advance was only a very small bite out of German-held territory. Cox divided the line in two and gave the left 600 yards to the 16th Battalion, supported by one company of the 14th Battalion, and the right half to the 13th Battalion, supported by one company of the 15th Battalion. The 13th Battalion had 16 Lewis guns and one Vickers gun to take into the attack, while the 16th Battalion, which had the more formidable task of capturing the Mouquet Farm compound, received 20 Lewis Guns and 4 Vickers guns. The infantry would at least be going into the battle more heavily armed than ever, and the German garrison in Mouquet Farm was receiving some serious attention.

The artillery barrage for this operation, as designed by corps, differed only very slightly from the operation of just a day or two before. Once again it conformed to what had become the norm. The lifts were very quick, just two minutes on each line, and in most places they were just 50-100 yards apart. The difference was that the final standing barrage this time was much closer to the final objective. In most places this meant about 50-100 yards from the objective, although around Point 12 it was danger-ously close – no more than 30 yards away – and to the left of the 13th Battalion's sector it was reasonably distant, being 2-300 yards to the north.

But by this stage many of the front line companies were so far forward that they came under their fire from their own field artillery regularly from the moment they arrived in the front line anyway. Heavy rain set in on the day of the operation and the heavy guns in Albert were firing short, probably as a result of the weather. The different atmospheric conditions of damp weather could affect the flight of the shell in the air as much as the rain, and cause it to fall in a completely different location than it would have on a sunny day. The 13th Battalion were alarmed to have two sixty-pound shells land within their lines without going off the afternoon before the operation, and the 16th Battalion also reported that in their sector "some of our own [heavy] shells lobbed as much as 200 yards in rear of our own lines".[3] But ambiguous messages sent from the front line meant that the artillery usually failed to receive enough specific information to make a change. When Captain Douglas Gray Marks sent back a message from the front line to say "many of the shells were falling too short and some fell in our trenches. Please ask artillery to lengthen range. This refers more particularly to Northern Sector of line held by us", a pencilled reply on the message indicates that this was "Very indefinite. No good result from such a message. Action taken however".[4] As predicted, the action taken was not very effective, and the infantry continued to take casualties from their own fire.

3   AWM: AWM 26/60/9: 'Our Operations:- 16th Battalion', 29 August 1916, Operations File Somme 1916, 4th Infantry Brigade.
4   AWM: AWM 26/60/9: Marks (13th Bn) to 4th Bde, 29 August 1916, 6.20pm,

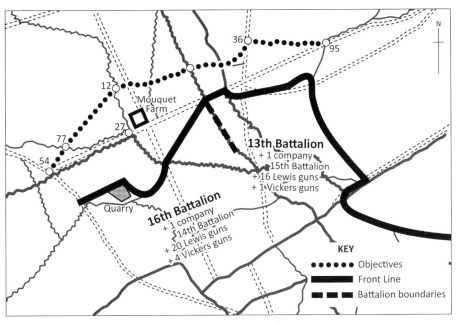

32 4th Division's operation, 29 August 1916.

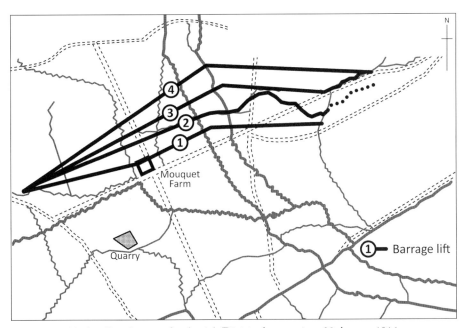

33 Artillery barrage for the 4th Division's operation, 29 August 1916.

Captain Douglas Marks was another reliable officer of the 13th Battalion who prioritised communication with the rear. (AWM P01150.004, detail)

Finally, though, the close proximity of the artillery barrages to the infantry did not go unnoticed. Major J.M.A. Durant, commanding the 13th Battalion sent a message on 29 August, the morning of the attack, to the 4th Brigade to say "I have just received the barrage – from personal observation I am sure that the first barrage is too close to our front line."[5] He later added:

Have just received the artillery order, and can well understand why they have caused us so many casualties (12) this afternoon. They were bombarding points with 9.2", 8" and 6" which were only 30 to 50 yards from our advanced sap heads. As the safety limit is 200 yards we should have been warned of this so that we could have temporarily withdrawn the garrisons of the posts affected. We did get a warning but it arrived too late (1.20pm). The men have had a shake-up, but I am sure they will rise to the occasion like the heroes they are.[6]

But this was not a matter of 'rising to the occasion like a hero'. No man, hero or not, could survive the blast of an artillery shell. Durant's men were sitting ducks under their own artillery fire. Finally the utter lunacy of ordering artillery barrages that could clearly be expected to hit their own men had been addressed directly and yet, as with other matters, no action was taken to rectify the situation and the 13th Battalion continued take casualties from their own fire. This state of affairs, which had become so commonplace as to be almost the norm, was treated as an unfortunate anomaly.

Operations File Somme 1916, 4th Infantry Brigade.
5   AWM: AWM 26/60/9: Durant (OC 13th Bn) to 4th Bde, 29 August 1916, 9.35am, Operations File Somme 1916, 4th Infantry Brigade.
6   AWM: AWM 26/60/9: Durant, (OC 13th Bn) to 4th Bde, 29 August 1916, 9.05pm, Operations File Somme 1916, 4th Infantry Brigade.

As mentioned, the infantry making the attack for this operation were heavily augmented with firepower in the form of machine guns, particularly by 1916 standards. On the right the 13th Battalion, attacking with an additional company of the 15th Battalion, took with them sixteen Lewis guns and one Vickers gun. On the left, the sector that included Mouquet Farm, the 16th Battalion and their additional company of the 14th Battalion were fortified with twenty Lewis guns and four Vickers guns. Brigadier-General Brand was given little directive as to how to attack the most formidable obstacle in his path, and so he determined:

> … [that] the attack on Mouquet Farm itself will be delivered by three companies distributed in depth with one company in immediate support and complete arrangements made for clearing the cellars and dugouts in, and immediately north of the Farm … as rapidly as possible.[7]

Apart from providing the infantry with additional firepower to carry with them during their assault, no further arrangements were made for strengthening this attack with artillery or trench mortars. When Brand passed the order down to the 16th Battalion, its commanding officer, Lieutenant-Colonel Drake-Brockman held a conference of company commanders and specialist infantry to discuss the attack on Mouquet Farm. There they decided that the battalion would approach the battle in the following manner. Each company was assigned a single objective. After taking it, they would then turn to its flanks to form a link with their neighbouring company. D Company would attack point 54 on the far left, and then turn to the left to make a defensive flank and to the right to reach the recently captured strongpoint at Point 77. Mouquet Farm itself would be attacked by B Company and the battalion bombing platoon, while A Company would attack another very small trench between Points 31 and 42 to the north east of the farm before turning to their right to make contact with the 13th Battalion at Point 73. C Company would attack a small trench running between Points 29 and 12 from the north-western corner of the old farm buildings before turning to both flanks to make contact with D Company on the left and A Company on the right. This was unmistakeably an infantry-based operation which once again closely resembled a large raid more than a small, set-piece battle.

The heavy rain during the day of the attack wreaked havoc with the front line. The mud created by the rain and mixed up by the shellfire was beyond the experience of the men of the 2nd Division. The 4th Brigade war diary observed:

> … soon reduced the trenches to little better than quagmire; the mud in most places being over knee deep while the parapets, weakened and softened by the wet, fell into the trenches when the slightest weight was put upon them. These conditions

---

7   AWM: AWM 26/60/9: '4th Australian Infantry Brigade Order No. 39A', 29 August 1916, Operations File Somme 1916, 4th Infantry Brigade.

obtained during the whole of the following day and night, making digging an impossibility and causing much discomfort and hardships to the troops.[8]

Birdwood later wrote:

> … never in my life have I seen such sights as the men presented when coming out of the trenches [after rain] – just one cake of mud from their head to their feet, giving them the appearance of having but one garment of mud only. It is perfectly marvellous how cheery they are under the circumstances and after a clean-up and a hot meal are quite ready to start fighting again when called on to do so.[9]

The problems of living, working and fighting caked in mud from head to toe did not seem to occur to Birdwood. Nor did it seem to matter in the slightest to the higher levels of command, and no delay seems to have been considered.

The attack – 29 August 1916

Nevertheless, somehow both the 13th Battalion and the 16th Battalion were able to get into position on time, and the attack began with the artillery barrage at 11.00pm. On the right the 13th Battalion reported that "each company reached its first objective but was forced to withdraw after hard fighting owing to weakened strength due to casualties".[10] The four companies of the 13th Battalion followed up the barrage closely. Although one message stated that "barrage fire last night [was] very good,"[11] in reality it was so thin that the German guns were not silenced at all. The battalion reported coming up against heavy machine-gun and rifle fire and "showers of bombs" as they advanced.[12] A patrol from the 13th Battalion which tried to connect with the 16th Battalion on the left met with heavy opposition from bombers. The men were in most cases forced to resort to hand-to-hand fighting for their successful entry into their objectives. Finally around midnight, the reserve company of the 15th Battalion was fed into the front line to reinforce an unstable situation. All company commanders were told to hold the objective they had reached and no more, but each of their companies were seriously depleted by casualties and the line they held was shaky at best.

---

8   AWM: AWM 26/60/9: 'Narrative of Operations by 4th Australian Infantry Brigade North-West of Pozières during Period 26th August – 2nd September 1916,' Operations File Somme 1916, 4th Infantry Brigade.
9   AWM: 3DRL/3376 3/1b: Birdwood to Lord Liverpool, 2 September 1916.
10 AWM: AWM 26/60/9: Message ST.425, Operations File Somme 1916, 4th Infantry Brigade.
11 AWM: AWM 26/60/9: Marks to 4th Bde, 30 August 1916, 2.55am, Operations File Somme 1916, 4th Infantry Brigade.
12 AWM: AWM 26/60/9: 'Appendix to War Diary No. B.1', 31 August 1916, Operations File Somme 1916, 4th Infantry Brigade.

On the left the 16th Battalion had been able to establish an good jumping-off position. They, too, reported that "the barrage of shrapnel was well delivered, but the volume was quite insufficient," but nevertheless:

> … [they] gained quite a considerable amount of ground during the barrage … at the lifting our men rushed the different objectives and in all cases reached the same except Point 12 North of Mouquet Farm.[13]

But the success was not to last. They stayed just an hour before retiring.[14] There were two main problems in maintaining their new forward positions. The first was a very heavy enemy barrage that fell on the old German front line almost as soon as the attack began. But worse was the attacking force of Germans who came out of tunnels in the Farm and attacked the men of the 16th Battalion from the rear. With considerable losses, the 16th Battalion had no other option but to retire. This then left the 13th dangerously unsupported with heavy machine gun fire enfilading their lines from Mouquet Farm and from a position on their right. They had suffered so many casualties both in the fighting and as a result of friendly fire that they could only hold the objective very thinly. Heavily shelled and aware of the withdrawal of the 16th Battalion, the 13th Battalion companies were also compelled to retire, too weak to hold the line. The 1st Anzac Corps was now conducting attacks that were failing because there simply was not enough troops available even to do no more than hold the captured line.

Renewed preparations

These operations had been the result of orders arising at 1st Anzac Corps headquarters. They had very little to do with Reserve Army's overall intent, and worse still, while these piecemeal attacks were going on, plans were afoot for a widespread British attack involving large portions of Fourth Army and Reserve Army's front. This would be the first operation on the Somme deliberately planned to be conducted on the same day by Reserve and Fourth Armies,[15] and 1st Anzac Corps would have to be involved, whether the battalions in the front line were exhausted and depleted by casualties or not. But that is not to say that cooperation with his right flank was Gough's foremost priority. Instead, Reserve Army's primary focus was on an attack on enemy trenches north and south of the River Ancre by the 49th and 39th Divisions, separated from Fourth Army by the frontages of II Corps and 1st Anzac Corps. Both II Corps and

---

13   Ibid.
14   AWM: AWM 26/60/9: 'Our Operations:- 16th Battalion', 29 August 1916, 29 August 1916, AWM: AWM 26/60/9.
15   Prior & Wilson *Somme*, p.173. Operations of 22/23 July, although conducted simultaneously by Reserve and Fourth Armies, were unintentionally coordinated, not by design.

1st Anzac Corps were meant to participate in the wider operation, but for the first time, their portion of the front was not the primary focus of Reserve Army operations, and any battle plans for them were delayed pending the results of their run of small operations. On 29 August 1916 Reserve Army Operation Order No. 24 finally issued objectives for both corps, five days after orders for the 49th and 39th Divisions appeared. Significantly, this order confirms that Gough's primary interest in this operation was his attack around the River Ancre, and not cooperation with Fourth Army on the right. II Corps and 1st Anzac Corps were to conduct very minor operations to extend Reserve Army's operations closer to the boundary with Fourth Army, but only just. II Corps' attack connected with neither the Ancre operation on their left, nor 1st Anzac Corps' attack against Mouquet Farm to their right. The 1st Anzac Corps, similarly, was to conduct its assigned operation in isolation, not being required to coordinate with either flank. While Reserve Army and Fourth Army were ostensibly coordinating a broad-fronted attack, in reality Gough was paying lip service to that plan while using the situation to further his own interests to the north.

This is supported by a closer examination of 1st Anzac Corps' objectives as defined by Reserve Army Operation Order No. 24. Their objective as given by Reserve Army was a line roughly 4-500 yards beyond Mouquet Farm at the southern point the network of German strongpoints known as the Zollern Redoubt, or Feste Zollern. Once again, this objective can only be effectively described by the use of maps because there was simply nothing of consequence there. The line, about 600 yards long, roughly correlated with a rumoured German trench, but in effect it had little tactical significance in real terms. What is important to note about this objective is that the direction of movement to achieve it is to the north west – towards Reserve Army's long-term goal of Thiepval and emphatically away from operations conducted by Fourth Army to the right. To confirm this, additional objectives for the operation were the clearance of a few small pockets of German trenches to the left of the current corps line. While the Australian operation was the closest to coordinating with Fourth Army, between the two lay the 1st Canadian Brigade between the Australians and the Army boundary (and not ordered to attack) and on the other side of the Army boundary III Corps, which also would not be conducting any offensive operation. So although this can be called the first real attempt to coordinate operations across the fronts of Reserve Army and Fourth Army, in reality the coordination was in no more than the timing of the two, not in any singularity of purpose or effort. By the time orders were passed down to 4th Australian Division, which would be conducting the operation for 1st Anzac Corps, they were given to understand that they would be participating in "a big attack by the allies between the Ancre and Somme from the N[orth], E[ast] and S[outh] of Thiepval," rather than an operation that extended into Fourth Army's sector and the French area of operations south of the Somme.[16]

16   AWM: AWM 26/59/11: 31 August 1916, Operations File Somme 1916, 4th Australian Division General Staff.

With Reserve Army's attention on a distant part of the line and an overall lack of focus, Birdwood seems to have had extra leeway to alter the orders given him. The first thing he did was to bring the objective much closer to the current 4th Division front line, once again in line with the current trend. 1st Anzac Corps Order No. 42 issued on 1 September 1916 gave Australian units first warning of the impending operation, and dramatically altered the objective as given by Reserve Army. Instead of attempting Reserve Army's projected advance of more than a quarter of a mile, Birdwood's objective was no more than 200 yards from the current position. The front of this attack was exactly the same as the objective for the recent unsuccessful attack by the 4th Division, making it twice as long as the objective ordered by Reserve Army. The general thrust, as feeble as it was, of the operation was more or less still to the northwest, but with gaps between the operations of 1st Anzac Corps and II Corps, the line became weaker through poor boundary connections threatened by German strongpoints. How this dramatic difference went through without Gough's notice or modification is unclear. However, the fact that the changes carried meant that either the modifications were decided by and agreed upon verbally between Gough and Birdwood, or the operation on this right flank was of such little significance to Gough that there was no need to comment. While the former is probably correct, the fact that such widespread changes to the original plan went through without formal comment is an indication that the objectives of this operation were of little material importance to the overall plan.

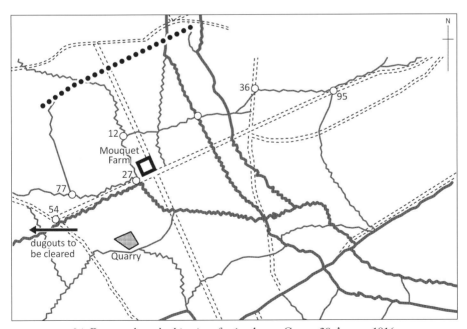

34 Reserve Army's objectives for 1st Anzac Corps, 29 August 1916.

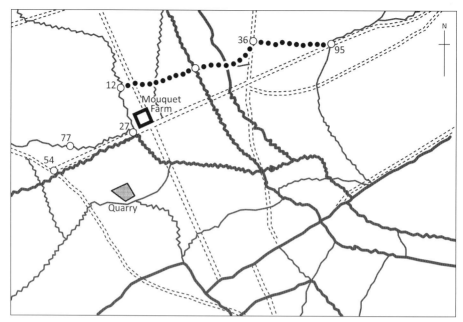

35 1st Anzac Corps' modified objective, 3 September 1916.

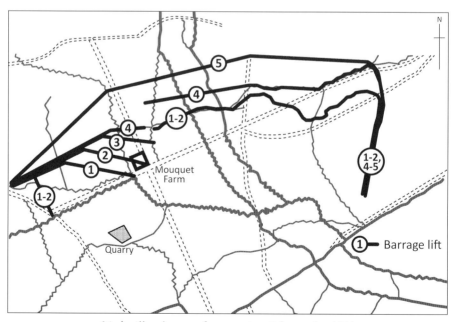

36 Artillery barrage for operation, 3 September 1916.

Even as the 4th Brigade was finishing the operation, reports were making their way through to 1st Anzac Corps from 2nd Division. Intelligence confirmed once again the fact that there were extensive cellars and bunkers under the farm holding at a minimum a number of German companies. A prisoner captured on 26 August told intelligence officers that the cellars beneath the farm were 8-10 metres deep and roofed with logs. He said that apart from one entrance, the cellars were absolutely undamaged, and held at least 150 men comfortably, a dressing station and two company headquarters. He also confirmed that the farm was connected by tunnels to German strongpoints above ground. Lieutenant James Stanley Rogers, the intelligence officer for the 4th Brigade, reported that the reason positions in the farm were lost was "owing to men being attacked in rear by Germans who must have come through tunnels".[17] Both this and another report by Rogers stated that he was "of the opinion that this place has been tunnelled underground and is practically a fortress".[18] The 4th Brigade's narrative of events recorded that "the enemy positions were held in such strength that it required a considerably stronger force to mop up the enemy in his dugouts and prevent him from attacking us in numbers."[19] There was no room left to doubt that Mouquet Farm was now the most formidable part of the line to be captured.

For the third time in a week and a half the artillery plan was almost unaltered, and continued to be light and fast-paced. The barrage for the attack of 3 September was designed to move through three objectives to its final standing barrage within eight minutes. This had not been modified in any way to account for the more detailed knowledge of the strength of the garrison at Mouquet Farm. There were no plans beyond this barrage to protect the infantry from counter-attack, which meant no plans to deal with the fact that Germans could reinforce local strongpoints underground, as it was now painfully clear they could do at will. This plan drew nothing on the lessons of recent operations, from the success of the barrage but the near-failure of Sinclair-Maclagan's overly intricate infantry movements at Pozières, to the obvious problems of relying too heavily on infantry in the operations of Legge's 2nd Division, or the repeatedly demonstrated difficulties in providing effective artillery cooperation for operations against close-range objectives. Nor did it take into account the better understanding the Australians now had of Mouquet Farm, its garrison and its defences. In short, it was a bizarrely inadequate attempt to advance the line a few hundred yards in a mildly useful direction, to the material benefit of neither the overall British operation of 3 September 1916, nor to the operations of Reserve Army, or even to operations of the neighbouring II Corps.

---

17   AWM: AWM 26/60/9. 4th Bde to 4th. Division, 31 August 1916, Operations File
      Somme 1916, 4th Infantry Brigade.
18   AWM: AWM 26/60/9: 'Our Operations:- 16th Battalion,' 29 August 1916, Operations
      File Somme 1916, 4th Infantry Brigade.
19   AWM: AWM 26/60/9: 'Narrative of Operations by 4th Australian Infantry Brigade
      North-West of Pozières during Period 26th August – 2nd September 1916,' Operations
      File Somme 1916, 4th Infantry Brigade.

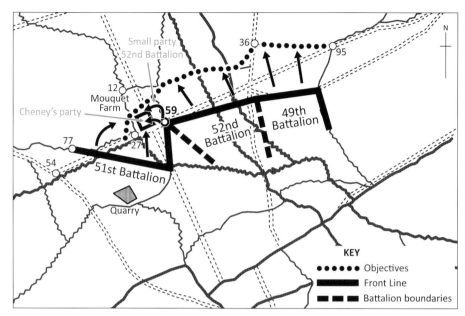

37 Conflicting directions of attack, 3 September 1916.

This new attack was to be conducted by the 13th Infantry Brigade. To do this, the front was divided equally between the 51st Battalion on the left, the 52nd in the centre, and the 49th on the right (with the 50th Battalion in Park Lane and Tom's Cut in reserve). The artillery barrage should really be considered two barrages that started together. The right two thirds of the barrage was to accompany the attacks of the 52nd and 49th Battalions in advancing in a north-north-westerly direction. Their attack would advance the line a small distance, capturing points like 42, 94, 36 and 95, which had The left third of the barrage was to cover the 51st Battalion in their advance on Mouquet Farm. The 51st's operation started from the most southerly point and they were to use this position to advance on the farm from a completely different direction to the rest of the operation. Neither flank of the 51st Battalion was particularly well connected with the neighbouring unit. On the left was the 13th Cheshire Battalion, 400 yards away, and on the right the 52nd Battalion was working in a different direction and would be ahead of the 51st's right flank from the start of the operation. A small party of the 52nd Battalion would enter the farm from a different direction, meeting the main force within the compound.

On 29 August Lieutenant Rogers, the Intelligence Officer of the 4th Brigade, had reported that "one Battalion could take [the farm] easily, our "B" Company took it without trouble, but it certainly requires another big Unit to mop it up"[20] – apparently

20   AWM: AWM 26/60/9: 'Our Operations:- 16th Battalion', 29 August 1916, Operations File Somme 1916, 4th Infantry Brigade.

Lieutenant Edward Cheney, 50th Battalion, led a raid on Mouquet Farm in the last days of 1st Anzac Corps' endeavour on Pozières Ridge. His party, consisting of thirty men, one bomb team and two Lewis guns, failed to capture the strongpoint. He died of wounds on 12 March 1918. (AWM P09291.063)

confusing 'taking' the farm with 'temporarily holding' it. But this plan was a far cry from using another big unit to mop it up. The most they would have would be a very small force consisting of 2/ Lieutenant Edward Lloyd Cheney of the 50th Battalion with 30 men, one bomb team and two Lewis Guns to be used if necessary, and another small party of the 52nd Battalion attacking from their objective once they had reached it. This plan was not taking into account what was known of the farm and its strength, or indeed lessons regarding overly complicated troop movements and their detrimental effect on the outcome of operations in the recent past. What this means is that the main attack against a German strongpoint recently described as 'practically a fortress' was to come from a single battalion on a front of no more than 400 yards, with no effective protection on either flank. Its potential for success was extremely limited.

Once again the ground would be more or less entirely unprepared in terms of a jumping-off trench and additional communication saps. The recent heavy rains continued to have a very bad effect on the state of the front line, but this should not have hampered any work, according to the 4th Division General Staff. On the 1st of September the division's war diary recorded:

> … reports received this morning of the work done last night is far from satisfactory – it is not quite clear, why – but whether it was the fault of the bad weather, and sodden state of the ground, and deep liquid mud in the trenches, or to the exhausted state of the troops – it shows a lack of determination on the part of certain officers to see the work through.[21]

21   AWM: AWM 26/59/11: Operations File Somme 1916, Fourth Australian Division General Staff.

Their answer was to call "certain officers" to divisional headquarters and exhorted to do better in the future. But like the 2nd Division, the 4th was exhausted. By the time they had been relieved from their last period in the front line in mid-August, the division had suffered four and a half thousand casualties. Not only was it weaker, but now back in the line in early September, the division reported they faced heavier opposition, recording that the enemy were thought to be present in considerably greater strength both in numbers and in firepower now than they had been when the division was in the line the previous month. And, of course, the weather meant that everything they had to achieve was that much harder. There was simply very little extra effort available to put in to the work that had to be done. The 14th Brigade had been in the line for only one night, but was in such poor condition that, combined with the expected severity of the coming battle, it had to be relieved in favour of a Canadian Brigade.

As previously mentioned, the 1st Canadian Infantry Brigade had entered the line taking over the far right of the line to the boundary with Fourth Division. These Canadian units had been placed under the command of the 4th Australian Division while the rest of the Canadian Division was in the process of moving into the sector. Some companies of the 13th Canadian Battalion were available in case of dire need, but the attacking force was still very thin. There were very few, if any, surplus reinforcements to provide carrying parties, mopping up parties or general reinforcement, and attacking battalions had to thin their troops to deliver these other requirements. In order to afford a reserve, the battalions taking part were ordered to leave "a small garrison – say one rifle per ten yards" in the front line.[22] This attack was making do with the bare minimum of men, preparation, artillery and supplies.

The 13th Brigade ordered the 51st Battalion to attack Mouquet Farm in an operation to be delivered in depth and strength. But with no 'big unit' allocated to help with mopping up the farm, the battalion had to provide its own "strong mopping-up party" to deal with dugouts and strongpoints in and around the farm. Lieutenant-Colonel Ross, commanding the battalion, chose to deploy all four of his companies on pre-laid tapes side by side across their allotted portion of the front, and have them follow the barrage together. B Company and the battalion bombing sections formed the spearhead of their attack, and would push through to Point 12. A Company's orders are less clear, but it appears they were to form a close support within the operation, probably to enter and assist with mopping up the dugouts below the farm. D Company, on entering the attack on the left, was to push through to Point 12 as well. In many respects theirs was the hardest task, because on the way through they had to turn back to the west to create a defensive flank facing Thiepval, with their backs to Mouquet Farm. C Company, on the right, was given the responsibility of making contact with

---

22   AWM: AWM 26/61/21: Glasfurd (OC 12th Bde) to 49th, 51st and 52nd Bns, 2 September 1916, 2pm, Operations File Somme 1916, 13th Infantry Brigade.

the 52nd Battalion. This included meeting up with Cheney's small party ordered to push into the Farm from Point 59 and to assist in mopping up.

The small raiding party of the 52nd Battalion that the advanced parties of the 51st Battalion were supposed to meet in the Farm was very small indeed. Lieutenant-Colonel Miles Fitzroy Beevor, commanding the 52nd Battalion, allotted just two platoons of B Company to directly participate in the attack on the farm from Point 59. Beevor would not lead his battalion in the attack. At about 4pm on the day before the operation was to go ahead he was wounded and command of the battalion fell to Major Denis Arthur Lane. The rest of 52nd Battalion's operation was to run along-side the line of the destroyed farm buildings but not enter the ruined compound itself because, it will be remembered, it ran in a different direction to the operation against the farm. Beevor had taken Brigade's orders and interpreted them in a very straight-forward manner. From left to right, C, A and D Companies would attack on fronts of less than 100 yards each side by side. C Company's attack ran alongside the farm, A Company was in the middle, and D Company was obliged to liaise with 49th Battalion on their right. Once each company had gained their objective, they were

Mervyn James Herbert, Miles Fitzroy Beevor, Francis Maxwell De Flayer Lorenzo, Stanley Price Weir: Maxwell Lorenzo as an officer of the 10th Battalion (seventh from right). The men are using a wagon as a grandstand to watch a battalion sports carnival at Mena Camp Egypt, Christmas 1914 (date on image is incorrect). Others would feature prominently in the fighting at Pozières, including (then Captain later Major) Mervyn Herbert, 50th Battalion (far left), Lieutenant-Colonel Stanley Price Weir, OC 10th Battalion (fourth from left), and Lieutenant-Colonel Miles Beevor, OC 52nd Battalion (sixth from left). (AWM P02321.004)

to send parties to bomb along German communication trenches running northward, and then stops would be put in to block German access.

To their right, however, the 49th Battalion commander, Lieutenant-Colonel Francis Maxwell de Flayer Lorenzo interpreted 13th Brigade's orders in a completely different manner. He assigned his advancing troops two objectives, the additional line being between 30 and 100 yards from the final objective. It should be noted that this was a straight line on a map, and once more did not correlate with any known features on the battlefield. It did, however, correlate to the first lift of the barrage. Lorenzo assigned A Company to attack and consolidate this newly-identified first objective, following which, all but one platoon of B Company would push through to form a screen in front of A Company's consolidation efforts. A second wave formed by C Company, which would attack the final objective, and D Company, which would provide another screen in the manner of B Company. Although these two battalions had received the same orders from 13th Brigade, once again their commanding officers had the leeway to interpret them in vastly different ways. While Lane's operation for the 52nd Battalion was very straightforward, Lorenzo chose to deploy his infantry in depth, putting four thin lines of infantry between his original jumping-off trench and the final objective.

There were two problems with Lorenzo's plan for the 49th Battalion. One was simply that having objectives that did not correlate with obvious geographical features made an operation incredibly difficult to keep on track. If the men were somehow successful in locating the correct position to capture and hold, they were obliged to dig their own defences under enemy fire to do so. Lorenzo assigned B and D Companies to carry picks and shovels through to each objective, dropping them there as they pushed through to provide their forward defensive screen. But these picks and shovels would be used to dig defensive positions under fire with only the protection afforded by a thin screen of troops to the front and a light, fast-moving barrage overhead. But a bigger problem facing the 49th Battalion was that although using waves of infantry had worked in the past, the tactic required coordination with an appropriate barrage to be of most use, and this one simply moved too quickly. 49th Battalion orders gave A Company, leading the charge, just three minutes (the time between the first and second lift of the barrage) to reach their intermediate objective line, have B Company move through to drop off picks and shovels, take them up use them to consolidate their line. Lorenzo carefully prepared his company commanders for the task ahead, personally taking them through:

> ... the work that each company had to do. Company Commanders then carefully explained to their platoon commanders, who then passed information on to all ranks so that every man in the attack knew approximately what he and the remainder of the Battalion had to do.[23]

23   AWM: AWM 4/23/66/4: 49th Battalion War Diary.

But this complicated operation was not taking into account the nature of plans at higher level, in particular artillery plans, and the infantry waves stood in danger of disintegrating without proper protection.

The potential for a real problem in the mismatched plans could not be overcome. The 49th Battalion had already experienced times in the lead up to the operation when the artillery fell short, causing casualties and damage to front line trenches. Wedging infantry waves into an attack where there was almost not enough room to fire a bombardment, much less accurately fire a lifting barrage in close coordination with the troops, was not going to provide them with enough protection, nor materially assist their operation. It was going to put them in danger of running into their own artillery fire, or running behind time. And, in the event, C Company of the 49th Battalion was indeed a little late to attack the second objective against all odds, although this seems to have surprised Lorenzo, who reported that they were delayed "for some reason not explainable".[24] As had happened so often in the past, somehow the 49th Battalion made this plan work to some degree. On the morning of 3 September 1916 the operation began on time at 5.10am. Lorenzo reported at 6.25, "have taken both objectives" – although not without problems, as the rest of his message reveals:

> Meeting with much bombing opposition from flanks both right and left. My front not in touch with 52nd. Casualties difficult yet to estimate. Am consolidating front line.[25]

The 49th Battalion was seriously depleted by the attack and could not sustain the advance. By 9am they reported "we have the whole line but not enough men to man trench. Please send some men if they can be spared."[26] Urgently in need of men, officers, supply and tools, the Battalion was finally forced back following the withdrawal of the left flank.

At the other end of the line, facing Mouquet Farm, the 51st Battalion was also reported to have gotten away punctually at 5.10am. The attacking force had been well prepared. Tapes had been pegged out on the line from which the attack was to be launched, and the entire battalion had filtered out between 11pm and 2am the night before to lie in the open in lines one behind the other. Each company was deployed in two waves – three platoons in the first wave and company headquarters, company bombers, the Lewis gun section and the final platoon carrying picks and shovels in the second wave. The units filtered into their attack positions one after the other. First came B Company, to make the furthest advance, then D Company with plans to swing to the left, C Company which was ordered to make contact with the 52nd Battalion and finally A Company in close support. The battalion had practiced their manoeuvres, and the men had had the plans carefully explained to them by officers.

Lieutenant-Colonel Arthur Murray Ross, commanding the 51st Battalion, later reported that "the barrage was perfect, and the waves followed up closely."[27] In fact, although laid out in waves as described by the battalion commander, the companies all moved off together when the assault began instead of staggering their departure from the tapes. Men of the 51st encountered very little opposition entering the farm compound, and within a very short time had managed to capture as many as sixty prisoners, clear three dugouts and destroy two machine guns.[28] Just over two hours into the operation, the 51st Battalion sent the message:

> Farm taken and at present held. Twelve prisoners taken and others in dugouts which are being dealt with … About 30 enemy killed in farm. Position beyond this obscure and have had no news of 52nd yet.[29]

But at around the same time the commanding officer of the small party of the 52nd Battalion, Major McPherson, was reporting "two platoons of B Company in Mouquet Farm. Five Prisoners captured including one with a machine gun … Not sure whether [Point] 42 is yet taken. Line very confusing." One thing he could be sure of, and added to his message, "PS: 51st Battalion in Mouquet Farm and beyond in some strength."[30]

The formidable nature of Mouquet Farm as a defensive position once again became apparent almost as soon as men entered the compound. Despite their numbers, the 51st Battalion was never able to entirely stamp out resistance. The first troops to enter the farm reported they were "being shelled from [a] source not yet apparent,"[31] and more confusion was to follow. Entrances to dugouts were extremely hard to discover in the pock-marked ground, an advantage the Germans used to fire machine guns or rifle grenades unexpectedly, or even lob 10lb bombs at the Australians trying to clear the compound, and then sink silently back into the ground. There was rifle fire and bombs coming from shell holes in every direction. It should be said there was a better

27   AWM: AWM 26/61/21. 'Report on Operation At Mouquet Farm 1st/4th September 1916', Operations File Somme 1916, 13th Infantry Brigade.
28   The first machine gun was destroyed deliberately, but the second machine gun was accidentally destroyed by shellfire after capture.
29   AWM: AWM 26/61/21: Ross (OC 51st Bn) to 13th Bde, 3 September 1916, Operations File Somme 1916, 13th Infantry Brigade.
30   AWM: AWM 26/61/21: McPherson (OC B Coy 52nd Bn), top of page torn off removing address, 3 September 1916, 7.25am, Operations File Somme 1916, 13th Infantry Brigade.
31   AWM: AWM 26/61/21: 'Tiger' (51st Bn) to 'Prize' (13th Bde), 3 September 1916, 6.40am, Operations File Somme 1916, 13th Infantry Brigade.

than reasonable chance that at least some of this fire came from other attacking units, given the three different attacks converging on the farm from different directions. Nevertheless, the German presence was strong, and from all reports, they made the most of their extensive dugouts.

Even worse was the increasing awareness that neither flank was supported or in touch with the unit on either side. Ross later claimed he had "not the slightest doubt" (his emphasis) that the advance went precisely as ordered and the 51st Battalion reached the correct objectives of Points 12 and 42 around Mouquet Farm.[32] He blamed the problems his battalion was facing on the 52nd Battalion for not meeting up with his right flank. By 9.30am the 51st Battalion commander reported his three most advanced companies:

> … will have to come in on to [the] Farm unless supported on [the] right as they are in the air. A few of [the] 52nd Battalion [are] in touch with my support line at Mouquet Farm front line [but we are] not joined to [the] 52nd. Communication trenches [are] being dug slowly but surely. All front line Lewis Guns are out of action. Shelling very severe. [The] 52nd Battalion are going back and exposing my right they appear to be very weak.[33]

This proved to be the last straw for the 51st Battalion's tenuous advance. At around 11am B Company of the 50th Battalion found that the 51st had largely left the farm and were in the nearby quarry, with an "isolated post near Mouquet Farm [from which] every party sent out so far has been wiped out".[34] Isolated on both flanks, and without substantial reinforcement, the attack of the 51st Battalion had failed.

What had happened in the centre? Both the 51st Battalion on the left and the 49th Battalion on the right had reported reaching their objectives in a timely fashion. Bean wrote in the Official History that "for some reason the commander of the 52nd … had not made his junior officers reconnoitre the ground over which they were to attack", hinting that this was the source of a problem for their advance.[35] But battalion reports indicate that on 1 September one officer and one non-commissioned officer from each company did indeed go out with the signalling officer to make a reconnaissance of the communication trenches and forward lines. This was probably the most the battalion could do with time permitting. When orders were issued at 1pm on 2 September, the commanding officer of the 52nd Battalion, Lieutenant-Colonel Miles Fitzroy Beevor, personally went through them with his company commanders. One

32   AWM: AWM 4/23/68/7: 'Report on Operation at Mouquet Farm 1st/4th September 1916,' 51st Battalion War Diary.
33   AWM: AWM 26/61/21: 51st Bn to 'Prize' (13th Bde), 2 September 1916, 9.30am, Operations File Somme 1916, 13th Infantry Brigade.
34   AWM: AWM 26/61/21: B Coy 50th Bn to HQ 50th Bn, 3 September 1916, 11.15am, Operations File Somme 1916, 13th Infantry Brigade.
35   Bean, *Vol. III*, p. 847.

of the first problems to strike the 52nd Battalion came the day before the attack, when Lieutenant-Colonel Beevor was wounded and had to be evacuated. He was replaced by Major Denis Arthur Lane.

Furthermore, the 52nd Battalion had taken equal – if not more – care in forming up as the other battalions. Their jumping-off trenches were described as "only trenches in name and afforded little cover [having been] heavily shelled during [the] night of 1st and 2nd September".[36] But each company was supplied with a guide to lead them out to their jumping-off position, and tapes were laid over open ground on the route in so that any loss of direction could be avoided. The battalion intelligence officer, Lieutenant Arthur Mainwaring Maxwell:

> … was sent along the companies [as they waited on the tapes], to synchronise watches for the second time, make certain all were in their correct positions and assist Company Commanders with any information required as to their front and objective.[37]

This was not without risk on his part, as Maxwell was 6ft 5in tall and must have had to take particular care to not present a target or warning the Germans as he crept along the jumping-off tapes. As with the left of the line, the battalion was broken into waves for the purpose of forming up prior to the assault, but the entire attacking force left the trenches at the same time. This time was reported as 5.14am – four minutes late. There is little to find in the final preparation and deployment of the 52nd Battalion to account for what happened next.

The battalion report states:

> … the assault was delivered with much spirit and dash, and in cases a short but fierce and bloody hand to hand conflict ensued, bayonets and rifle butts coming into free play.[38]

But this blithe report of spirit and adventure masked a darker truth. The battalion had not fared well at all. The first reports to come through from Major Lane were urgent requests for more men. At 7.07am he asked for a "fatigue party of as many men as are available for taking up ammunition etc. to firing line" and marked the message "<u>urgent</u>".[39] Around the same time Lieutenant Duncan Struan Maxwell, Arthur's

---

36 AWM: AWM 26/61/21: '52nd Battalion 13th Australian Infantry Brigade, Report on ATTACK on MOUQUET FARM,' 9 September 1916, Operations File Somme 1916, 13th Infantry Brigade.
37 Ibid.
38 Ibid.
39 AWM: AWM 26/61/21: Lane (OC 52nd Bn) to Officer in Charge, Pioneer Bn, 3 September 1916, 7.07am, Operations File Somme 1916, 13th Infantry Brigade. His request does not seem to have been met.

brother and commanding officer of A Company, confirmed they were in touch with the 49th Battalion and had captured a number of prisoners. But he, too, ended his message with a simple but telling request: "want more bombs and men".[40]

In fact, the messages from A Company were almost the only messages received by battalion headquarters during the operation. Few, if any came from the other companies in the line. In fact C and D Companies of the 52nd Battalion went into the attack and all but disappeared. It took nearly a week of investigation to determine what had happened to them. It was later discovered that C Company on the left, the closest to Mouquet Farm and, therefore, the 51st Battalion's operation, had pushed too far forward and found themselves under their own artillery barrage. Their company commander, the grandly-named Captain Ralph Ratnevelu Raymond Ekin-Smyth, was able to regain control and begin to draw his men back towards their objective, but he was mortally wounded in the process. Both of his legs were shot off, and it was later reported that he lay on the ground shouting and waving to his men to try to get them back in to position. He died before he could be taken for help. Desperate messages were sent forward, but as the Major Lane, now the commanding officer of the 52nd Battalion, later reported, "the company again pressed forward and as an organised unit ceased to exist".[41]

On the right of the 52nd Battalion's operation, D Company fared worse. The company began from the correct position, and Lieutenant Duncan Maxwell, with A Company, reported that he saw Captain Harry Edward Moncrieff Massey, D Company's commander, about 20 yards from their objective. But, he added

> They should be on our right but apparently their officers became casualties … that is the last I have seen of him – and with the loss of direction which followed they entered the new trench with us. We were held up for perhaps half an hour, and then succeeded in pushing to the right through D Company's objective and joining up with the 49th.[42]

It appears that every officer in D Company became a casualty within the first two hours of battle. Like C Company, D Company of the 52nd Battalion ceased to exist as a tactical unit. But in the case of D Company, there were not enough survivors to even accurately piece together what had gone wrong. And so while the Battalion report states that ach company seized the objective, this claim simply cannot be true.

40   AWM: AWM 26/61/21: Maxwell (OC A Coy 52nd Bn) to HQ 52nd Bn, 3 September 1916, Operations File Somme 1916, 13th Infantry Brigade.
41   AWM: AWM 26/61/21: '52nd Battalion 13th Australian Infantry Brigade, Report on ATTACK on MOUQUET FARM,' 9 September 1916, Operations File Somme 1916, 13th Infantry Brigade.
42   AWM: AWM 26/61/21: Message from Maxwell (OC A Coy 52nd Bn) Addressee taped over in file, 3 September 1916, 3.52pm, Operations File Somme 1916, 13th Infantry Brigade. Massey was later determined to have been killed in action.

A Company alone persisted in the attack. Its commander, Lieutenant Maxwell became the focus of the operation, because many of the messages intended for the destroyed C or D Companies made their way through to him. With exceptional courage and attention to maintaining the plan, Maxwell pushed his company through to what he believed was the objective by 7.50 in the morning. Unsurprisingly, he failed to gain touch on either flank, and was forced to distribute his desperately weakened company along as much as his battalion's front as he was able. He managed to cover A and D Company's sectors, but could not reach much further to the left, accounting for the few sightings of 52nd Battalion men by the 51st in Mouquet Farm. At around 11am he reported:

> … we have about 2 officers, 8 sergeants, 81 others. Can give you no casualty list as most casualties occurred in No Man's Land. Captain Littler is I believe Dead. Sgt. Swift is dead … You can see by our frontage and number of men we want reinforcements. Are we to expect relief tonight? … want reinforcements if we are to hold tonight.[43]

Relief would take two days, and Maxwell's small force, augmented by one company of the 13th Canadian Battalion, somehow managed to hold the line. Maxwell continued to make clear, concise and frequent reports – as previously demonstrated an invaluable task for a company commander to undertake during battle – and reportedly "carried on without rest from 2nd to 5th of September under exceedingly trying conditions".[44] Maxwell was later awarded the Military Cross for his conspicuous gallantry, particularly in holding his position through three German counter-attacks and for displaying "great courage and initiative throughout, and set[ting] a splendid example to his men".[45]

Although Maxwell had reported that he had gained the objective, his only had been lost when the man carrying it was killed. The following day Maxwell met Captain Fortesque of the 49th Battalion. Fortesque was carrying an aerial photograph of the battlefield, and Maxwell realised he was much further east of his objective than he had initially thought. All messages sent by him the previous day were based on this error. Fortesque ordered the company commander to move forward to his original objective, but Maxwell refused for two reasons. He wrote, "firstly, our own artillery

43   AWM: AWM 26/61/21: Maxwell (OC A Coy 52nd Bn) to OC 52nd Bn, 3 September 1916, 10.52am, Operations File Somme 1916, 13th Infantry Brigade.

44   AWM: AWM 26/61/21: '52nd Battalion 13th Australian Infantry Brigade, Report on Attack on Mouquet Farm,' 9 September 1916, Operations File Somme 1916, 13th Infantry Brigade.

45   NAA: B883, NX12610: 'Notification of award of Military Cross, Base Records Office AIF,' 25 April 1917. Duncan Maxwell went on to serve in the Second World War as brigadier commanding 27th Brigade of the 8th Division, was taken prisoner by the Japanese in Singapore, and spent four years in prisoner of war camps in Taiwan and Japan.

was shelling it; secondly, I believe it to be occupied by Germans … [and] … I do not think I have sufficient men to occupy, hold and improve it, even if it were possible by reason of our artillery merely stopping shelling."[46] Not only that, but the small advance would leave him unable to signal aircraft and would leave his left flank in a more precarious position than it already was. His company was massively stretched by trying to hold as much of the battalion's front as possible and never managed to stretch the whole way to make contact with the 51st in Mouquet Farm. Maxwell and his men were forced to fall back towards the 49th Battalion by 4.30pm on 4 September 1916, and were relieved the following day.

Through the success of the 49th Battalion and the efforts of Lieutenant Maxwell's A Company, the right of this attack managed to hold the line for some time. But the 49th suffered heavy casualties, particularly among its Lewis gun crews. Under pressure, Lieutenant-Colonel Lorenzo suggested that the "Canadians be asked to string out and take over my line … This will relieve pressure on me".[47] Maxwell could not spread his force out towards Mouquet Farm because, as he reported, "we have all we can hold in event of a counter-attack now".[48] Lorenzo, as commander of this overall force managed to get the position consolidated, the defences on the captured German trenches turned around and some communication trenches under construction during the day following the operation. This was remarkable given how weakly the line was held. Efforts to reinforce it were largely unsuccessful. A Company of the 50th Battalion under Captain David Todd was sent forward with 150 tools to help consolidate the line. They went forward under a heavy enemy artillery barrage falling between the front line and support trenches. Only about 35 men joined the 49th Battalion in the front line. Lorenzo was largely unsuccessful in getting messages through, and the 13th Brigade resorted to sending messages to the 1st Canadian Brigade asking if they could "give us any information about [the] 49th Battalion [as] we haven't heard [from them] for some time."[49] Lieutenant Maxwell continued to be the main conduit of information to brigade from the front line, deliberately going out to find as much as he could about other units in order to provide the best picture of the situation possible to 13th Brigade Headquarters.

Each of these operations saw some success, but each time it was short-lived. Each time the operations were to take close-range objectives under a light and fast artillery

---

46   AWM: AWM 26/61/22: Message from Lieutenant Duncan Struan Maxwell, OC "A" Company, 52nd Battalion. Dated 4 September 1916, Operations File Somme 1916, 13th Infantry Brigade.

47   AWM: AWM 26/61/21: Lorenzo (OC 49th Bn) to 13th Bde, 3 September 1916, 12.27pm, Operations File Somme 1916, 13th Infantry Brigade.

48   AWM: AWM 26/61/21: Maxwell (OC A Coy 52nd Bn), top off message with address torn off, 3 September 1916, 12.37pm, Operations File Somme 1916, 13th Infantry Brigade.

49   AWM: AWM 26/61/21: Ridley (13th Bde) to 4th Division, 3 September 1916, 2.12pm, Operations File Somme 1916, 13th Infantry Brigade.

barrage. The Germans were usually not forced to keep their heads down and stop firing during these barrages, and the infantry were forced into desperate hand-to-hand fighting to gain ground. Many units were crippled by casualties, and at least two were reported to have 'ceased to exist'. And yet there were very little changes to the basic approach in the last weeks of 1st Anzac Corps' tenancy of the line. Because the infantry could get into their objective there was a tendency to assume a lack of moral fibre was the only reason they could have been ejected by German counter-attacks, and so the basic offensive approach did not appear to need examination. And when given a request to try something different, as with Reserve Army's longer-range objective for the operation of 3 September 1916, Birdwood demonstrated his marked preference to try to take no more than the next trench by dramatically reducing the line. This operational approach was the sum of learning by 1st Anzac Corps during the Battle of Pozières and is a sad indictment on Birdwood's understanding of fighting at the Somme, and of his willingness to sacrifice his men rather than take advice from subordinates like Gellibrand or Durant, or re-examine his own methods. The learning process would have to happen elsewhere.

Conclusion

The Battle of Pozières Ridge lasted precisely six weeks. In that time the 1st Anzac Corps advanced the British line just over a mile and a half in a north-westerly direction, from a position just south east of the village of Pozières up to the edge of Mouquet Farm to the north of the village. The most successful phase of the battle was its first when the village of Pozières was captured, but as operations along the ridge wore on the bar by which success was measured was steadily lowered. First the corps captured a village, then the major German trenches in the sector, then a series of trenches towards Reserve Army's stated aims, then some strongpoints just ahead of the front line. At times the corps failed to attack the major defences ahead of them appropriately – when capturing Pozières 1st Anzac Corps nearly fell apart through not giving the capture of the OG Lines the emphasis it deserved, and for weeks steadfastly refused to address the problem of Mouquet Farm. While in July the advance could be measured by hundreds of yards, by late August it was not unheard of for a battalion to evacuate its front line to facilitate an artillery barrage and then 'attack' and 'capture' the front line it had just left. The situation became farcical, and the overall strategy lost in a flurry of hurried, small-scale operations with inappropriate artillery support.

The infantry themselves, slowly detached from their main form of firepower support and having to fend for themselves in the field, were put under further pressure by the hurried, small-scale series of operations thrust upon them. Because the next operation was rarely more than a day or two away the men in the front line were forced to make preparations as quickly as possible, digging new jumping-off trenches, repairing damaged ones, making reconnaissance patrols and forming working and carrying parties. All of this was conducted under some of the heaviest shellfire experienced anywhere on the Western Front. Lieutenant-Colonel Jess, in command of the 7th Battalion wrote that he "personally was a witness on one occasion when the strongpoint was blown in, and can realise the nerve wracking effect of such frequent occurrences".[1] The horror of this situation should not be underestimated. Men were buried by shell blast, dug up and buried again. Others dug through corpses, old and new, to reach them. Extended periods of heavy shellfire had a soporific effect, creating

---

1   AWM: AWM 26/54/7: '7th Battalion AIF Report on Operations 15th/21st August 1915 [*sic*],' 26 August 1916, Operations File Somme 1916, 2nd Infantry Brigade.

men effectively sleepwalking through their duties. Grown men cried like babies without knowing why. Shellshock, nerves, the shakes, all were treated with respect and understanding from men who understood the arbitrary human response to living within a roaring inferno. Men in the front line were also often poorly supplied, particularly with water, as a result of shellfire cutting supply lines to the most forward positions. They were more often than not remarkably valiant in the face of extreme adversity. But their morale was seriously tested, and on at least one occasion broke down as a result of the cumulative effect of these ongoing problems.

Some of these problems were the responsibility of Gough and his headquarters at Reserve Army. Gough's impetuosity was largely responsible for the push to hurry operations through, particularly in the early days. Only on a very few occasions was it possible to convince him to slow down – notably when Walker insisted on extra days to prepare for the attack on Pozières before 23 July, and when Haig intervened following the dramatic failure of Legge's first operation on the night of 28 July. But generally the rush to attack went unmodified and gradually became a feature of operations generated at corps and lower levels. There became a kind of culture of rapidity within the corps. And yet Reserve Army paid lip service to the need for thorough and careful preparation, and many of its memoranda "conceded that preparation must be thorough and careful" as in Gough's Memorandum of 3 August 1916. This was truly no more than lip service however – the most important point to be had from that document was that units of Reserve Army must 'press the enemy constantly and … continue to gain ground as rapidly as possible', which was totally at odds to the slower, methodical process implied through 'thorough and careful preparation'. The real problem arose when, in the same document, Gough gave his approval to having 'Subordinate Commanders … think out and suggest enterprises instead of waiting for orders from above'.[2] This gave Birdwood and others the opportunity to press ahead with their small-scale operations with minimal reference to the overall plan. By this simple directive, Gough effectively removed himself from organising a broad operational strategy in favour of urging haste on a small, disjointed scale. This gave more than enough scope for 1st Anzac Corps' deterioration into its confusing, muddled rush of small-scale operations.

And yet on a number of occasions Reserve Army issued orders to the 1st Anzac Corps for operations which had a number of elements that were slowly being demonstrated as being key to success. The most noticeable of these was the operation against Pozières which, as mentioned, had good distances between its objectives, maintained defence in depth as the operation went ahead, and achieved a significant gain in terms of territory. On subsequent occasions when Reserve Army issued similar orders they were always changed, particularly in terms of territorial advance, by corps or divisional commanders. This was a particular failure of 1st Anzac Corps and Birdwood, who was

2   AWM: AWM 26/42/1: Reserve Army SG.43/0/1, 3 August 1916, Operations File Somme 1916, Reserve Army General Staff.

in fact quite tentative about making a determined advance in any direction, or indeed to attack any major obstacle, such as Mouquet Farm. He always failed to intervene, particularly in gaining extra preparation time for his divisional commanders. The only time he did intervene was in the case of Gordon Legge, when, in order to retain the confidence of the Australian Government, he insisted that Legge not be replaced. This was a decision that was not based on any particular operational factor at all; at other times Birdwood seemed to agree with Gough that Legge was inexperienced and directly responsible for the failed attack.

1st Anzac Corps was also particularly responsible for the deterioration of artillery tactics such as the lifting barrage. It is clear from this short period of time that Birdwood was out of his depth as a commander, but able to manage through a policy of meekly passing on orders from Army and leaving it to divisional commanders to make alterations, or making the alterations himself in favour of shorter objectives and apparently easier to reach targets. The increasing number of smaller operations was particularly suited to Birdwood's tentativeness because it meant that his corps could regularly report success – even if only very localised – without running the risk of a large-scale, unmistakable failure. With Gough satisfied that at least Birdwood was impressing upon his subordinate leaders the necessity for the energetic measures and

General Sir William Birdwood (left of group in foreground) chatting with divisional commanders at the unveiling ceremony of the 1st Australian Division Memorial at Pozières. Major-General Harold Walker is to the right of the man with his back to the camera, and Major-General Nevill Smyth is on the right edge of the photograph facing the camera.
(AWM EZ0134)

offensive action which the present situation required, despite gaining no significant territory, Birdwood had little incentive to reassess his method of command or the tactics of his corps.

The three divisional commanders of 1st Anzac Corps displayed quite different approaches to the operations assigned them by Army and corps. Walker, in command of the 1st Australian Division, was perhaps the most proficient of the three. Certainly he was the most outspoken, and stood up to Gough when the Army commander tried to rush his division into action before it was adequately prepared. But on other occasions he did not stand up to Birdwood or succeed in gaining more time for preparation while his division was in its second period in the front line. Walker had confidence in his brigade commanders and left them to organise their infantry plans as they saw fit. His orders demonstrate a solid understanding of the role artillery could play in the actions of the infantry, but again too often he allowed his concerns regarding orders from corps or Army to be overridden by Birdwood. The clarity of purpose he displayed in the attack against Pozières diminished over time, and the general confusion of 1st Anzac Corps' later period in the line about Pozières affected his division as well.

Nevertheless Walker's overall approach was quite different to Legge's approach to command of the 2nd Australian Division. Legge micro-managed his brigade commanders by issuing orders that gave them very little leeway in interpretation or application. He also demonstrated a poor understanding of the mechanics of the attack in trench warfare, with a serious underestimation of the importance of firepower in advancing across no man's land and far too heavy an emphasis on the role of the infantry. His tactics cost his division dearly in both the lives of his men, and the esteem of his senior commanders. However, although he was closely monitored following the failure of his division's first operation against the OG Lines in late July, his basic problem of overcrowded infantry lines and diminished artillery barrages was never directly addressed.

Cox of the 4th Australian Division was perhaps the most interesting of the three. Every operation of his division was conducted behind an artillery barrage, which seems to indicate that he more than anyone clearly understood the important role firepower had to play in breaking the deadlock on the Western Front. And yet most of the barrages fired during his time in the line were completely inappropriate and, as discussed, did not coordinate with the infantry action at all. Cox was also the first to preside over the small raid-like attacks that became the norm during the latter part of 1st Anzac Corps' approach to operations, and he seemed to struggle to appreciate the role broad-fronted, deep assaults – like that on Pozières – had in gaining significant amounts of territory.

Just as divisional commanders demonstrated a marked ability to act as individuals, brigade commanders, too, could demonstrate initiative and individuality in their role. And as divisional commanders were limited by corps command, brigade commanders were limited by the division in which their formation belonged. However, at this level the scope within which brigade commanders could work was much more limited, and depended heavily on the actions of their divisional commander. Brigade commanders in the 1st Division benefited from Walker's hands-off command style, which gave them leeway to interpret their orders in different ways. As a result we have the example of Smyth and Sinclair-Maclagan at Pozières who, given the same orders from division, deployed their infantry in very different ways – to the detriment of Sinclair-Maclagan's 3rd Brigade. But again, they were absolutely at the mercy of the plan they were given to work within. Legge's brigade commanders were much more restricted by the orders they received and could do little in terms of innovation or individual interpretation of those orders. This was due both to the detail of the orders in terms of infantry movement – the composition and action of each infantry wave was detailed by division – and also struggled to achieve success because of the poor preparatory bombardments and lifting barrages of the artillery. In some cases, the preparation work of the brigadier had a latent effect on their brigades when in battle. The 4th Infantry Brigade materially benefited from Monash's extensive and detailed training programs which were continued by his successor, Brand. In contrast, the 13th Infantry Brigade, like the 4th Brigade a member of the 4th Australian Division, was not trained in such minute detail by its commander, and a comparison of the two demonstrates a noticeable difference, particularly in the ability of individuals in the field to understand their role as circumstances evolved during battle.

Battalion commanders are often considered to have little impact on the course of the battle once it began, having lost control as soon as the whistle sounded for their men to leave their jumping-off trenches. But during the Battle of Pozières Ridge many battalion commanders demonstrated that they were able to keep close control of their men and have a material effect on the outcome of the battle. The most stellar example was that of Heane and Howell-Price at Pozières. These two battalion commanders were able to cooperate within the same sector to excellent effect, and their battalions made the greatest advance on 23 July 1916. Heane left his headquarters on at least one occasion to make a personal reconnaissance of the front line to be better able to command his men, and Howell-Price paused his force in no man's land and personally made sure his wave of infantry was in the correct formation before joining the assault. Certainly other battalion commanders were not as active in their role, some preferring to stay in headquarters and wait for reports. In other cases, notably that of the 50th Battalion, problems with battalion command streamed down into companies. When Lieutenant-Colonel Frederick Hurcombe was evacuated with shellshock the battalion felt the impact of his loss. Major Ross Jacob had some difficulty adjusting to his sudden promotion to battalion commander, and some of his company commanders, such as Major Mervyn Herbert, struggled to maintain their morale. Battalion command was in many ways one of the most dynamic on the field because it was the first to encounter reports of companies being blocked or of counter-attacks arising in the field, and therefore the first to respond. Battalion commanders could have a significant effect on events, or very little as in the case of Lieutenant-Colonel Arthur Stevens at Pozières, whose headquarters was overrun by another battalion, leaving him out of the loop and disconnected from events. The experience and influence of the battalion commander during the Battle of Pozières was not at all uniform across the corps.

The infantry in the field during the battle had to contend with an enormous number of variables – many of which were thrust upon them as a consequence of orders given at higher levels of command. So many good junior officers, non-commissioned officers and ordinary soldiers were lost simply because of the hazardous situation in which many ill-thought-out schemes placed them. Major Durant, the officer commanding the 13th Battalion, once said that he was sure his men would be able to "rise to the occasion like the heroes they are", which was hardly realistic in the face of modern technological warfare.[3] Many men were killed in the process of behaving like heroes, like Lieutenant Victor Warry, a company commander of the 25th who was mown down by machine gun fire while standing at a gap in the wire in front of the OG Lines trying to lead his men through. And yet, if the artillery barrage suppressed the German defenders sufficiently, and the men could find shelter from the constant shell-fire, there was scope for individuals in the field to materially alter the course of events. The right flank at Pozières was in serious danger of breaking down completely but was saved by the actions of Captain Ferdinand Medcalf, who organised several strong-points and short lines of defence before acting as the primary conduit of messages into and out of the front line in that sector. Captain Hugh Pulling similarly took control of the 13th Battalion's sector in early August in the face of two of his fellow commanders struggling in their role. He, too, became the focus of all information into and out of the field, and was commended for sending reports in much sooner than those of his neighbouring battalions. He provided a stabilising and cohesive influence. Even at the lowest ebb of the 50th Battalion, individuals like Captain Harold Armitage and Captain Murray Fowler were able to stop a panicky retreat of men from a completely demoralised company and re-form the front line. While these individuals were reliant on so many factors being right before they could survive for any significant period in the front line, with each factor being in their favour they could have an extraordinarily disproportionate influence on events.

One of the problematic aspects of studying an operation like the Battle of Pozières Ridge is that in the end there is almost no evidence of learning from this experience. Certainly there were countless memoranda, notes and messages written with clearly expressed 'lessons learned'. But these written notes resulted in no practical examples which indicated that what was being written about was actually being absorbed and implemented. While Gordon Legge wrote in his report on the action of 28/29 July that it was a mistake to crowd many men into a line, there is no evidence that he made any effort to modify the numbers of men in operations in either the first or the second period of time the 2nd Division spent in the front line. Similarly 'lessons learned' on objective distances, artillery barrages, infantry waves and myriad other parts of battle have almost no examples of having been carried out even after the problems were clearly noted. Each operation marks a deterioration – in artillery application, in

3   AWM: AWM 26/60/9: Durant (OC 13th Bn) to 4th Bde. 29 August 1916, 9.35am, Operations File Somme 1916, 4th Infantry Brigade.

infantry deployment, in the scope of the operation both in depth and breadth, and in preparation times – from the one before. It is a matter for further study to see if the articulated 'lessons' were digested and employed at a more distant remove from events here, but it can be certain that even though many potential improvements were clearly articulated during the six weeks of the battle, they were not implemented in any plans.

Equally those individuals who demonstrated a high degree of understanding or competence at various times, such as Walker, or the many company or battalion commanders who have been noted as particularly competent, did not seem to learn anything during the course of the battle. They brought their already-established skills to the operation, and remained as they were, unable to extend their positive influence beyond their personal sphere of operations. The constant, desperate rush to attack as quickly as possible seems to have been largely responsible for the failure of any number of commanding officers at all levels to digest the results of recent events and modify their actions, sensibly or otherwise, in response.

Mouquet Farm itself was not captured until 26 September. Although initially not involved in active offensive operations towards the farm, eventually the Canadian Division that replaced the Australian divisions was also drawn into a number of small-scale operations in the same direction. And yet Mouquet Farm was not captured until the position was overtaken by an advance in the lines to either side of it. On 26 September the 6th East Yorkshire Pioneer Battalion was working in the vicinity of the farm digging communication trenches. The farm's downfall was ignominious to say the least:

> No. 16 [platoon] under Lieutenant Coultas could not start work owing to the Mouquet Farm being still held by the enemy. He therefore attacked the farm in order to try and [get] them out, eventually after about four hours and smoke bombs had been thrown down the entrances of the farm, one officer and 35 other ranks gave themselves up.[4]

Mouquet Farm was finally, irrevocably, in the hands of the British. In the effort, Lieutenant Coultas was another to lose his life. If Pozières Ridge was part of the battle that had to happen on the way to success, it was a costly path indeed.

The Battle of the Somme is largely told and remembered through its longer set-piece battles – 1 July, 14 July, 15 September. But for its other 138 days this was not how the battle was fought. At Longueval, Pozières, Mouquet Farm, Delville Wood, Ginchy, Guillemont, High Wood, and Intermediate Trench the Somme was characterised by small-scale, disjointed, interminable attacks as described in the Mouquet Farm operations. This was the warfare that most soldiers on most days of this battle were required to fight. That is, if there is a typical day on the Somme it was characterised by small groups of men struggling forwards towards ill-defined objectives on

---

4   TNA: WO 95/1804: 6th Battalion East Yorkshire Regiment (Pioneers) War Diary.

a moonscape battlefield. These troops might or might not be protected by artillery fire but were almost as likely to find their own shells landing among them as those of the enemy. Their task was to winkle out machine guns and enemy troops in undisclosed positions, firing from head-on or from a flank in numbers that were usually unknown. In the course of these actions they would be subjected to fire from enemy artillery batteries whose location and number would also be unknown to them and were even unknown to their own artillery. The attacking troops were more often than not exhausted before they began, forced by the haste with which most operations were mounted to work hard to prepare their jumping-off positions before going 'over the top'. Although the attacking force might start in appropriate strength, it would almost always suffer casualties to such a degree that it dwindled away to pitifully small numbers with no hope of holding the front captured. Or the infantry waves were so thickly packed that they formed excellent targets for enemy machine guns or riflemen, and larger numbers were lost to a similar end result. The fronts of attack were usually too narrow or so disjointed, and again operations so rushed that it was never possible to deploy into the measured attack formations adopted for the large set-piece battles. In these battles men would scamper forward over a shell-cratered wilderness in the faint hope that they would have some support their right and left.

It must be hammered home that on the Somme *this* was the war the infantry knew. And the war they knew had three overwhelming features. The first was that the nature of the operations they were unfortunate enough to be required to conduct were so rushed, so disjointed, so ill thought out, so badly integrated with firepower, that on most occasions they did not stand a decent chance of success. The orders, whether they come from on high or from more proximate levels of command were impossible to fulfil. This was not the way to fight a battle or even a war. The infantry in the Mouquet Farm battles were martyrs rather than soldiers – required by cloud-cuckoo-land plans to lay down their lives without, in many cases, even getting to grips with the enemy. The second feature of these battles is equally lamentable. Even if by some miracle an objective was captured and the line was advanced, it was all to no purpose. It did not matter a jot to the overall campaign if Mouquet Farm fell or not. It was not the key to Thiepval (which was still in enemy hands after Mouquet Farm was captured) or to anywhere else. When it was eventually captured nothing followed. The German line in this sector did not collapse, or withdraw. Thiepval was captured from a completely different direction. The capture of Mouquet Farm was inconsequential.

The third factor goes to the intention of the operation. The campaign was decidedly not in the accepted sense one of attrition. In attrition the aim is to wear the enemy down at a faster rate than one's own troops. This could not be the case in these hastily arranged battles. The fact is that they were prepared in such haste that there could be no over-arching aim. The number of men committed to battle was never at any time carefully chosen to further the aims of attrition. Those who fought were those who happened to be there. While very occasionally reports spoke of heavy German casualties, these were the consolation of a failed operation, not the success of a pre-planned attritional battle. Attrition in fact requires careful planning to induce or force the enemy to commit sufficient forces to create an imbalance of sacrifice. An imbalance was achieved here, but almost certainly on the wrong side. It was the enemy who could commit just enough machine guns, riflemen and artillery to hold up an attack; the attackers committed whatever they had available. Mouquet Farm, in terms of planning, objectives and casualties, was not even a road to nowhere. If continued it was the road to oblivion. The 1st Anzac Corps could here hardly recover from such an experience with any speed. None of Haig's armies could recover if this went on too long. New methods would have to be employed or the war would be ended by attrition – but not in a way that favoured the Allies.

Appendix

1st Anzac Corps Order of Battle 23 July – 3 September 1916

1st Australian Division	**Major-General Harold Bridgwood Walker**
1st Infantry Brigade	**Brigadier-General Nevill Maskelyne Smyth**
1st Battalion	Lieutenant-Colonel James Heane
2nd Battalion	Lieutenant-Colonel Arthur Borlase Stevens
3rd Battalion	Lieutenant-Colonel Owen Glendower Howell-Price
4th Battalion	Lieutenant-Colonel Iven Giffard Mackay
2nd Infantry Brigade	**Lieutenant-Colonel Henry Gordon Bennett**
5th Battalion	Lieutenant-Colonel Frank William Le Maistre
6th Battalion	Lieutenant-Colonel Clarence Wells Didier Daly
7th Battalion	Lieutenant-Colonel Care Herman Jess
8th Battalion	Lieutenant-Colonel Graham Coulter
3rd Infantry Brigade	**Brigadier-General Ewen George Sinclair Maclagan**
9th Battalion	Lieutenant-Colonel James Campbell Robertson
10th Battalion	Lieutenant-Colonel Stanley Price Weir
11th Battalion	Lieutenant-Colonel Stephen Harricks Roberts
12th Battalion	Lieutenant-Colonel Charles Hazell Elliott
2nd Australian Division	**Lieutenant-General James Gordon Legge**
5th Infantry Brigade	**Brigadier-General William Holmes**
17th Battalion	Lieutenant-Colonel Edward Fowell Martin
18th Battalion	Lieutenant-Colonel Evan Alexander Wisdom
19th Battalion	Lieutenant-Colonel William Kenneth Seaforth Mackenzie
20th Battalion	Lieutenant-Colonel Alexander Windeyan Ralston

6th Infantry Brigade	**Brigadier-General John Gellibrand**
21st Battalion	Lieutenant-Colonel William Dempster Forbes
22nd Battalion	Lieutenant-Colonel Robert Smith
23rd Battalion	Lieutenant-Colonel Wilfred Kent Fethers
24th Battalion	Lieutenant-Colonel William Walker Russell Watson
7th Infantry Brigade	**Brigadier-General John Paton**
25th Battalion	Lieutenant-Colonel James Walker
26th Battalion	Lieutenant-Colonel George Ferguson
27th Battalion	Lieutenant-Colonel Walter Dollman
28th Battalion	Major Alan William Leane
4th Australian Division	**Major-General Herbert Vaughan Cox**
4th Infantry Brigade	**Brigadier-General Charles Henry Brand**
13th Battalion	Lieutenant-Colonel Leslie Edward Tilney
14th Battalion	Lieutenant-Colonel Charles Morland Dare
15th Battalion	Lieutenant-Colonel James Cannan
16th Battalion	Lieutenant-Colonel Edmund Alfred Drake-Brockman
12th Infantry Brigade	**Brigadier-General Duncan John Glasfurd**
45th Battalion	Lieutenant-Colonel Sydney Charles Edgar Herring
46th Battalion	Lieutenant-Colonel Geoffrey Trollope Lee
47th Battalion	Lieutenant-Colonel Robert Eccles Snowden
48th Battalion	Lieutenant-Colonel Raymond Lionel Leane
13th Infantry Brigade	**Brigadier-General Thomas William Glasgow**
49th Battalion	Lieutenant-Colonel Francis Maxwell de Flayer Lorenzo
50th Battalion	Lieutenant-Colonel Frederick William Hurcombe (later Major Ross Blyth Jacob)
51st Battalion	Lieutenant-Colonel Arthur Murray Ross
52nd Battalion	Lieutenant-Colonel Miles Fitzroy Beevor

Bibliography

Australian War Memorial, Canberra

AWM 4	**Australian Imperial Force Unit War Diaries, 1914-1918 War**
——1/29/6	1st Anzac Corps General Staff – July 1916
——1/29/7 Pt. 2	1st Anzac Corps General Staff – August 1916
——1/29/8	1st Anzac Corps General Staff – September 1916
——1/30/7 Pt. 2	1st Anzac Corps Intelligence – August 1916
——1/42/18 Pt. 1	1st Australian Division General Staff – July 1916
——1/42/18 Pt. 2	1st Australian Division General Staff – July 1916
——1/42/19 Pt. 1	1st Australian Division General Staff – August 1916
——1/43/9	1st Australian Division Administrative Staff – August 1916
——1/48/5 Pt. 2	4th Australian Division – August 1916
——1/48/5 Pt. 3	4th Australian Division – August 1916
——13/10/22	1st Australian Divisional Artillery – July 1916
——13/10/23	1st Australian Divisional Artillery – August 1916
——13/10/26	1st Australian Divisional Artillery – August 1916
——23/1/12	1st Infantry Brigade – July 1916
——23/1/13	1st Infantry Brigade – August 1916
——23/2/16	2nd Infantry Brigade – August 1916
——23/3/9	3rd Infantry Brigade – July 1916
——23/4/11	4th Infantry Brigade – August 1916
——23/5/13	5th Infantry Brigade – July 1916
——23/6/12	6th Infantry Brigade – August 1916
——23/13/6	13th Infantry Brigade – July 1916
——23/13/7	13th Infantry Brigade – August 1916
——23/18/9	1st Infantry Battalion – July 1916
——23/21/17	4th Infantry Battalion – July 1916
——23/22/17	5th Infantry Battalion – July 1916
——23/24/17	7th Infantry Battalion – July 1916

——23/26/19	9th Infantry Battalion – July 1916
——23/25/19	8th Infantry Battalion – July 1916
——23/27/9	10th Infantry Battalion – July 1916
——23/28/16	11th Infantry Battalion – July 1916
——23/29/17	12th Infantry Battalion – July 1916
——23/29/18	12th Infantry Battalion – August 1916
——23/30/22	13th Infantry Battalion – August 1916
——23/32/17	15th Infantry Battalion – August 1916
——23/37/12	20th Infantry Battalion – July 1916
——23/38/12	21st Infantry Battalion – August 1916
——23/40/11	23rd Infantry Battalion – August 1916
——23/41/12	24th Infantry Battalion – August 1916
——23/42/12	25th Infantry Battalion – July 1916
——23/45/16	28th Infantry Battalion – July 1916
——23/66/4	49th Infantry Battalion – September 1916
——23/68/6	51st Infantry Battalion – August 1916
——23/68/7	51st Infantry Battalion – September 1916
AWM 26	**Operations Files, 1914-1918 War. [Somme 1916]**
——40/1	British Expeditionary Force General Staff, 10 – 17 July 1916
——40/3	British Expeditionary Force General Staff, 27 July – 6 August 1916
——40/4	British Expeditionary Force General Staff, 7 – 15 August 1916
——41/60	Reserve Army General Staff, 18 – 22 July 1916
——41/61	Reserve Army General Staff, 18 – 22 July 1916
——42/1	Reserve Army General Staff, 27 July – 6 August 1916
——42/3	Reserve Army General Staff, 7 – 15 August 1916
——42/4	Reserve Army General Staff, 16 – 22 August 1916
——42/6	Reserve Army General Staff, 23 – 27 August 1916
——43/37	Summaries of Operations of Reserve Army, 1 July – 8 September 1916
——46/22	1st Canadian Division General Staff, 28 August – 3 September 1916
——46/24	1st Canadian Infantry Brigade, 28 August – 3 September 1916
——50/15	1st Anzac Corps General Staff, 27 July – 6 August 1916
——50/16	1st Anzac Corps General Staff, 7 – 15 August 1916
——50/17	1st Anzac Corps General Staff, 16 – 22 August 1916
——50/18	1st Anzac Corps General Staff, 23 – 27 August 1916
——51/26	1st Australian Division General Staff, 23 – 26 July 1916

——51/30	1st Australian Division, General Staff, 16 – 22 August 1916
——52/4	1st Anzac Corps, Intelligence, 7 – 15 August 1916
——52/17	1st Anzac Corps, GOCRA, 27 July – 6 August 1916
——52/18	1st Anzac Corps, GOCRA, 7 – 15 August 1916
——52/20	1st Anzac Corps, GOCRA, 23 – 27 August 1916
——52/25	1st Anzac Corps BGHA, 27 July – 6 August 1916
——52/28	1st Anzac Corps BGHA, 23 – 27 August 1916
——53/2	1st Australian Divisional Artillery, 27 July – 6 August 1916
——53/21	1st Infantry Brigade, 23 – 26 July 1916
——53/24	1st Infantry Brigade, 16 – 22 August 1916
——54/3	2nd Infantry Brigade, 23 to 26 July 1916
——54/7	2nd Infantry Brigade, 16 – 22 August 1916
——54/12	3rd Infantry Brigade, 23 – 26 July 1916
——55/1	3rd Infantry Brigade, 23 – 26 July 1916
——55/4	3rd Infantry Brigade, 16 – 22 August 1916
——55/6	3rd Infantry Brigade, 23 – 29 August 1916
——56/4	2nd Australian Division General Staff, 27 July – 6 August 1916
——56/5	2nd Australian Division General Staff, 27 July – 6 August 1916
——56/8	2nd Australian Division General Staff, 23 – 27 August 1916
——56/9	2nd Australian Division General Staff, 23 – 27 August 1916
——57/22	5th Infantry Brigade, 23 – 27 August 1916
——57/27	6th Infantry Brigade & Battalions, 27 July – 6 August 1916
——58/3	6th Infantry Brigade, 23 – 27 August 1916
——58/9	7th Infantry Brigade and Battalions, 27 July – 6 August 1916
——59/6	4th Australian Division General Staff, 7 – 15 August 1916
——59/9	4th Australian Division General Staff, 23 – 27 August 1916
——59/11	4th Australian Division General Staff, 28 August – 3 September 1916
——60/6	4th Infantry Brigade, 7 – 15 August 1916
——60/9	4th Infantry Brigade, 28 August – 3 September 1916
——61/15	13th Infantry Brigade, 7 – 15 August 1916
——61/21	13th Infantry Brigade, 28 August – 3 September 1916
——61/22	13th Infantry Brigade, 4 – 8 September 1916
——63/11	Supplementary unbound records, File 11
AWM 28	**Recommendation File for Honours & Awards, AIF 1914-1918**
——1/5 Part 3	1st Australian Division, 23 to 26 July 1916

——1/6   1st Australian Division, 27 July to 6 August 1916
——1/69   2nd Australian Division, 27 July to 6 August 1916
——1/72   2nd Australian Division, 23 – 27 August 1916
——1/180   4th Australian Division, 7 – 15 August 1916
——2/81   4th Australian Division, 1916, 1917, 1918
——2/305   11th Battalion AIF, Item 2, Army Book 72
AWM 1DRL/0428   **Australian Red Cross Society Wounded and Missing**
                     Enquiry Bureau files, 1914-18 War
EXDOC   **Exhibition Documents**
——019   Pulling, Hugh Douglas (Major), MC
——020   Pulling, Hugh Douglas
——021   Barton, Francis Maxwell (Captain), 1893-1916
——022   Marks, Douglas Gray (Captain), DSO, MC, 1895 -1920
——023   Marks, Douglas Gray (Captain), DSO, MC, 1895 -1920
——026   Smythe, Edward Vivian (Lieutenant), 1891-1968
G5831.S65   **Trench Maps**
——Sheet 7:14:2   Hand-drawn of Pozières by A.E. Scammell, 1:5,000
——Sheet 7:15:8   Ferme du Mouquet, 1:5,000

The National Archives (Kew)
CAB 45   **Post-war Official History Correspondence**
WO 95   **Operational War Diaries**
——5   General Staff, Operations Section, General Headquarters, 1 –
                     31 July 1916
——518   Headquarters Branches and Services: General Staff, April –
                     December, 1916
——1823   12th Imperial Division War Diary, 1 January – 31 August
                     1916
——1847   35th Infantry Brigade War Diary, 1 July – 31 December 1916
——1852   7th (Service) Battalion Suffolk Regiment War Diary, 1916
——2745   48th Imperial Division War Diary, 1 April 1915 – 31
                     December 1916
——2755   1/5 Battalion Royal Warwickshire Regiment War Diary, July
                     1916
——2760   145 Infantry Brigade Headquarters War Diary, 1916
WO 153   **Battle of the Somme (Battles of Guillemont & Ginchy)**
                     Maps & Plans
WO 158   **Miscellaneous Operations Files**

——21	Commander-in-Chief, British Armies and Chief of Imperial General Staff and Secretary of State, War Office: Correspondence
——333	"Scheme D"
——334	"Scheme F"

Liddell Hart Centre for Military Archives, King's College, London

6/2/161 Philip Howell papers

National Archives of Australia

NAA: B2455 ARMITAGE H E S	Service record
NAA:B2455 HERBERT M J MAJOR	Service record
NAA: B2455 LE NAY LOUIS LEON	Service record
NAA: B2455 MEDCALF FERDINAND GEORGE	Service record
NAA: B2455 PULLING HUGH DOUGLAS	Service record
NAA: B2455 SMYTH RALPH RATNEVELUE RAYMOND EKIN	Service record
NAA: B2455 ROGERSON EDWARD	Service record
NAA: B883, NX12610	Service record of Duncan Struan Maxwell

Diaries & Memoirs

Bean, C.E.W., *Two Men I Knew: William Bridges and Brudenell White, Founders of the AIF* (Sydney: Angus & Robertson, 1957).

Blake, Robert (ed), *The Private Papers of Douglas Haig 1914-1919* (London: Eyre & Spottiswoode, 1952).

Lloyd George, David, *War Memoirs of David Lloyd George, Vol. II,* (London: Odhams Press, 1938).

Manning, Frederic, *Her Privates, We* (London: Peter Davies, 1930).

Sheffield, Gary & John Bourne (eds), *Douglas Haig: War Diaries and Letters 1914-1918*, (London: Weidenfield & Nicolson, 2005).

Newspaper Articles

'11th Battalion History', *Western Mail*, Perth, 30 July 1936, p.2.

'16th Battalion History', *The Daily News*, Perth, 23 November 1929, p.6.

'The "Dinkums": History of the 27th Battalion', *The Mail*, Adelaide, 29 April 1922, p.3.

'Toxites' (Pseudonym of Captain Walter C. Belford), 'Unit Histories', *Western Mail*, Perth, 22 February 1940, p.2.

'Twelfth Battalion History', *Examiner*, Launceston, 17 March 1924, p.4.

Official Histories

Bean, C.E.W., *Official History of Australia in the War of 1914-1918. Vol. III: The AIF in France* (Sydney: Angus & Robertson, 1929).

—— *The Official History of Australia in the War of 1914-1918. Vol. IV: The AIF in France, 1917* (Sydney: Angus & Robertson, 1933).

Belford, Walter C., *Legs-Eleven: Being the Story of the 11th Battalion (AIF) in the Great War of 1914-1918* (Perth, W.A., Imperial Printing Company, 1940).

Edmonds, J.E. (ed), *Military Operations: France and Belgium, 1916 Vol. I, Appendices* (London: Macmillan, 1932).

Miles, Captain Wilfrid, *Military Operations: France and Belgium, 1916 Vol. II* (London: Macmillan, 1938).

Books

Beckett, Ian F.W. & Steven J. Corvi (eds), *Haig's Generals* (Barnsley: Pen & Sword, 2009).

Bennett, Scott, *Pozières: The Anzac Story* (Carlton North, Victoria: Scribe, 2011).

Bond, Brian et al, *'Look to Your Front': Studies in the First World War* (Padstow: TJ Press International, 1999).

Clark, Alan, *The Donkeys* (London: Hutchison, 1961).

Charlton, Peter, *Pozières 1916: Australians on the Somme* (London: Lee Cooper in association with Secker & Warburg, 1986).

Coulthard-Clark, C.D., *No Australian Need Apply: The Troubled Career of Lieutenant-General Gordon Legge* (Sydney: Allen & Unwin, 1988).

Dewar, George A.B. (with Lieut.-Col. J.H. Boraston), *Sir Douglas Haig's Command. Vol. I* (London, Bombay & Sydney: Constable & Company, 1922).

Farrar-Hockley, A.H., *The Somme* (London: Pan, 1966).

Freeman, R.R., *Hurcombe's Hungry Half Hundred: A Memorial History of the 50th Battalion AIF 1916-1919* (Norwood: Peacock Publications, 1991).

Gammage, Bill, 'Introduction' in C.E.W. Bean, *Official History of Australia in the War of 1914-1918. Vol. IV: The AIF in France 1917* (St. Lucia: Queensland UP, 1983).

—— *The Broken Years: Australian Soldiers in the Great War* (Australia: Penguin, 1974).

Gliddon, Gerald, *The Battle of the Somme: A Topographical History* (Stroud: Alan Sutton Publishing, 1994).

Griffith, Paddy, *Battle Tactics of the Western Front: The British Army's Art of Attack 1916-18* (New Haven & London: Yale University Press, 1994).

Hart, Peter, *The Somme* (London: Weidenfeld & Nicolson, 2005).

Hughes, Colin, *Mametz: Lloyd George's Welsh Army at the Battle of the Somme* (Gerards Cross: Orion, 1982).

Laffin, John, *British Butchers and Bunglers of World War One* (Gloucester & Wolfeboro: Sutton Publishing, 1992).

Liddell Hart, B.H., *Reputations* (London: John Murray, 1928).

—— *The Real War* (London: Faber, 1930). [Subsequently published as *A History of the World War* (Boston: Little & Brown, 1934)].

Lupfer, Timothy T., *The Dynamics of Doctrine: The Changes in German Tactical Doctrine During the First World War* (Fort Leavenworth, Kansas: US Army Command & General Staff College, 1981).

Macdonald, Lyn, *Somme* (London: Michael Joseph, 1983).

Lt.-Gen. Sir John Monash, *The Australian Victories in France in 1918* (London, Hutchinson & Co., 1920).

Norman, Terry, *The Hell They Called High Wood* (London: William Kimber, 1984).

Philpott, William, *Bloody Victory: The Sacrifice on the Somme and the Making of the Twentieth Century* (Great Britain: Little, Brown, 2009).

Prior, Robin & Trevor Wilson, *Command on the Western Front: The Military Career of Sir Henry Rawlinson 1914-1918* (Oxford: Blackwell, 1992).

—— *The Somme.* (Sydney: University of New South Wales Press, 2005).

Sheffield, G.D., "The Australians at Pozières: Command and Control on the Somme, 1916." David French & Brian Holden Reid (eds.) *The British General Staff: Reform & Innovation* (London: Routledge, 2002), pp.112-126.

Sheffield, Gary, *The Somme* (Great Britain: Cassell, 2003).

Simpson, Andy, *Directing Operations: British Corps Command on the Western Front 1914-18* (London: Spellmount, 2005).

Terraine, John, *Douglas Haig: The Educated Soldier* (London: Hutchison, 1963).

—— *The Smoke and the Fire: Myths and Anti-Myths of War 1861-1945* (London: Sidgwick & Jackson, 1980).

Tolstoy, Leo, *War and Peace* (London: Penguin Books, 2005).

Travers, T., *How the War Was Won: Factors that led to Victory in World War One* (Barnsley: Pen & Sword, 2005).

Van Hartesveldt, Fred, *The Battles of the Somme, 1916: Historiography and Annotated Bibliography* (Westport, Connecticut: Greenwood Press, 1996).

Winter, Jay & Antoine Prost, *The Great War in History: Debates and Controversies, 1914 to the Present* (Cambridge: Cambridge University Press, 2005).

Journal Articles

Bean, C.E.W. 'The Writing of the Australian Official History of the Great War – Sources, Methods and Some Conclusions.' *Royal Australian Historical Society Journal & Proceedings,* 24:2 (1938), pp.85-112.

Howard, Michael. 'World War One: The Crisis in European History – the Role of the Military Historian.' *The Journal of Military History*. 57:5 (Special Issue, October 1993).

Ponterotto, 'Joseph G. Brief Note on the Origins, Evolution, and Meaning of the Qualitative Resesarch Concept "Thick Description",' *The Qualitative Report*, Vol. 11, No. 3 (Sept. 2006).

Unpublished Theses

Hughes, Jackson, 'The Monstrous Anger of the Guns: The Development of British Artillery Tactics, 1914-1918', PhD thesis: University of Adelaide, 1994).

Index

PEOPLE

PLACES

FORMATIONS & UNITS

Armies & Army Corps

Fourth Army xx-xxi, 29, 32-33, 57-59, 87, 90-91, 101, 138-139, 148, 189-190

Reserve Army ix-x, xiv, xxi, xxviii, 30-31, 34, 36-37, 46, 52, 57-60, 62-63, 75, 80-81, 85, 87-93, 105, 108-109, 112, 114, 117-120, 123, 135-136, 138, 141, 143-144, 156, 164-167, 189-191, 193, 206-208, 219

1st Anzac Corps iii, v, viii, x, xvi, xviii, xx, xxiii, xxvi-xxviii, 31-32, 57-62, 64, 67, 75-76, 78, 80-81, 85, 87-90, 92-96, 98-99, 101, 103-104, 108-110, 112-114, 116-124, 129, 135-141, 143-144, 147, 154-156, 159, 163-168, 171-173, 181-183, 189-193, 195, 206-210, 215-216, 218-220, 228

II Corps 58-59, 76, 87, 93, 103, 108, 114, 116-120, 136-138, 164, 189-191, 193

III Corps 76, 190

Divisions

1st Australian Division v, viii, ix, xvi, 29, 31-38, 40, 44, 46-47, 51-53, 60, 62-63, 65, 67, 73, 81, 95-96, 136, 138-141, 145, 148, 153, 160, 162-164, 168, 170, 182, 209-211, 216, 218-221

2nd Australian Division v, ix, 58, 60-61, 63-69, 73, 75-79, 79-82, 83-86, 86-87, 89, 94, 96, 104, 136, 164-165, 167-176, 180-183, 187, 193, 196, 210, 212, 216, 220-221

4th Australian Division ix-x, 87, 89-91, 93-94, 97-99, 103-104, 107-112, 114-116, 119, 121, 123, 130, 133, 135-136, 138-139, 142-143, 165, 182-183, 185, 190-191, 195-196, 205, 210-211, 217-218, 220-221

12th (Eastern) Division 59, 76, 87, 109, 120, 138

23rd (New Army) Division 76, 87

48th (South Midland) Division 44, 136, 164

Brigades

1st Australian Brigade ix, xvi, 36-37, 40, 44-45, 52-53, 141, 144-149, 152-153, 155, 216, 218, 220

1st Australian Brigade 38, 40, 44-45, 52-53, 141, 143-144, 146-149, 152.

1st Canadian Brigade 190, 196, 205, 219

2nd Australian Brigade vi, xvi, 38, 42, 48, 148-153, 156, 161-163, 207, 216, 218, 220

3rd Australian Brigade vi-vii, xxvi, 36-38, 45-53, 74, 153-160, 161-163, 211, 216, 218, 220

4th Australian Brigade v, ix, 87, 90, 93-94, 96-97, 100-106, 107-109, 111-115, 120, 122, 125-131, 136, 183-184, 186-188, 193-194, 211-212, 217-218, 220

5th Australian Brigade 60, 63, 66-68, 73-74, 77, 167, 216, 218, 220

6th Australian Brigade 60, 66-69, 71-72, 75, 77, 168-169, 172, 175, 177-183, 217-218, 220

7th Australian Brigade iv, vii, ix, 60, 65-75, 77, 79, 82-83, 168, 217, 220

13th Australian Brigade v, 108, 111, 114, 125-127, 129, 132, 134-135, 194, 196, 198-205, 211, 217-218, 220

14th Australian Brigade 108, 196

35th Brigade 98, 100-102, 109-110

37th Brigade 109

44th Brigade 148, 152

145th Brigade 119, 141

Battalions & Regiments

1st Australian Battalion vi-vii, xvi, 38, 40, 42-44, 141, 146, 216

2nd Australian Battalion vi, 38-41, 43, 54, 144, 160, 216

3rd Australian Battalion vii, 38, 42-43, 141, 145-147, 216

4th Australian Battalion vi, xvi, 38, 40-41, 52, 141, 144-147, 216

5th Australian Battalion 44, 55, 161, 216

Miscellaneous

Wolverhampton Military Studies

www.helion.co.uk/wolverhamptonmilitarystudies

Editorial board

Professor Stephen Badsey
Wolverhampton University

Professor Michael Bechthold
Wilfred Laurier University

Professor John Buckley
Wolverhampton University

Major General (Retired) John Drewienkiewicz

Ashley Ekins
Australian War Memorial

Dr Howard Fuller
Wolverhampton University

Dr Spencer Jones
Wolverhampton University

Nigel de Lee
Norwegian War Academy

Major General (Retired) Mungo Melvin President
of the British Commission for Military History

Dr Michael Neiberg
US Army War College

Dr Eamonn O'Kane
Wolverhampton University

Professor Fransjohan Pretorius
University of Pretoria

Dr Simon Robbins
Imperial War Museum

Professor Gary Sheffield
Wolverhampton University

Commander Steve Tatham PhD
Royal Navy
The Influence Advisory Panel

Professor Malcolm Wanklyn
Wolverhampton University

Professor Andrew Wiest
University of Southern Mississippi

Submissions

The publishers would be pleased to receive submissions for this series. Please contact us via email (info@helion.co.uk), or in writing to Helion & Company Limited, 26 Willow Road, Solihull, West Midlands, B91 1UE.

Titles

No.1 *Stemming the Tide. Officers and Leadership in the British Expeditionary Force 1914* Edited by Spencer Jones (ISBN 978-1-909384-45-3)

No.2 *'Theirs Not To Reason Why'. Horsing the British Army 1875–1925* Graham Winton (ISBN 978-1-909384-48-4)

No.3 *A Military Transformed? Adaptation and Innovation in the British Military, 1792–1945* Edited by Michael LoCicero, Ross Mahoney and Stuart Mitchell (ISBN 978-1-909384-46-0)